Cords That Cannot Be Broken

A Study of Twin Souls

by

JUDITH MERVILLE

Regency Press (London & New York) Ltd.
125 High Holborn, London WC1V 6QA

ISBN 0 7212 0906 8

Printed and bound in Great Britain by
Buckland Press Ltd., Dover, Kent.

DEDICATION

This book is dedicated to all those who suffer. That they might find consolation both in the knowledge of God's eternal Love, and through being of service to others who are suffering too. Also to my own twin soul, with a big THANK YOU for his inspiration past and present, and always remembering that whether or not we meet on the Earth's plane is of little importance.

CONTENTS

ACKNOWDGEMENTS   9

INTRODUCTION   11

CHAPTER I –   Twin Souls in History   21
                El Morya and Lady Miriam
                St. Germain and Lady Portia
                St. Francis and St. Clare
                Edgar Cayce and Gladys Davis Turner
                Joan Grant and Esmond
                Elizabeth Taylor and Richard Burton

CHAPTER II –   Twin Souls teach one another Lessons   32
                The story of Angela and Bruce

CHAPTER III – The Ties can never be Cut   57
                The story of Carol and Dan

CHAPTER IV –   Twin Souls are often very Telepathic   72
                The story of Ellen and Fred

CHAPTER V –   Twin Souls often find that they do similar things 79
                at the same time
                The story of Graham and Helen

CHAPTER VI –   Sometimes the strong attraction can cause feelings of 93
                Guilt and Confusion
                The story of Iris and Joe

CHAPTER VII – When Twin Souls are together it increases their strength 106
                The stories of Kenneth and Lucinda
                and Mary and Norman

CHAPTER VIII – Twin Souls always catch one another up spiritually 127
                The story of Oliver and Polly

CHAPTER IX –   If one partner gets left behind spiritually, their   134
               power may be transferred to the other partner
                   The story of Quentin and Rosie

CHAPTER X –   Twin Souls are sometimes the Same Sex   143
                   The story of Susie and Tessa

CHAPTER XI –   When Twin Souls are together they tend to find that   152
               they gain one another's talents as well as amplifying
               their own
                   The story of Ursula and Victor

CHAPTER XII – Sometimes Twin Souls have to separate for their Growth 164
                   The stories of Winifred and Xavier
                   and Yvonne and Zachary

CHAPTER XIII – Twin Souls who are very evolved sometimes   184
               come together in order to do important work
                   Harmon and June Bro
                   Aron and Doris Abrahamsen
                   Dr. Michael Newton and Peggy
                   Anne and Daniel Meurois-Givaudan

CHAPTER XIV – Twin Souls do not need to be together physically   192
                   A clairvoyant counsellor
                   My friend "John"
                   Edwin Courtenay
                   Ann and Ken Evans
                   Marlo Morgan

CHAPTER XV –   Conclusion – The Message   200

POSTSCRIPT   211

ACKNOWLEDGEMENTS

I should like to express my thanks firstly to Edwin Courtenay, my clairvoyant friend and adviser, who – owing to the research I had done into the subject during the course of writing my first book – first suggested that I write a book about Twin Souls. Also to Lilla Bek, who encouraged me in embarking on the project, having herself taught me much on the subject. My sister, Philippa Merivale[1], too, is well versed in spiritual matters, and has always been ready to lend a listening ear and offer invaluable advice. It goes without saying that the debt to all the subjects of my study is immense – not only for the time that they gave me for the interviews, but also for reading through and commenting on the chapters in which they figured. Being myself no artist, it was my daughter, Alice, who kindly did the illustrations in Chapter III. Heartfelt thanks are due to John Thorpe of Regency Press for his immense speed, efficiency and general co-operation throughout the course of production of the book. I should also like to thank Roy Stemman, the editor of the magazine *Reincarnation International*, firstly for introducing me (when I was already three quarters of the way through writing this one) to Joudry and Pressman's wonderful book on Twinsoulship[2], from which I have quoted liberally, and secondly for publishing my article on the subject, which generated much interest. And last, but by no means least, I am grateful to my husband, who has not only put up with hastily-put-together meals over the last months, but also listened carefully to my reading, and made constructive criticism, of some of the chapters.

Notes
1. Philippa Merivale's book – Experience of Aura Soma – is to be published in May 1998 by Element Books, Shaftesbury, Dorset.
2. Twin Souls – A Guide to Finding Your True Spiritual Partner by Patricia Joudry and Maurie D. Pressman, M.D., is also published by Element Books.

INTRODUCTION

This book is an attempt to deal with just one aspect of our soul journey – not by any means the most important aspect of it, but one on which there seems at present to be on the one hand a great thirst for information, and on the other hand something of a dearth of written material. I feel that part of the reason for this dearth is that esoteric science has been making such rapid advances in the last few years that it has not been easy for those with both the interest in it and the ability to write to keep up with the developments. Also, however, Patricia Joudry and Maurie D. Pressman, M.D., in their comparatively recent book entitled *Twin Souls – A Guide to finding your True Spiritual Partner*[1], make the important point that up until now the world has not been ready for this information. Now, with the general raising of consciousness as our planet is preparing to take a major step upwards in spiritual development, more and more of us are getting ready for reunion with our twin souls, and this knowledge is consequently of great importance to us.

Many people talk about "soulmates", and there are a number of books on the subject, of which the best known is probably that of Jess Stearn[2]; but "soulmate" is rather a broad term, which includes both twin souls and other types of close spiritual or spiritual and sexual relationship. Owing to the above-mentioned dearth of writing on the subject, it has taken me a considerable amount of research (partly through reading, but mainly through questioning of psychics) to obtain a full understanding of the concept of twin souls (or "twin flames", to use another popular connotation), and this is why, now that I believe I have finally got to the bottom of the question, I feel a desire to share the knowledge I have gained with as many people as possible. Some of my research must have been done at about the same time as Joudry and Pressman were publishing their book, but the latter only became known to me when I was near to completing this one. Joudry and Pressman's book is an <u>excellent</u> introduction to the subject, but many readers will want to take the matter further. In fact Patricia Joudry says herself in her Introduction: *What we have written here is hardly the last word on twinsoulship; it is only a beginning. There is much more to be discovered on this beneficent law of love . . .* While these authors do of course cite individual experiences, my own book is based on case histories as living examples of the spiritual principles concerning twin souls being acted out in concrete reality.

11

Dick Sutphen is a well-known American hypnotherapist who uses past-life regression therapy and has published several books. In, for instance, *You Were Born Again to be Together*[3] he speaks much of soulmates (including his own wife, Tara), but he makes no distinction at all between the various types. Jess Stearn, on the other hand, clearly distinguishes three types of soulmate and echoes what Edgar Cayce said: that one can easily have up to about twenty soulmates, but one has only one twin soul.

So let us begin with some definitions. Stearn's three different types are "companion soulmates", "karmic soulmates" and "twin souls". A companion soulmate (in Cayce's terms also) is someone with whom one has built up a good and close relationship over many lifetimes (very likely not always as man and wife, but sometimes perhaps as brother and sister or parent and child) and with whom one can consequently very easily fall in love and make an extremely happy and successful marriage. Edgar Cayce and his beloved wife, Gertrude, were a perfect example of this and, in view of the fact that Stearn is one of Cayce's biographers[4], I find it very surprising that in his book entitled *Soulmates* he erroneously describes Gertrude as Cayce's twin soul, with scarcely a mention of Gladys David-Turner, his devoted secretary, who was, as was well known to all three of them, in reality his twin soul. (For the accurate story I recommend Harmon Bro's biography of Cayce[5].)

A "karmic soulmate" is someone with whom one falls in love on account of a debt or some other piece of uncompleted karma. Stearn has among his stories of married couples a fascinating one about a black girl whose husband is white, and who only fully understood the reason for their love (so much frowned upon in that society) when she was regressed and discovered herself to have previously been her great aunt Regina, who had been murdered by the white man with whom she had refused to make love. This same man was in her present life of course now the black girl's devoted husband! In the case of "karmic soulmates", the close sexual relationship often does not extend beyond a single lifetime.

The nature of the relationship between twin souls being the subject of this book, this will be examined in much greater depth in the ensuing chapters. For the moment let us confine ourselves to a definition. Students of the esoteric will be aware that the original and true nature of the human being is spirit. (On this subject I recommend *Récits d'un Voyageur de l'Astral* by Anne and Daniel Meurois-Givaudan[6].) The physical body is the vehicle of which we make use while we are on earth, the soul is the body we use in the astral realms, while the spirit (generally referred to as the "Higher Self") of each one of us remains permanently in the spiritual realms, where it is our aim and destiny ultimately to rejoin it.

In the beginning, after we had all broken away from God and were starting on the lengthy journey back to the Source, each spirit gave birth to two souls, representing the masculine and feminine energies, mirror images one of the other, complementing one another, and consequently invariably attracted to one another. Each pair of twin souls normally incarnated together the first time (or alternatively one stayed behind in spirit to serve the other as a guide), but subsequently we parted, going separate ways in order to increase the totality of our experience, and each enjoying the enrichment of (as Lilla Bek puts it) "dancing with other souls". This dancing with other souls has, over the aeons, built up much karma for us all to work out, and for that reason, though we do now and again meet up with our twin soul, we can spend centuries of lifetimes in which we are never together.

Only when we have paid all our debts, worked out all our karma, and achieved total detachment from the material world, will we be ready after death to transcend the astral realms and rejoin our essential being in the realms of spirit. Since twin souls have all been born of the same spirit as each other, they will need ultimately to fuse and then rejoin their spirit partner together. This means that they need always to keep more or less at the same level of development. If one partner refuses at some point to evolve spiritually, the other will be held back also; but on the other hand, since they are so very closely connected, if in a particular lifetime one soul makes a massive leap ahead, her partner will inevitably catch up before too long.

This ultimate fusion of twin souls is an aspect of the subject not touched on by Jess Stearn in his book entitled *Soulmates*[2], but after learning about it directly from the mouths of psychics, I found it described very beautifully by Daniel Meurois-Givaudan in the second of his and his wife Anne's two wonderful books about their lives as Essenes at the time of Christ. Anne and Daniel (on whose writings I comment further in Chapter Twelve) are twin souls who were among the early disciples. They were husband and wife also in the lifetime in which they knew Christ, and these two books, *De Mémoire d'Essénien*, of which volume one is subtitled *L'Autre Visage de Jésus*[7], and volume two *Chemins de ce Temps-là*[8], are written (like Joan Grant's "far memory autobiographies"[9]) from readings of the Akashic Records made while out of their bodies, this being the most effective way in which to do it.

Daniel, as "Simon" in the earlier incarnation, was trained as a young boy by the monks of the "Krmel" in order to prepare him for the discipleship and when, in volume two, he is beginning to recover from his beloved "Myriam's" death, he recalls the teaching he had received as a child on the subject of twin souls. Since this is both the fullest and the most beautiful explanation of twin souls that I have yet seen in writing, I quote it in full, (with apologies for any inadequacy in my translation). These are the words of the monk Moshab as remembered by Simon.

"The story of love between man and woman is the story of a long-lived nostalgia. In its utmost depths, in its very root, the human being clothed in flesh is both male and female. This root is the spirit, and the spirit, which animates each one of us, was created androgynous in the image of the Nameless One.

Our separation from the Nameless One, our distancing, has shattered the unity we once enjoyed and dissolved the original marriage. In the beginning, each spirit gave birth to two souls; two souls destined to sail across the worlds, over the lands, one clothed by the moon, the other by the sun. That is why each moon seeks its sun, and why each sun weeps for a moon the ideal image of which it keeps locked in the depths of its heart. Human love, in its attempt to recreate that unique vessel of the spirit, is beautiful, so beautiful. You must appreciate, however, that this love is only a recollection; that it is nothing other than nostalgia for another Love so much more beautiful. A love whose radiance is so immeasurable that not one of us can even begin to conceive of its true nature.

The man and woman who seek one another are like the right and left eyes of the same face. They need to learn to look in exactly the same direction, without either one of them taking precedence over the other. Ultimately, they are called to fuse into a single eye; then will they be the One Lamp shining on the brow of the enlightened being, of him who has remembered, has recognised . . .

Throughout the vast expanse of different worlds, my brothers, there are myriads of souls travelling together. Souls who meet with each other over and over throughout the ages. These we call 'companion soulmates'. They make up large families journeying through time in order to learn who they are, sometimes loving one another, sometimes tearing one another apart. These must not be confused with twin souls. Twin souls only find each other again when their heart and their consciousness have achieved the great awakening. They are the same being twice over, and their union seals the end of the pact which they needed to make with the world of flesh. Such marriages are the ultimate transmutation from which the True Person can prepare to be born."

This piece of writing shows, as do the books of Joan Grant (particularly *Eyes of Horus*[9]), that, far from being a "new discovery", the information that is now available on the subject of twin souls is simply a return to knowledge that was held by such great peoples as the Ancient Egyptians and the Essenes. Its return has, however, been gradual. Violet Mary Penry-Evans (née Firth), the Freudian psycho-analyst and esotericist who wrote in the twenties and thirties under the pseudonym of Dion Fortune, had much understanding of spiritual relationships, and her book *The Esoteric Philosophy of Love and Marriage*[10] has been reprinted fairly recently by Aquarian Press ("because there is still much of value in them and because they can act as valuable pointers to seekers", despite the fact that "since then a great deal more has been understood and realised so that many of the ideas then expressed are not now necessarily acceptable").

The above book deals briefly with twin souls and partially recognises the nature of the spiritual link between them. The author says, "Such people may even fancy that they are not two separate entities, but the halves of a single whole. The close sympathy and perfect rapport between two such minds causes every mood to find its reflection in the other, so that the grief of one will plunge both in sorrow, and joy rejoice them equally." Fortune believes, however, that this unity is achieved only through a succession of shared lives (i.e. what we would now call "companion soulmates"), for she also says that "Esoteric science does not teach that souls are created as twins, but that such unions are built in the course of many incarnations."

Despite the fact that it is slightly outdated, Dion Fortune's book on marriage is very well worth reading for its insight into the spiritual ideals for which we need to aim and its guidance on how to set about it. Chapters Five and Six explain the seven planes of existence and how they are each contained within us, while Chapters Eighteen and Nineteen discuss the ties between souls and the choosing of a mate, pointing out that for a union to be "perfect" the links need to be made on all seven levels. She said that such unions were rare – as indeed they still are. (Though this point has no great relevance to our subject, it is interesting to note that Violet Firth – who lived from 1890 till 1946 – did not follow Freud a hundred per cent, since she found that his philosophy did not explain everything, and certainly not her own psychism.)

In my own research I have experienced a certain reticence on the part of psychics over the question of twin souls. (When Edgar Cayce was asked *"Does a soul have one other special soul it is meant to be with whenever possible?"*, the answer which came through was *"This it shall learn for itself."*) The reason for this, I have come to realise, is that it is very rightly felt that many of us too easily get "hung up" on the search for our twin soul, when, more often than not, that is not what this particular lifetime was supposed to be about. In actual fact, since the spiritual connection between twin souls is so close, whether or not they are physically together in any particular lifetime is a complete irrelevance. The work that we do on the spiritual level is of even greater importance than that which we do on the physical level. The more evolved we are, the more work we do out of our bodies; and when we are at a high level of evolution, not only do we meet up with our twin soul when out of our body at night in order to do important work together, we also practise fusing with them at those times in preparation for our ultimate joint return to spirit.

Lilla Bek, who is well known as a counsellor as well as an author and lecturer, says that she receives countless numbers of letters from people who are seeking their *soul partner*, but none at all from people who are seeking their *spirit partner*. Her thesis is that, if we concentrate on perfecting ourselves and helping others with the aim of hastening everyone's return to the world of spirit, our soul partner will be working with us anyway, whether we are aware of it or not, and in any case, the more evolved we become, the higher we will go, and at the highest levels *we all merge into one fire*.

This latter phrase comes from Lilla's reply to a letter addressed to her as *Grandma Elder* in the *Agony Aunt's* column of the magazine *Caduceus*[11]. The writer's question is a simple one: *"People talk about twin souls. Does this phenomenon really exist?"*, yet had I not already been conversant with Lilla's

15

view on the subject, I might have been hard put to deduce it from the reply she has given. The reason for her lack of straightforwardness is, however, clear. She says: *Most of the time we are longing for some uplift. Often it is psychological – we need something that the other person has . . . We would miss out if we spent all the time looking for our twin soul . . .*

Lilla's reply to the *Caduceus* reader's question is also very good because it makes clear Dion Fortune's point mentioned above: the fact that a true meeting at soul level is rare on earth. This is because, as she says, *Not everybody manifests their soul. Your soul cannot rule your life or your body unless you are very evolved.* And when people are that evolved, firstly they can stand on their own without needing to be constantly with their twin soul (as *The Prophet*[12] says of Marriage . . .

And stand together yet not too near together,
For the pillars of the temple stand apart,
And the oak tree and the cypress grow not in each other's shadow)

and secondly, they become, as Lilla says more collective, i.e. more full of love for <u>everybody</u> and more ready to *merge with the Ultimate in completion of Self.*

I also have personal experience of this reticence on the part of psychics. When I had only recently become convinced of the fact of reincarnation and was eager to begin an exploration of my own karma, I asked in a request for a past-life reading whether I was acquainted with my twin soul. The psychic whom I had approached completely ignored that question, but included in the list of purposes of my present incarnation firstly the fact that I had come as a writer, and secondly that my first priority should be the care of my husband (a companion soulmate!) and our three children. He did, however, since it had some bearing on my present incarnation, tell me about a lifetime in which the man who I have subsequently been able to identify as my twin soul had been in love with me and I with him, mentioning him by his present name!

A question which is of course fundamental to those seeking, or objectively interested in, the "perfect unions" such as the soul unions mentioned by Dion Fortune and Lilla Bek, is how twin souls can be identified. Lilla's answer to this is "instinct", but for those of us without her psychic powers the matter is much less simple! Edwin Courtenay, another well-known clairvoyant, says that the auras of twin souls are very similar, and that when they are seated side by side these merge and become virtually indistinguishable. Vicky Wall, the founder of the fast-spreading new therapy *Aura Soma*, had auric sight even after she had gone blind, and in her fascinating autobiography, *The Miracle of Colour Healing*[13], she mentions her own observation of this fusion of the auras of what she describes as "true soulmates". Another method of identifying twin souls is discussed by Jess Stearn, and that is astrology. Rather than going into this here myself, I would refer readers to Chapter Fourteen of *Soulmates*[2]. Still other pointers – available to the "ordinary person" – will be discussed in my concluding chapter.

Although Jess Stearn emphasises the fact that in order to meet a soulmate one should work on oneself rather than simply going out looking (and his book mentions classes on "Finding a Soulmate" which teach this too), the tenor of his and other books on the subject is to some extent "finding the perfect partner in order to live happily ever after". There is of course no doubt that this is what most of us dream of, but one of the aims of this book is to show firstly that finding one's twin soul does not necessarily entail "happiness ever after", and secondly that we all, as part of our learning experience, have to go through lives which are by no means predominantly blissful ones.

For the important thing to remember is that we are all human, we have all come a long way from the "perfect spirits" that God originally created; otherwise we would not still need to be here. In Moshab's explanation of twin souls quoted above, he says that each sun keeps the *ideal image* of its moon locked up in the depths of its heart. And from what does this "ideal image" come? It is the subconscious memory of its "other half", stored away from the time when the two souls were first created, aeons and aeons ago. During those aeons, as we well know, we have all strayed a long way from the ideal.

So, when twin souls meet and recognise one another on the Earth's plane (which they normally, though not invariably, do more or less at first sight or fairly soon after), the memory that is first triggered off is of the ideal, but of course the person frequently falls far short of that ideal. Hence, as will be seen in our ensuing pages, the cause of much heartache, pain, and even infidelity or ill treatment.

Chet Snow, another American hypnotherapist who has written on the subject of regression, and also "progression"[14] (i.e. into future lives), shows an awareness of the fundamentally spiritual nature of twin souls. In one of his progressions into a future life induced by Helen Wambach (the initiator of this practice) he finds himself married to "Louise", whom he had already identified as his twin soul from a regression, but he is puzzled by an awareness of being filled with tremendous love for what are apparently two "twin souls". He then realises that the second person with whom he feels this strong bond of love is actually Christ, who is, as it were, the "twin soul" of everyone on our planet, and for whose return to Earth Chet had been (in this future life) instrumental in preparing.

Jesus said (Matthew 19:9): "Now I say this to you: the man who divorces his wife – I am not speaking of fornication – and marries another, is guilty of adultery." Sticking to the same partner for life seems to be rather unfashionable these days (perhaps particularly in New Age circles!), but I personally go along with Edgar Cayce's view that it is better to do so except in extreme circumstances of incompatibility, or where there is abuse, when staying in a relationship prevents growth. For, if one moves from relationship to relationship, what almost invariably happens? Firstly there is pain, and when we have been responsible for causing pain this only gives us yet another karmic debt to have to come back for. And secondly, when there are children involved, to the pain is added emotional insecurity, which, as research has shown, often leads later to further broken marriages.

So many of us seek relationships in order to fill a void or because of a lack of independence. Yet, whether they are twin souls or not, such partnerships of co-dependence are never the most satisfactory. The spirit being Ramtha, speaking through J. Z. Burnett, says, *The soulmate is a mirror, and the mirror reflects itself perfectly. The neurotic reaches out for the neurotic, the negative for the negative and so forth. That is why marriages fail. They have not prepared themselves. Looking for their counterpart, they find it . . . Love thyself, for in so loving you find all that you love as well.* And a woman who had found her twin soul, whom Jess Stearn met in a class on Soulmates, said, *"If I had met this person ten years ago, I wouldn't have been ready. I had some growing by myself to do first."*[2]

This same woman understood too the requirements for a good relationship between twin souls, for she also said, *"It's a matter of loving unconditionally. You have to cast out your doubts, your fears of being hurt, you have to let yourself go. In spite of the things that sometimes drive you up the wall. As I see it, you are one but for some reason, from the past, you had to separate and do things apart, so you could appreciate each other more when you came together again."*[2] Does not *The Prophet*[12] also say of Sorrow and Joy, *The deeper that Sorrow carves into your being, the more joy you can contain?*

All of us in our many lives have experienced both great sorrow and intense joy at the hands of (or in the arms of!) our twin soul. My own story has been told in my first book, *A Memory Stirred*[15]. For this present book I owe immense gratitude to all those who have so willingly shared their stories with me. (In order to preserve anonymity where it was desired, I have disguised the characters concerned as well as not using their names, but in each case they have vetted what I wrote for accuracy of the essence of their story.) The stories vary greatly in length for the simple reason that people vary greatly. Some had more to tell me than others; others wanted to tell me more.

There are many aspects to this complex question. Although I have headed each chapter with one particular aspect in order to try to outline them all, there is of course much overlap, i.e. each couple's story could very likely have been placed under more than one heading.

Psychics tell us that, with the dawning of the New Age, more and more twin souls will be coming together. This is because twin souls working together are a stronger force for good, and also because, as has already been stated, fusion before returning to spirit is our ultimate aim. We need all, therefore, to be preparing ourselves for this. I hope that this book will make clear that the best way in which to prepare ourselves is not through searching to the ends of the

Earth for our twin soul, but rather through endeavouring to find out what was our purpose for this particular lifetime, fulfilling that purpose to the best of our ability, and (to use the words of John Walsh of the Edgar Cayce Centre) "changing the consciousness of the cells of our bodies into a God consciousness; by doing this we raise our vibrations, and this process helps us to help all other souls in creation to get back to God: our source".

Notes

1. *Twin Souls – A Guide to finding your True Spiritual Partner* by Patricia Joudry and Maurie D. Pressman, M.D., published by Element Books, Shaftesbury, Dorset.
2. *Soul Mates* by Jess Stearn, published by Bantam.
3. *You Were Born Again to be Together* by Dick Sutphen, published by Pocket Books.
4. *The Sleeping Prophet* by Jess Stearn, published by Bantam.
5. *A Seer Out of Season* by Harmon Bro, published both by Signet and by Thorsons.
6. *Tales of an Astral Traveller* by Anne and Daniel Meurois-Givaudan, to be published in America by "Vent d'Ouest". Original *(Récits d'un Voyageur de l'Astral)* published by Editions Amrita.
7. This has been published by Destiny Books as *The Way of the Essenes – Christ's Hidden Life Remembered*.
8. This has not yet been translated into English, but the authors have given me permission to do so. I am at present seeking a partner for this difficult task prior to seeking a publisher.
9. All Joan Grant's books are published by Ariel Press.
10. *The Esoteric Philosophy of Love and Marriage* by Dion Fortune, published by Aquarian Press 1988.
11. *Caduceus* issue number 28.
12. *The Prophet* by Kahlil Gibran, published by Mandarin.
13. *The Miracle of Colour Healing* by Vicky Wall, published by Aquarian Press.
14. *Mass Dreams of the Future* by Chet Snow, published by Deep Forest Press, U.S.A.
15. *A Memory Stirred – One Person's Spiritual Journey: A Universal Message* by Judith Merville. At present being considered by Regency Press.

Chapter I

TWIN SOULS IN HISTORY

There must be innumerable stories of famous people who have had, throughout the ages, good or bad relationships with their twin souls. Those mentioned by Patricia Joudry and Maurie D. Pressman in their book[1] all had excellent relationships, and my only reason for adding to their list is that I believe the subject to hold much interest and relevance to people in difficulties over the question today. I shall list my own examples in chronological order.

EL MORYA AND LADY MIRIAM

I can claim no expertise on the subject of the Ascended Masters and so, for the benefit of the uninitiated, I will simply explain that they are very powerful beings who have long since "made it" back to spirit and now have positions as teachers to the rest of us who are still caught up in *samsara* (the "wheel of karma"), and I would also refer readers to Edwin Courtenay's book *The Ascended Master Book of Ritual and Ceremony,* which is due to be published in 1997 in both Germany and the USA. These Masters, having finished all their incarnations, have of course fused with their twin souls, and so their spirits each manifest the aspects of two souls (not to mention all the personalities that these two souls took on over the aeons during which they repeatedly came to Earth).

El Morya, according to Edmund Harold, the well-known Australian clairvoyant, is the father of Numerology and Astrology and *heads all schools of esoteric thought world-wide*[2]. For Edwin Courtenay he is *the Master whose job it is to enforce the will of God, and he was once both King Arthur and the famous Lancelot with whom Guinevere was unfaithful to her devoted husband.* What made this possible is a phenomenon which is described by clairvoyants such as Edwin Courtenay as "psychic twinning"[3]. Though Dr. Michael Newton, an American past-life regression therapist, speaks in his fascinating book *Journey of Souls*[4], of "parallel lives", this is not, it appears, a very common occurrence. It simply means that, in order to increase the experience, the Higher Self sometimes decides to send down, more or less simultaneously, two (or occasionally even more), as it were, "parcels of soul", which immediately join

21

up again on returning to the astral realms. It is important to appreciate that this is a very different thing from the two completely separate (twin) souls which only finally fuse when they are both ready to return to spirit.

In the lifetime in which Lady Miriam was known as Guinevere, this soul suffered the torment of being attracted to two apparently different people, who were in fact one and the same soul – both of them "the other half of her being". Her story might perhaps have been different had she been given a choice in the beginning, i.e. had she not been forced to marry Arthur. Now, however, we need have no fears for this "unhappy trio", who are all very happily united in the great personality of El Morya. (In Aura Soma the *El Morya* bottle is pale blue over pale blue, and described in Vicky Wall's book[5] as *The power behind the throne of consciousness.* Blue being the colour of the throat chakra, this bottle is useful for communication, which is perhaps one of the reasons why I personally like it so much!)

ST. GERMAIN AND LADY PORTIA
The name of St. Germain is probably better known to many than that of El Morya, since he is regarded as the Master of the New Age. (Edmund Harold, however, prefers to call him "Rakoczy", which is a name he had in an earlier incarnation. Edmund Harold does wonderful meditations using "Rakoczy's violet flame", and the St. Germain Aura Soma bottle is indeed violet over violet.) Once again, I would refer readers to Edwin Courtenay's book on the Masters. There is also, however, another channelled book – *St. Germain – Twin Souls and Soulmates*[6] – which gives some information about this Master in the lifetime during which he was St. Germain.

Another previous incarnation of St. Germain was the celebrated Merlin, and his consort, Lady Portia, was at that time Morgan le Fay. In that lifetime they were more "enemies" than "lovers", since they were on opposite sides in the battle for the Kingdom. This is a role that twin souls sometimes play for one another: providing opposition in order to fortify them in their mission.

ST. FRANCIS AND ST. CLARE
St. Francis of Assisi and St. Clare are perhaps the best known "spiritual lovers" in the whole of history! I feel that they serve as an example of the type of love for which we should all be aiming.

Some centuries before he incarnated as the personality who became one of the greatest and most popular saints of the Catholic Church, this same soul was that of the great Greek, Pythagoras. It is fascinating, when reading the lives of these two men, to note the large number of parallels between them. But that is by the way; our concern here is to note the remarkable parallels between the lives of Francis and Clare, when they both rejected the wealth of their families and founded respectively the famous order of the Franciscans and the "twin" order of the Poor Clares. These parallels were very well summed up by

22

Sister Frances Teresa in an article in the Catholic journal *The Tablet*[7], entitled *Lady of Light.*
  Their lives ran parallel in so many ways. Each of them had broken dramatically and painfully with their families. Each of them was granted an insight into the Gospel which led them, from different starting-points, to honour poverty and "minoritas", or lesser-ness, in place of power and glory. Each set out to be brother or sister to the whole world, cutting across all the divisions of society. Each of them was filled with a deep, tender love for Christ, for the Eucharist, for the poor and vulnerable.
  Clare outlived Francis by a good many years. She knew that she still had work to do on Earth but (again in the words of Sister Frances Teresa): *At every turn Francis filled her thoughts even though he was long dead. He had profoundly influenced her relationship with Christ, although she was already committed long before she met him. He taught her absolute and radical love. He fanned the flame which set her ablaze for the rest of her life, speaking to her about Jesus Christ and conversing in words she was waiting to hear. On the most profound level they had heard the same call . . . When we recall the story in which the burning love between Francis, Clare and Christ seemed to set fire to the whole wood around St. Mary of the Angels, we glimpse the power of a love rooted and founded in Christ.*
  Clearly a couple who had already reached the point described by Lilla Bek as *more collective . . . more ready to merge with the Ultimate in completion of Self.* Most Roman Catholics, however, who pray to St. Francis and St. Clare, would be very surprised to discover that their prayers were addressed to a single being! (Now generally recognised as the Ascended Master Kuthumi.)

EDGAR CAYCE AND GLADYS DAVIS TURNER
These two are perhaps not <u>so</u> different from the above, since this famous Christian prophet, too, founded his entire life on service to God and to his fellows, and in fact probably died sooner than he needed to on account of the way in which he sacrificed himself to his work. He of course, as already mentioned in our Introduction, was extremely happily married to Gertrude, a companion soulmate, but the work that the two of them were doing together (furnishing thousands of people the world over with medical or past-life readings, on top of his profession as a photographer and bringing up their family) needed the added strength of Edgar's twin soul for it finally to flourish as it did.
  Gladys was twenty odd years younger than Cayce, and took up her position as his secretary at a very early age, remaining completely devoted to the work until his death. The fact that the three of them were able to form such a strong trio, without an iota of jealousy between the two women, is indicative of their godliness. For Cayce, much though he loved his wife, was never impervious to the charms of other women, and Gladys was by all accounts a very attractive

young lady. The twin soul bond must undoubtedly have tugged at both of them from time to time, and it is worth noting that Gladys did not marry until after Cayce's death.

Another interesting point about the Cayce family is that Gertrude's twin soul was their elder son, Hugh Lynn (not Sally, Hugh Lynn's wife, as Jess Stearn suggests in his book *Soulmates*[8]). Joudry and Pressman assert – clearly erroneously – that twin souls never incarnate into the same family. It is certainly unusual for them to incarnate as parent and child, but I have heard of a couple of other instances of it, and in this one it no doubt served as an additional means of giving strength, for Hugh Lynn did an immense amount to perpetuate his father's work after his death.

One of Cayce's many prophecies was that he himself would return in 1998. It will be interesting for any of us who are around when he gets old enough in his next life to see whether or not he marries Gladys, but whatever this advanced soul does next time round will clearly be part of the Divine Plan for the New Age!

JOAN GRANT AND ESMOND

Joan Grant, well known for her beautiful "far memory" books written from readings of the Akashic Records made while out of her body, suffered the immense misfortune of being engaged to her twin soul, who accidentally killed himself while cleaning his shotgun! The fact that she subsequently married three times is probably indicative of the difficulty for anyone who has known their twin soul in their current incarnation in forming a completely satisfactory relationship with anyone else. (Her third marriage, however, to Denys Kelsey, was obviously very successful, and they worked together in past-life regression therapy.)

It is therefore hardly surprising that the "twin soul theme" is strong in Joan Grant's writing. Her first book – and the one which is commonly regarded as her masterpiece – was *Winged Pharaoh*[9], but for me *Life as Carola*[9] is equally powerful. This, very brief, Italian life was one quite extraordinarily full of tragedies, of which the last was the loss of her lover, the sailor Alcestes. Though Carola does not actually say so in this book, it seems to me extremely likely that Alcestes was her twin soul. They had similar backgrounds, since both had been abandoned by their fathers and subsequently orphaned, and they both had a very great wander lust (this being the thing which in due course caused Alcestes' death). Their relationship was not an easy one, since Carola was nominally married to Alcestes' godfather, the elderly widower who had taken her under his wing after she had narrowly escaped death as a heretical nun. Carola was telepathic and knew not only the moment but also the manner of Alcestes' death, and a parallel with this can be seen in Joan Grant's most recent life, described in her autobiography *Far Memory*[9].

The twin soul theme is, however, stronger in *Eyes of Horus*[9], together with its sequel *Lord of the Horizon*[9]. Again, this book has a parallel with Joan's most recent life, for she broke off her first engagement after falling in love with

24

Esmond when out of her body at night. (It is easy to imagine her parents' reaction when she told them shortly before the wedding that she had fallen in love with a man whom she had met only in dreams!) She met Esmond in the flesh quite soon after incurring her parents' wrath for calling off her wedding, and he stared at her for a long time and then said, "It really is you. I have dreamed with you for nearly two years. Do you recognise me too?" She replied, "Of course I do", and they were engaged more or less within minutes!

As the young man, Ra-ab-Hotep, son of the Nomarch of the Oryx, Joan took rather longer to find "his" twin soul in the flesh and, though "he" never got engaged to anyone else, he told his father that he would not marry the girl he had thought of for him, who was a *stranger*, because he hoped to meet *the girl of his dreams*. Meri, who described the two of them as *two petals of the same flower*, in fact assured him when they met *on the other side of the river*, that they would in due course meet physically, and that he would recognise her even if she was fat and ugly. Ra-ab is eighteen when they finally meet (which is quite old for marriage by Ancient Egyptian standards), and Meri (who turns out to be slim and beautiful!) lives in another Nome, whose customs are much less "Christian" (for want of a better word!) than those of the Oryx. Their life as a married couple, however, is a superb example of "twin souls coming together in order to work for good". Both this book and Joan Grant's autobiography are also interesting because they show how twin soul meetings (like other important ones of course) are planned in the spirit world <u>before</u> they take place on Earth.

In *Scarlet Feather*[9], the twin soul connection is made earlier still, as Piyanah (as Joan then was) and Raki are cousins, who are suckled together after Raki's mother's death, and brought up as twins by Piyanah's mother (who had been exiled from the tribe for having committed the "unforgivable crime" of loving Piyanah's father and wanting to live with him instead of in the Squaws' teepee). When the two of them were very young, Piyanah's mother sometimes took them to sleep in the mountains when the weather was hot and, sleeping under the stars, she would tell stories about them: *how each star was a torch set in the sky by someone who had entered the land beyond the Sunset, and how the larger ones were two torches that belonged to two people who loved each other very much, so we knew there would only be one new star when Raki and I were dead.* (Note here the similarity with Moshab's definition of twin souls quoted in our Introduction!)

I love all Joan Grant's books, but *Scarlet Feather* is the most relevant of all of them to our subject. (I also have to admit to a great partiality for books which have a happy ending!) For, at least as much as Ra-ab and Meri, Piyanah and Raki are a supreme example of twin souls coming together for strength and to "bring more light into the world". Piyanah's mother dies when they are still children, and her father, Na-ka-chek, only admits to his love for her years later, after she has appeared to and spoken with him. Only then does he recognise her wisdom and, as a means of making atonement to her, he decides that Raki and Piyanah should succeed him jointly as chief, and that they should found a new

25

tribe based on love and on equality of the sexes. This is finally achieved after innumerable tribulations and trials of endurance (all of which make the most gripping reading).

I find it most interesting that *Scarlet Feather* was first published in 1945, when I doubt very much whether many people in England were discussing the subject of twin souls. Yet (unlike Dion Fortune's book written a decade or so earlier[10]), this book contains it <u>all</u>. When Piyanah is undergoing one of her endurance tests, she says, *Because of Raki I am stronger than the cold! He is my fire, my sun, my warmth; for love is stronger than cold, and separation and darkness. . . The light and heat that were part of Raki soaked into me and gave me their strength.* Then later, during their marriage ceremony, Na-ka-chek says, *Because you loved each other, you were able to love yourselves. Because you loved yourselves, you knew yourselves, and in that knowing came an echo of the Before People, who long ago drove the Sorrow Bird from the land where they lived in peace. To this love shall you pledge your oath, and each day at dawn, and at noon and at sunset, you will say, "I love us both, the male and the female: I love myself, the male and the female: and with eyes that are open to that love will I see others, the male and the female . . ." This oath shall endure after your bodies return to dust . . . Raki and Piyanah are <u>of one spirit on the other side of the water.</u>*

Nearer the end of the book Piyanah says: *I tried to explain that I was a very ordinary woman, who had no magic except that she belonged to a tribe who recognised that man and woman are the <u>right eye and the left eye,</u> the left hand and the right hand, the left foot and the right foot, <u>of a third, who is man and woman, and so greater than either.</u>* Note again, in the words that I have underlined, the similarity with Moshab's definition.

Reading Joan Grant's books, one might find it difficult not to wonder why she needed to come back again. There seems to be <u>nothing</u> that she hasn't done or experienced in her previous lives! Edmund Harold, however, is of the opinion that we are all going to have to keep coming back for another billion years – until we have transformed this planet into a "light planet" and <u>all</u> reached perfection as Ascended Masters. On the other hand, Paul, the spirit surgeon who works through Ray Brown, maintains that we can <u>always</u> have the choice of remaining in spirit in order to work out our karma, rather than returning to Earth where, he says, we only accrue yet more karma. We can but wait and see!

ELIZABETH TAYLOR AND RICHARD BURTON

My final example of a famous pair is not exactly "historical", since one of the two is still alive, but their relationship has undoubtedly already made history, and in any case a contemporary story is perhaps more within our grasp than the preceding "case histories". It was Lilla Bek who voiced to me her opinion that Elizabeth Taylor and Richard Burton were twin souls, and reading biographies of each of them[11] has certainly confirmed to me this view. In fact Melvyn Bragg, in his biography of Burton entitled *Rich*, actually says (though I don't suppose for a moment that he was aware of the full implication of his words), *Strange, in some ways unreal creatures, Burton and Taylor recognised twin souls.*

This, rather tragic, pair are to my mind the epitome of a pair of twin souls who simply could not make it together because of immaturity, lack of spiritual values and an inability to stand on their own, yet who, through all their problems with each other and numerous relationships with other people, recognised both the strength and the immortality of their mutual love. Bragg says in the Foreword to his book: *In part, these* (=Richard's Notebooks) *record the life of a man obsessed with one woman – Elizabeth Taylor. The switchback course of this obsession, its often unbearable frankness and its extraordinary passion testify to the uniqueness of a marriage which, for many years, mesmerised the public.*

It will be seen through the course of this book that twin souls often incarnate into similar circumstances and have similar experiences. Despite some very obvious differences – Richard being the penultimate son of an enormous, poor, Welsh mining family, and Elizabeth the elder child of only two in a family of higher social standing – their early lives bear many striking similarities. Among the most obvious of these are the two which must surely have been at the root of their many problems: firstly parental deprivation, and secondly excessive adulation from a very early age.

Elizabeth's deprivation took the form not of insufficient mothering, but of a surfeit of it. Her mother's ambitions as an actress were thwarted by her marriage, and she consequently transferred them totally and relentlessly to her daughter, whose beauty brought her fame from a painfully early age. Though in later life Elizabeth won Oscars on her own merits as an actress, it was initially her looks combined with her mother's pushiness that were responsible for her success. Her mother went everywhere with her, and when she was a teenager would even answer for Elizabeth when people addressed questions to her. All this, inevitably, put a great strain on the marriage, and Elizabeth's father was but a shadowy figure in her life. A rift eventually came when Elizabeth began to find her mother's possessiveness and dominance unbearable. (This rift was, however, healed many years later, when Elizabeth nearly died and called for her mother to come to the hospital. The latter maintained that it was the healing of their relationship, her prayers and her faith in Christian Science that saved Elizabeth's life.)

Richard was the twelfth of thirteen children, of whom eleven survived, and his mother died when he was only two, within days of giving birth to his younger brother. His father had a severe drink problem and, since there was no way he could cope with so many young children, Richard was immediately taken in by his eldest sister, Cecilia ("Cis"), who had recently married. Cis worked slavishly and self-sacrificingly to maintain the two households, not withholding any motherly love from Richard even after the birth of her own two daughters. Mr. Jenkins was just as much a shadow of a father to Richard as was Mr. Taylor to Elizabeth, and most of the fathering that he received was from his brother, Ivor, nineteen years his senior.

Just like Elizabeth's, Richard's extraordinary good looks brought him adulation from a very early age, but a difference between them was that Richard also very obviously had exceptional intelligence and innate talent. The family's immense poverty forced Richard to leave school and go to work, but he was "rescued" by one of his teachers, Philip Burton, who (like Elizabeth's mother) transferred his own ambitions in the field of acting to the younger person. Philip Burton went so far as to make himself Richard's legal guardian, take him to live with him and send him back to school. Richard's changing his name by deed poll from Jenkins to Burton is indicative of the strength of the bond between them. From school he went to Oxford for six months, with the intention (never to be fulfilled) of returning there after his stint in the Army. During this period at Oxford he made an instant success in acting and, like Elizabeth, his rise to fame and wealth was rapid.

While Richard had a large and lively family, as well as two former teachers and Emlyn Williams, to give him the adulation which must have done so much to boost his confidence at the start of his career, Elizabeth's world-renowned beauty made her the prize coveted by countless numbers of men, and she has remained a spoilt child, totally unable to look after herself or even to toilet train her beloved dogs. Both craved fame and wealth above all else, and both became victims of these once they had achieved them. Both were always irresistible to the opposite sex, had apparently insatiable appetites for sex, could never bear to be without a partner for a single moment, and had innumerable affairs in addition to several marriages. And their appetites, alas, were not confined to sex: both always drank to excess and, while alcohol led to Richard's downfall and he was also addicted to smoking, Elizabeth's partiality for food has given her both health and weight problems. In fact, extremely bad health is another thing that they always had in common, and both at some point had operations on their spines and consequent immense back trouble.

While Elizabeth's first marriage was very short lived, Richard was strangely faithful to his first wife, Sybil, despite frequent infidelities. Until she married Mike Todd (her fourth husband), whose death in a plane crash was an appalling shock to her, and since the dissolution of her second marriage to Richard, Elizabeth has cast off husbands and lovers more or less as she has her dresses. Richard, on the other hand, kept swearing that he would "never leave Sybil" even after his very public affair with Elizabeth had started. Being utterly devoted, and used to his "comings and goings", Sybil did not initially take the threat of Richard's affair with Elizabeth very seriously; and Richard's family all took her side and did their utmost to support Sybil and the two daughters.

Despite Elizabeth's reputation as a "wrecker of marriages" and Richard's usual lack of conscience about his infidelities, the pair were initially afflicted with the feelings of guilt that is common to twin souls who are not free when they meet and experience the "fatal attraction" that is the almost inevitable consequence of the strong link between them. Another thing that they had in common was owning homes in Switzerland and, after filming *Cleopatra* in Rome and causing worldwide scandal in the process, they made a sincere effort to return to their respective spouses. Living in the same country, however, proved too much for their willpower and, after many months of meetings and agonisings, they decided both to file for divorce. (Richard said, *I knew it would cause havoc in my private life. With my wife, and children, and brothers and sisters. But that is finally, painfully, unavoidable.*[12]) The rest of the story is so well known that it does not seem necessary for me to repeat it.

Richard's drink problem was undoubtedly the main cause of the difficulties between them (and also the cause of the dissolution of his third marriage, to Susan Hunt). To my mind, however (though Elizabeth appears latterly to have made considerable progress in this direction), it was their lack of spiritual ideals that prevented them from ever being able to act in marriage as twin souls should: in perfect unison and harmony, always putting the interests of the partner before their own. Richard, though being what many would consider quite revoltingly rich, was immensely generous (particularly to all his siblings), and of course the gifts – especially of enormous jewels – that he made to Elizabeth are famous. Yet he could not bear it if she was earning more than he was, or even if her name was put before his on the posters advertising one of their films! Nor did their habit of being unfaithful to their spouses cease even when they were married to each other.

While, as we have said, Elizabeth has had a life-long habit of casting off husbands uncaringly, she was never able to do that with Richard. When they separated, no one believed that it would be permanent. When he told her to go after a brief reunion, she said that it was only the second sad day in her life (the first having been that of the death of Mike Todd). *I don't want to be that much in love ever again. I don't want to give as much of myself. It hurts. I didn't reserve anything. I gave everything away . . . my soul, my being, everything . . . And it got bruised and hurt.*[13]

As for Richard, his fortieth birthday present to Elizabeth was a $50,000 heart-shaped diamond inscribed with a promise of everlasting love. A promise that he kept until death despite his two subsequent marriages. The phone calls from Elizabeth, frequent when he was first living with Susan Hunt, dwindled but never ceased all together; and there were subsequent films (for instance *Private Lives*) in which they co-starred. Richard's brother, David Jenkins, says in his biography, *More than once Richard told me, in the confidential small hours, "If I live to be a hundred, I'll always love that woman."* When David showed Sally, Richard's last wife, a magazine article saying that Elizabeth had been admitted to a Los Angeles clinic for treatment and drying out, she begged him not to show it to Richard, *or we shall be bloody flying out to see her.* It was only

Sally's feelings that kept Elizabeth away from Richard's funeral in Céligny (near Geneva), and she turned up at the graveside a couple of days later. His family gave her a warm welcome soon afterwards in Wales, and Sally was put out at seeing her seated amongst them at the Memorial Service in London.

Twin souls who are in alignment tend to acquire one another's talents in addition to their own, and it can probably be said that acting together enhanced each of their performance. Also, while Elizabeth, unlike Richard, was never an intellectual or a great woman of literature, under his influence she took to poetry. They were opposites in many ways – he punctilious, she slovenly and notoriously and invariably late for everything – but at the same time they shared too many flaws, and this sharing no doubt intensified them.

Of the two, Richard seems to have been the more impressive personality, tremendously loved and admired despite his faults. Elizabeth, however, cannot be blamed entirely for her selfishness and self-centredness when one considers her upbringing and her "unreal" lifestyle. Melvyn Bragg sums it up very well: *It is as easy to dismiss her as appearing spoilt, greedy, selfish and mean as it is to dismiss Burton as seeming boastful, faithless, a poseur and a drunk. Far too easy. For we must recognise that these two people were subject to seductive and ravishing opportunities, to strains beyond the comprehension of most, to temptations of the flesh, the press, the purse. They go where few could or dare to go . . .*[14]

It is so often said, however, that suffering is our greatest teacher, and – what with her *terrible illnesses, destructive addictions, broken marriages*[15], not to mention the deaths of one of her favourite husbands (Mike Todd) and other close friends – Elizabeth has undoubtedly had a very large share of suffering in this lifetime. And the result appears to have been quite a big step upwards in her spiritual development. For, following the death of her close friend Rock Hudson, she became a founder member of the American Foundation for Aids Research and now regularly attends AIDS benefit events worldwide, being thought to have contributed about ten million pounds to charities of this nature. In fact the article in *Catholic Life* containing the above quotation claims that she *now shuns Hollywood parties and the glittering celebrity circuit in favour of fundraising*[15]. A further article in the magazine *Hello*[16] describes her recent recovery from brain surgery and her courageous determination to win the fight for life, even postponing the operation in order to be present for her sixty-fifth birthday fundraising show for the AIDS Foundation.

Elizabeth is also one of the many people I have read about to have obviously benefited from a near-death-experience. When she had hers she met Mike Todd at the end of the celebrated tunnel, and it was he who told her that she was to carry on living. She said, *And I have lived. If the knife slips while I'm on that operating table tomorrow and I never wake up in this world again, I'll die knowing I've had an extraordinary life*[16]. People who have N-D-Es always appear to return to the world with increased faith, and Elizabeth says, *The power of love is a gift from God . . . It's so easy to forget that life is a gift from God.*[16]

Had Elizabeth and Richard been ready for each other when they were married in the ways that I am attempting to describe in this book, they could certainly have "made" one another this time round. As it is, she has gone on learning her necessary lessons since their final separation and his death, and this will obviously be of benefit to them both for a future lifetime. So I wish them joy in their next lifetime together – a joy which they will find easier to obtain if their efforts then are directed more towards helping others than to achieving fame and wealth for themselves!

Notes

1. *Twin Souls – A Guide to Finding your True Spiritual Partner* by Patricia Joudry and Maurie D. Pressman, M.D., published by Element Books, Shaftesbury, Dorset.
2. See *Master your Vibration* by Edmund Harold, published by Grail Publications, Australia.
3. Edwin Courtenay himself at present shares a house with the two men who he believes to be his "psychic twins", and the three of them find themselves to be a strong power base for one another.
4. *Journey of Souls* by Michael Newton, M.D., published by Llewellyn, USA.
5. *The Miracle of Colour Healing* by Vicky Wall, published by Aquarian Press.
6. *St. Germain: Twin Souls and Soulmates* channelled through Azena Ramanda and Claire Heartsong, published by Triad.
7. *The Tablet* of 13 August 1994.
8. *Soulmates* by Jess Stearn, published by Bantam.
9. All Joan Grant's books are published by Ariel Press.
10. *The Esoteric Philosophy of Love and Marriage* by Dion Fortune, published by Aquarian Press.
11. *Rich* by Melvyn Bragg, published by Hodder and Stoughton; *Richard Burton – A Brother Remembered* by David Jenkins, published by Century; and *Elizabeth Taylor – The Last Star* by Kitty Kelley, published by Michael Joseph.
12. *Rich* by Melvyn Bragg.
13. *Elizabeth Taylor – The Last Star* by Kitty Kelley.
14. *Rich* by Melvyn Bragg.
15. *Catholic Life* March/April 1997.
16. *Hello,* 22 March 1997.

Chapter II

TWIN SOULS TEACH ONE ANOTHER LESSONS
The story of Angela and Bruce

"It was like a nightmare," Angela said. "I couldn't believe it was really happening. It was just like a nightmare, and I knew one always woke up from nightmares; but this time I was awake all the time and so there was nothing to wake up from. It wasn't till the Monday morning, after I'd got home again, that the truth really dawned. Then, when I was doing my meditation, the tears suddenly started streaming uncontrollably as I realised that it really had happened; that Bruce and I had been at the same conference for a whole weekend and not even said 'Hullo' to one another. The pain was quite unlike anything I had previously experienced, and I wondered what I had done to deserve it. But then I remembered a horrendous Elizabethan lifetime I had discovered through hypnotic regression and, although I knew that I myself had already paid that particular karmic debt, I had been told that Bruce had not yet fully recovered from it. So that was sufficient explanation for the behaviour which seemed so out of character for him, and I also reflected that I had been let off extremely lightly."

Angela, who is a strong character and a mature soul who has had a very large number of lifetimes, chose quite a difficult incarnation this time round, but she realises now that the purpose of it was to take her into the career of a healer. The painful childhood she endured on account of being made by her father to feel that she was "no good" did not completely stifle her innate desire to help people, and, following some initial difficulties in finding a career, she became a social worker at a comparatively early age. It was not, however, until she was in her fifties that she discovered her true vocation, and before that she had to work through quite a number of emotional problems.

Angela fell in love with Bruce, her twin soul and a teacher of social workers, when she was in her forties. Since they are both practising Christians and he had for long been married, she never for a moment entertained the hope that he would leave his wife for her, but she did realise from the first instant they met that he was somebody totally unique and important for her. In their beautiful book about twin souls[1], Joudry and Pressman make two points which are very relevant here. I quote:–

A man in a distinguished position, married, and with a family could understandably be thrown into turmoil when suddenly confronted with the other half of his soul. In such a case there may be refusal to acknowledge the twinship. Yet souls come together at the choosing of destiny. They meet at the exact point in their evolution when the polarities must unite.

This is exactly what happened in this case, and Bruce's natural refusal to acknowledge even the attraction, let alone the twinship, caused Angela immense and inevitable pain. She accepted it, however, not only because of her Christian faith, but also because of her acknowledgement of the fact that no upright man will abandon his family responsibilities for another love, even that for a twin. To quote Joudry and Pressman again:–

In this case the partner will feel compelled <u>all the more</u> to honour the needs of those to whom he or she is committed. This is the real meaning of honour, conforming to karmic law as our conscious dictates. When we hear of a man or a woman walking out on dependants because the twin soul has appeared, <u>we can be fairly sure the twinsoulship was false.</u> (My underlinings.)

Joudry and Pressman make another point which is particularly relevant to Angela: that the reason why knowledge of twinsoulship is only now coming to the surface is that, as mentioned in the Introduction, previously we were not ready for it. As Moshab says in his definition quoted in our Introduction, it is only when we have perfected ourselves that we can be ready for fusion with our twin, and this general readiness is an important part of the dawning of the New Age. Before all the comings together on Earth and the fusions in spirit can take place, however, there clearly has to be a raising of awareness of the fact that we each have a twin – a "perfect partner" with whom, and only with whom, we can be totally happy – and Angela is one of those people who was born with this awareness even though she and Bruce were not destined to be together this time round. Their meeting, and being attracted to one another, comparatively late in life, happened at the exact point (Joudry and Pressman's *choosing of destiny*) when each of their <u>souls</u> was ready to make the connection. Angela explains: "I was fat and ugly when I was younger, and so, if we'd met before he got married, he wouldn't have noticed me; and, although I would certainly have found him attractive, I would have been much too nervous to have been able to address a single word to him!"

One of the features I have discovered in my research into twin souls is that they frequently incarnate into similar circumstances, and this was certainly the case with Angela and Bruce. She was the eldest of a large family, while he just had two younger sisters, but they both felt that they had to shoulder quite a lot of responsibility as the first born. Angela's father was a surgeon, Bruce's a teacher, both were Cambridge graduates and both gave education a high priority, sending their sons to church boarding schools and their daughters also to private schools. Their respective childhoods were often filled with periods of great loneliness, caused by feeling alone mentally.

While Bruce felt fairly distant from his mother, who was quite hard on him, though she expected great things of him (especially since he displayed an excellent brain from a very early age), he had a good relationship with his father, whom he admired. Angela on the other hand had rather more difficulty at home, as her father was a tyrant and her mother, much though she loved all her children, was unable to defend them from him. Angela suffered particularly as a girl, since her father despised women and, as we have said, he did an excellent job of making her believe herself to be no good at all.

Angela consequently grew up thinking initially not of a career but only of matrimony. Though her father had brainwashed her into believing herself to be unattractive, she dreamed constantly of her "Mr. Right" who would see through her plain features to the loving, kindly soul within and bring her "happiness ever after" as well as several children who would be loved as she and her brothers and sisters had never been loved. Though she considered herself a good Christian and listened regularly in church to the biblical passage about there being no marriage in Heaven, she could never remove from her mind the deep conviction that for her there was – somewhere in the world – just one man who was meant for her, whom she could really love with her whole heart and soul and that, having found him, they would continue to love one another for all eternity.

When Angela went to bed at night she would escape from her father's cruelty into daydreams about her "Mr. Right", and by the time she was about sixteen and getting ready to leave school, she had formed a very clear picture of him in her mind. She says: "He was tall, not particularly good looking, but with a kindly face which revealed his gentle nature, very gentlemanly in manner, sensitive and considerate. He would be extremely intelligent, yet not mind that I was stupid, and he would also have a wonderful sense of humour. His profession was not totally clear to me, though I knew I'd prefer it if he were an academic, but he had unquestionably to be an Oxford graduate. I'd been to Oxford many times with my family, and one of my greatest yearnings was to get there myself, but I knew there was no hope of that. The only other vital requirements I had for my Mr. Right were firstly that he would share my taste in music, and secondly that he would also be a Methodist." It was over thirty years later that Angela was to discover that the picture she had drawn in her imagination was actually dictated by her subconscious acquaintanceship with and knowledge of Bruce! This, however, is less surprising when one realises that we often meet with our twin soul at night, when we are out of our bodies (frequently, when we are sufficiently evolved, doing important work together).

The subconscious memory which has been influencing Angela most in her current incarnation is of a lifetime when they were wife and husband in England in the Middle Ages. This was not a particularly significant lifetime in historical terms, as they were simple peasants, but it is important in Angela's subconscious for the memory she carries from it of an exceedingly happy marriage. Bruce had a small piece of land, which he farmed in order to support his family, and the two of them were deeply in love and completely devoted to one another from the day they first met in the prime of their youth. This strong bond of love enabled them to surmount the immense difficulty of caring for a large family on extremely slender means. For they were very fertile and – as was so often the case in that period of history – Angela would get pregnant again as soon as one baby was weaned.

Bruce was the most wonderful father as well as a very devoted husband and, during the few hours of the week that he found time to rest from his labours, the children would badger him endlessly to play games with them. He never complained, however, as he loved them so dearly and this was his only form of relaxation, and he would simply go to bed when they grew weary, fitting in as much sleep as he could before having to get up again. Angela worried about Bruce having to work so hard outside the house, while he worried about her having to work so hard inside it, but they both felt that their joy in one another's company mattered more to them than their many hardships.

Despite their long hours of work, they never missed Mass on Sundays, and they all prayed together daily as a family. As the children grew, Bruce taught the boys to grow and tend crops, while Angela taught the girls to cook and other "womanly" chores, and gradually the couple became able to delegate some of their responsibilities. In their old age Angela and Bruce were well cared for by their children and were also able to find much joy and take immense pride in their many grandchildren. Their Christian faith remained strong until they died (only a few months apart, as is so often the case with twin souls), and they were both confident of being reunited immediately in Heaven.

Bruce, however, is unfortunately more influenced in his current incarnation by the lifetime a few centuries later (mentioned in our first paragraph), during the Elizabethan era, when the two of them were married again in exceedingly different circumstances. This time Angela was once more the woman and Bruce the man, but neither was at all spiritual and Angela was an extremely unpleasant person. They were married not from love but because their parents had arranged it. She was a member of an exceedingly well-to-do family, while his was much less well off, and consequently Bruce and his parents felt that they had been very fortunate in achieving such a match. As the years went by, however, he considered himself less and less fortunate, as not only was Angela very domineering, she also looked down on him on account of his lowlier status and never allowed him to forget it.

Being at that time not at all religious, and suffering so much from being married to such an unpleasant woman, Bruce not unnaturally had a series of affairs with other women. He managed to do this for several years without Angela finding out, but suddenly one day word came to her ears about his carryings on with a certain noblewoman. Angela had already been harbouring suspicions about him having had a relationship with one of their own servant girls, but had tried to dismiss the notion as her imagination. For, although theirs had not been a love match, nothing can ever weaken the bond between twin souls and, despite all that he suffered at her hands, Bruce totally accepted Angela's attitude that he was her personal property and, although she looked down on him and was overbearing or even cruel to him, she too could not help feeling his sexual attraction very strongly. So the thought of his spending even a moment in the arms of another woman was completely intolerable to her.

The story of Bruce's affair with the noblewoman seemed, however, to be incontrovertible, and he returned home shortly after the news of it had reached Angela. She waited until he was seated at the dinner table and then stood over him accusingly. Being taken so unawares and always in awe of his wife, Bruce was too terrified to attempt a denial, and in any case he was basically an honest man at heart. His admittance filled her with uncontrollable fury and she promptly questioned him fiercely about the servant girl. Again Bruce's honesty prevailed, and Angela became so beside herself with rage that she seized the carving knife and plunged it straight into the back of his neck. To her horror, and that of the servants present, he died instantly, but she, having great presence of mind when it was a question of saving her own skin, saw an obvious culprit in the servant girl whom Bruce had just admitted to having previously taken as his mistress.

Angela's money gave her a power that nothing else can give and, since the only witnesses of her act were the household servants, she threatened them all with a similar fate if they betrayed her. The poor jilted servant girl was, as we have just said, an obvious scapegoat, and Angela promptly fabricated a very convincing story about the girl's jealousy on hearing of Bruce's affair with the noblewoman. For the rest of that lifetime Angela mourned her twin soul's loss not as a lover mourns her beloved, but as a miser mourns the loss of his most treasured possession, and she carried the bitterness of hatred with her to the grave. For is not hatred always intricately bound up with love until the latter has been purified?

Part of the karma from this lifetime was worked out a century or so later, when Angela and Bruce both took on masculine incarnations in Italy, and both became priests who went out as missionaries to America at the time of the Pilgrim Fathers. This time Bruce was some years Angela's senior, and he was also his superior. While Angela felt the twin soul bond very strongly, was completely devoted to Bruce and carried out all his orders scrupulously, he felt rather less affection and treated his twin soul very much as his inferior.

Angela and Bruce have probably not been incarnate together since that period in history, but in their present lifetime she is quite sure that she incarnated with a determination to find Bruce after what she felt to be too long a separation, whether or not they would be able to marry. He incarnated about six years before her, and for him this time round the spiritual path was uppermost and marriage was to be of secondary importance. Whereas she, as we have said, has now paid the karmic debt of the terrible murder she committed and cleared that memory from her conscience, he has – perhaps hardly surprisingly! – not yet recovered from it subconsciously, and consequently has a very natural fear of affairs of the heart. This fear made him choose a mother whose nature was such that it would be impossible for him to be close to her and, as all psychologists will tell one, this inevitably governed his later relationships with women. The feminine side of his own character is, however, very well developed, which makes him show much caring towards the many women he encounters during the course of his work, and is one of the characteristics which most attracted Angela to him.

Bruce married quite late and, like Angela, he took some time to find out what was the right career for him, changing from a first degree in Science to a second one in Theology, and then subsequently training in Sociology and Criminology. Thanks to his academic prowess, he soon got a job at a London college teaching social workers. His wife, whom we shall refer to as "Briony", is a primary school teacher and they have two daughters. They are both Methodists and, though she is by no means passionately in love with Bruce, she has always performed the duties of wife and mother to perfection, and before he first met Angela, he had managed to convince both himself and those around him that his life was all that could be desired. Briony returned to her own career as soon as their daughters were old enough and, though she had a certain amount of appreciation of the importance of her husband's work, she took no real interest in it, and to a certain extent their lives became very separate. This suited Bruce, who became more and more engrossed in his work, which quite often took him away from London, and he enjoyed the security of knowing that there would always be a meal ready for him when he came home late and tired.

During the years in which Bruce was successfully settling into his career and family life, Angela tried a number of different jobs while waiting for her "Mr. Right" to come along and rescue her into matrimony and from the need to earn her own living. Eventually she gave up hope of this and, wanting to do something worth while with her life, she qualified as a social worker and then got a job in Manchester. She did not have Bruce's academic abilities, but, finally out of range of her father's criticism, she found nevertheless that she had talents she had never dreamt of on the practical level.

To the outside world, therefore, Angela (like Bruce) presented a façade of total contentment. Deep down, however, though she loved her work and felt a profound desire to be helping those less fortunate than herself, she was far from being really happy. She says, "I'd always suffered very badly from PMT, and often I was still filled with self-hatred and yearning for the Mr. Right who I imagined would solve all my problems. So it wasn't surprising that, when a member of my church congregation who was undergoing marital difficulties started paying me attention, I promptly fell in love with him. The relationship was doomed to failure from the start, as 'Julian' would never have had the guts to leave his wife, although the marriage was so disastrous, but I was so hungry

37

for love that, although my Christianity gave me guilty feelings about divorce, I clung for two years to the thread of hope that Julian gave me."

During the course of the next two years they met fairly infrequently on account of Julian's fear of being found out. Then Angela went away for a summer holiday and on her return found a letter awaiting her in which Julian said he had got a job abroad. He said that he'd realised that his wife would never let him go and, since he knew Angela would never be happy with less than marriage and her own family, he had decided it was better that they did not meet again. "I was completely devastated. Though Julian in no way resembled the ideal man I'd created in my imagination, he was good looking and charming and his attentions had made me for the first time believe in my attractiveness as a woman. Now when I looked at myself in the mirror I could again only see the plain girl that my father had thought 'good for nothing'.

Then I thought back to my university days at home in Reading, when I was very unhappy living at home and the person who helped me the most through my emotional difficulties was the University Methodist chaplain. He tried to convince me that getting a boyfriend was not the answer, and that I needed to learn to love myself. I believed that to be impossible, however, and, although I took seriously what he said about God's love for me, I felt that I would only ever be able to feel the reality of it when it was shown to me through a human being (a male human being of course!). So I tried very hard again to think about God's love for me, but the fact of Julian having let me down made God seem more remote than ever. I prayed hard for another man to enter my life, but nothing happened until my boss suggested that I attend the annual national conference on Criminology.

Bruce had been one of the prime instigators of this event a few years previously and, though he was not one of the speakers on that particular occasion, he was the chief organiser, and so several times through the weekend he rose to make some announcement. As soon as I set eyes on him I <u>knew</u> that he was the Mr. Right of my imagination. By this time I'd <u>completely</u> given up any thought of matrimony, and in any case once when Bruce stood up I was near enough to notice that he wore a wedding ring. It was during a meal time, and the person I was sitting next to happened to mention that she and Bruce had been to Oxford together! That clinched it, and at the very next meal he came and sat down next to me. I felt my heart throb in a way I'd never felt before. Although Julian had cast a sort of spell over me, I'd never regarded him as <u>objectively</u> attractive, but Bruce was by miles the most attractive man I'd ever set eyes on. I felt stupid, nervous and tongue-tied, and didn't even expect him to notice me, as a newcomer, when the table was full of his old friends and acquaintances, but he brought me into the conversation in the most gentlemanly manner imaginable, and I felt that he was speaking to me almost as an old friend, certainly as someone who he knew would see eye to eye with him on everything. The thing that struck me most was that he was treating me with the utmost respect <u>as a woman</u> and suddenly, for the first time in my life, I found myself almost wanting to shout aloud, 'It's good to be me! I like being me!' During that lunchtime conversation I discovered too that Bruce was a keen Methodist, <u>and</u> that his favourite pastimes were listening to music and singing in the church choir!"

This first meeting is significant, as it will be seen throughout the course of this book that one of the feelings most frequently experienced by twin souls is that of "instant recognition". In cases of people who are already conversant with the concept of reincarnation, the recognition will tend to take the form of a realisation of having known the person before. Angela, however, with her strictly Christian upbringing, did not at this point believe that we have more than one life, and so for her the "recognition" simply took the form of an overwhelmingly strong feeling of attraction. She says that she has no way of knowing what <u>he</u> experienced then, but it is unlikely that he would not also have felt some attraction, even if it was less strong.

Angela did not talk to Bruce again that weekend, but on the last evening he stood up and made an announcement about a day of lectures and workshops that he was organising in London a few months later. She made a mental note of the date, thinking that she could combine it with a visit to her widowed mother in Reading. Once back at work, Angela's thoughts turned rarely to Bruce, but the weekend had given her a renewed enthusiasm for her work and increased her sense of her own worth and her self-confidence. For such is often the purpose of meetings between twin souls.

Angela looked forward to the day school a few months later, for reasons none other than work ones, but she says: "On my arrival, almost the first person I saw was Bruce, who gave me a warm smile of recognition, and I was again gob-smacked by his attractiveness. In the morning there were a couple of excellent talks by leading criminologists, and in the afternoon the participants were divided into two groups for workshops. Over lunch I chatted to various, very friendly people, and all together I felt in my element. When it was time for the workshops, I felt slightly overawed at finding myself put into the one led by Bruce, thinking that I'd be scared to open my mouth in case I made a fool of myself, but he put me completely at my ease from the moment of the introductions, and as the time went on I found myself able to contribute to the discussion with a certain amount of confidence, and the appreciative manner in which Bruce listened to my comments did even more to make me feel valued. I had to leave five minutes early in order to be sure of catching my train for Reading, and as I left the room I was very conscious of Bruce's eyes following me.

During the next three days I was kept quite busy doing things for my sick mother, but the memory of the day, which had also taught me a lot that was useful for my work, together with strong thoughts of Bruce, gave me a pleasant, warm feeling I'd never had before. Because I knew that we had the same ideals and were, in a sense, working together even though it was at a distance." This, again, is quite normal: Joudry and Pressman say in their beautiful book on the subject that twin souls *will have in common a faith in life, in the goodness behind all things; for if they did not believe in the supremacy of goodness, they would not be ready for the great good of each other* . . . And also, *Our experiences have shown that twin souls, more often than not, will be engaged in complementary aspects of the same work.*

When, the following year, the time came for the next annual conference of Criminologists, it was taken for granted that Angela would again represent her office. She says, "I really looked forward to it and, on the way there, it crossed my mind that I'd probably see Bruce again. Sure enough, on the Friday evening, he came and sat down right next to me at the dinner table. To my horror I realised that my face had immediately turned lobster colour! I felt so embarrassed that I didn't know what to do or say, and so I made some inane comment to the effect that I remembered who he was but he probably wouldn't remember me from the previous conferences. He replied that I was quite right, that he didn't remember me, and then started talking defensively about his wife, turning as soon as he decently could to the person at his other side and those opposite him. It was horrible! For the rest of the meal he didn't look my way again, and I convinced myself that, having noticed my red face, he was thinking of me as a harlot. I went to bed that evening feeling incredibly miserable and didn't sleep very well at all."

By the following evening, however, Angela had completely regained her composure. "I told myself that it was quite ridiculous to allow myself to be thought of as a harlot – I didn't even feel particularly interested in sex; it was spiritual love, companionship and children that I'd always yearned for in the past – and I thought that Bruce should remember from our conversation the previous year that I was a good Methodist like him and realise that I'd never dream of trying to come between him and his wife. Anyway, I hadn't <u>done</u> ANYTHING, and it wasn't my fault that my face had changed colour. So, when the bar was open and Bruce was waiting to be served, I went boldly up to him in order to strike up a conversation. This was made slightly easier by the fact that the woman he was standing next to was someone I'd spoken to already and found friendly, so I addressed my first question to her. Then I turned to Bruce as naturally as I could and asked him what family he had. He replied coldly that he had two teenage daughters, in a way that made me feel that he thought it was none of my business, and then he bought drinks for himself and the other woman. I felt really left out and miserable, so I just bought myself a drink and soon gave up the attempt at pursuing the conversation with Bruce. Then I moved to another part of the room telling myself that I'd lost what might have been a lovely friendship on account of my foolishness, but that it didn't really matter that much since Bruce was married anyway."

Of course the reader might well remark that blushing is very natural when one is attracted to someone. With mature twin souls, however, who are coming near to the end of their incarnations, such a problem is increased when they do not live together. This is because their souls tend to practise fusing at night when they meet up for the work that they do together, and the consequent confusion caused by the subconscious yearning for fusion, and the conscious necessity to hold back, can cause "strange symptoms" such as blushing, trembling and even a feeling of sickness. It is very natural that Bruce, as a married man, should feel alarmed by Angela's physical display of feelings at what was only their third meeting, and want to detach himself from her. This should not, however, be seen as a reason for it being important for twin souls to be together physically, because, whereas twin souls who live together are sometimes lazy about fusing at night, the yearning of those who are separated on the Earth's plane actually helps spiritual fusion, and this can therefore accelerate the final return to spirit.

A few months later Angela's boss asked her to attend a special meeting in London, and when she got there she found that it was being chaired by Bruce. As the various women members arrived, Bruce embraced all those he already knew, and she could not help feeling a pang of envy. One of Bruce's colleagues, with whom she had talked quite a lot at the previous conference, asked him, "Do you know Angela?" and he replied rather sheepishly, "Yes, we have met," and then turned his head hastily the other way. Angela found she had a lot to contribute to the meeting, and so she was able to tell herself that her work was the most important thing to her and so Bruce's behaving almost as though she didn't exist didn't matter a scrap.

She imagined that to be the end of the story, but twin soul connections never work like that! The following year circumstances forced Angela to arrive a little bit late for the annual conference. On entering the hall she found that Bruce was facing her, and he gave her the most enormous smile of greeting. Once again her heart missed a beat, and at the end of the talk which had already started, he came up to her and spoke in an extremely friendly way. They spoke once or twice more during the course of that weekend, and this time after getting back to Manchester she found she could not put Bruce out of her mind.

Angela went back to Manchester marvelling that it was only a bit over three years since she and Bruce had first met, because she felt as though she had always known him (not realising, of course, at this point, that she had always known him!). Over the next few years there were occasional meetings in London in addition to the annual conference, and Angela went to them whenever she was given the chance – because she found it useful for her work and interesting, but also always with the hope of seeing Bruce again. Now he always greeted her with a kiss just the same as the other women he had known for years, and she felt that he always made very sure of kissing her "goodbye" too, even if he was leaving in a hurry. The evening when she knew for sure that she was absolutely head over heels in love with him was one Saturday in the middle of a conference, when the customary social event took the form of a barn dance. Angela was shy about dancing and nobody asked her to do so, but Bruce

41

danced enthusiastically with partner after partner. He had been sitting beside her before getting up to dance and had left his file on the chair. Returning to pick it up on his way to bed, he asked her, "Did you dance?" and when she replied negatively, he said teasingly, "You're a coward!" She murmured, "Yes . . . I am," and as she did so, he held her eyes firmly in his for a long moment, giving her a look of such tenderness and love that she says she felt as though she were in Heaven. ("A feeling such as I had never felt before, and which I had never really believed possible for me!" she comments.)

Reflecting now on the denial both of love and of the twinship, which happened later, when they had got to know one another much better, Angela says that, were he to be confronted with it, Bruce could rightly say that he had never told her that he loved her. He did, however, during those intervening years, give Angela much indication of love in ways other than words, and one of the lessons that he needs to learn at present is that giving love entails responsibility. For there is nothing more painful than being told that the love one had been shown was not real. It is even worse than the death of love (something that happens frequently when a particular piece of karma has been completed), because it completely undermines a person's sense of their own worth. Bruce, however, as we shall see, was through this particular action teaching Angela her most needed lesson.

Over the next few years life carried on in some ways much the same for Angela, her infrequent meetings with Bruce causing her always a mixture of very intense joy and pain, but in other ways this was a time for her of very great change. For menopausal headaches and the failure of conventional medicine to cure them drove her, on the advice of a friend, to a homoeopath, who led her gradually first to Yoga classes and then to the books of Louise Hay[2]. These in turn led her to a passionate interest in healing and the integration into her Christian faith of belief in reincarnation.

Her Christianity made her resist this latter belief for quite some time, but eventually, on the advice of Malcolm, her homoeopath, she went to a hypnotherapist in search of a karmic cause of her headaches. The first session was an absolute revelation to Angela. She found herself plunged straight into a lifetime many centuries previously in which she had been married to Julian, who accidentally wounded her very badly by hitting her over the head while in a temper. The whole thing was so real to Angela that she found there was no longer any way she could resist believing in reincarnation, and she also subsequently found a big improvement in her headaches. She started to read avidly on the subject of reincarnation and realised that, as her friends had predicted, it helped her Christianity rather than contradicting it, giving her at last an understanding of how God could be totally just, as well as an explanation for all the suffering in the world.

Further regression sessions with Moira revealed a number of lifetimes she had shared with Bruce, but not yet the one in which she had murdered him.

Angela consequently discussed with her the concept of twin souls, with which she had become familiar through her reading on Edgar Cayce. Moira, who is quite psychic as well as very skilled at her job, assured Angela that Bruce must be her twin soul, and she says, "I was so excited I could hardly contain myself! Whereas for the previous several years I'd been through agonies thinking that I was, as it were, 'destined' for Bruce yet it could never happen, now I felt that my present lifetime was relatively unimportant since we'd been together many times in the past and would inevitably come together again in the future. Feeling that this information would perhaps make Bruce happy too, I longed to tell him a bit about it, but first of all I wanted some confirmation."

Well, the friends who had introduced Angela to the concept of reincarnation had also converted her to astrology. It so happened that the next time she met Bruce he told her that he was about to be sixty, and she managed to find out his birthday by confiding to one of his colleagues that she wanted to send him a card. The astrologer who was recommended to her was sufficiently psychic not to need Bruce's time and place of birth, and he confirmed that they were quite definitely twin souls. He also said a number of things which rang very true for Angela (such as Bruce's fear of affairs of the heart), and which she found extremely helpful. He told her that she needed to see him as a man rather than an ideal, and this made her realise the extent to which she had always put him on a pedestal, and also made her resolve in future to be less nervous about meeting him.

Angela had never mentioned Bruce to Malcolm, but he had for some time suspected that she was in love with someone, and after she had finished the hypnotherapy sessions and seen the astrologer, he wheedled the information out of her. As soon as Malcolm found out that Angela knew who her twin soul was, it gave him greater insight into the emotional problems she was undergoing, and he changed her homoeopathic remedy accordingly. He encouraged her in her desire gradually to share her new knowledge with Bruce, realising the implications of the situation for him as well, and he also asked her whether she had ever thought of changing her career. She admitted to a certain amount of disillusionment and frustration with her job, caused by the Conservative government's attitude to prisons and prisoners, said that she was becoming increasingly interested in healing, and told him about a past life she had been regressed to in which she had worked as a healer. Malcolm then said that he had sometimes felt that she had the makings of a healer, and suggested that she try to perform healing with her hands.

This took Angela completely by surprise as, though she was now accustomed to receiving hands on healing from Malcolm, it had never occurred to her that anyone who wasn't "very special" might be able to do it. A few days later, however, a colleague was complaining of acute stomach cramps, and so, knowing her to be open-minded about such things, she volunteered to try putting her hands on her. To their mutual amazement it worked within a few minutes and Angela found that her hands had become red hot. She then started to read a lot about healing and to practise it as much as she could.

Before telling Bruce about her healing powers, about which she was <u>sure</u> he would be sceptical, Angela decided to tackle him on the reincarnation question. Despite her resolution, she was still nervous about talking to him on any subject, but a church conference they both attended gave her an excellent opportunity, when the subject came up of how God could be totally just. He agreed to go home with one of her books on Edgar Cayce, and she felt sure that he would find it convincing just as she had done. The next time she saw Bruce she lent him a book on astrology, and the time after that she lent him her copy of *Life Between Life*[3], which shows how we plan our incarnations and principal relationships, enclosing in the envelope a letter in which she expressed something of her love and also told him that she had a reason for wanting him in particular to understand about reincarnation, and that she planned to disclose "the whole truth" to him eventually.

On this third occasion (her confidence gradually increasing), Angela also told Bruce about her new interest in healing and, as she had feared, he did look rather sceptical. He made no comment about the books, however, and so she remained hopeful about his conversion. Her reasons for desiring this conversion were really threefold: firstly, as we have said above, she thought that the idea of their being able to marry in a future lifetime might please him too, secondly this new conviction meant so much to her now and she hated the thought of his thinking her "mad" in any way, and thirdly she knew that twin souls had to develop spiritually together. She was beginning to weary of the Earthly realm and, having read so much about other realms, was getting impatient to return there permanently, but thought that she could not finish her incarnations until Bruce was ready to as well, which would necessitate his increasing his spiritual awareness. (It wasn't that he was any less spiritual than she – far from it – just that he was still very caught up in traditional Church belief and consequently a bit rigid in certain ways, which would slow down his readiness to return to spirit.)

They still met rarely, Bruce still had not made any comment about the books, and Angela was becoming more and more sure that she wanted to leave her job and go into healing full time. She had become very interested in crystal healing and wanted to train in that, and was also thinking of learning to do Shiatsu. She knew that it would not be easy to get started in the healing profession, but her mother had now died and left her some money, so that giving up her social work would not render her immediately destitute. One thing she dreaded about leaving her job, however, was the thought of no more Criminology meetings and conferences where she would meet Bruce, but on the other hand, she realised too that he was now not very far off retirement.

Angela confided these worries to Malcolm, and he asked her, "What <u>exactly</u>

is it you want from him, if you say that there's no chance of his ever marrying you?" She thought hard and then replied, "I'd like to be in a situation where I knew I could still see him, say once a year or even two years, even after he's retired, to exchange Christmas cards with a brief update on each other's news, perhaps to be able to ring him up once in a blue moon (or he me), and – ideally – to acknowledge our feelings for one another."

"In that case," said Malcolm, "I think you should come up front and tell him so. I'm sure it wouldn't be easy for a man in his position, and with his religious convictions, to express his feelings, but suppressed emotion is _very_ bad for the health and can even cause such things as cancer. Honesty and openness would be _much_ better for both of you, and once things are clear you'll be in a better position to move into your new career as a healer."

Well, Angela quite took Malcolm's point, but she didn't think it would be nearly as easy as he made it sound. For one thing there was the difficulty of her ever being able to talk to Bruce at any length at all when they only ever met briefly at conferences; for another, he had recently told her that he was shortly taking a long-overdue sabbatical, which would obviously mean his missing some future meetings; and last but not least of course was the problem of her shyness at talking to him – particularly over anything involving feelings. She therefore felt that she could only possibly put her desires over after building up the relationship very gradually.

At the next conference Angela gathered all her courage and asked Bruce to go out for a meal with her on the Saturday evening, on the pretext of feeling a need to tell him about her new career plans and also find out his views on reincarnation. To her relief he agreed and, though they were both distinctly nervous and slightly ill at ease, the evening went off better than she had dared hope, despite the fact that Bruce told her he must return her books as he simply could not find the time to read them. They discussed the question of reincarnation a bit, she doing her best to explain the points on which he was unclear, but he still would not budge an inch from the traditional Christian position. However, her fears of his disapproval over her intended new career ("abandoning the thing that was so dear to them both") were unfounded. "Everyone should follow their own inner voice," he said, "and I respect what you are trying to do even though I personally prefer to stick to traditional medicine."

After that Angela didn't quite know what should be her next step. Bruce wouldn't make time to read her books (well, she _knew_ how overworked he was), he refused to believe in reincarnation, yet she still wanted, and Malcolm still thought it would be best, if she told him that he was her twin soul. Even if he rejected the information, it would still reach him at _some_ level, she and Malcolm reflected, which would inevitably help their long-term coming together, and in any case she desperately wanted him to know what was going on for _her_ and why she was so much happier. She had hinted when they went out for the meal at the fact that she had something very important to tell him, and he had said, "Well, why don't you just come out with it then?" but there was no way she could do that. The whole thing felt so embarrassing, especially when she knew it would seem ridiculously far fetched to someone who could not even accept reincarnation. The only way to put it over to him, she decided, was on paper, so this she did.

Now the problem was how to give Bruce what she had written, as alas no further conference or meeting was in the offing. So she plucked up courage and wrote, saying that she was coming to London to stay with her brother (which was true) and could they have a meal together again so that she could tell him "this important thing"? When he failed to reply, she plucked up even more courage and phoned him at work, which was the most difficult thing she had ever done in her whole life. He was somewhat reluctant to agree to her proposition, but not unfriendly, and finally agreed because she was so insistent.

Before the meeting took place, Angela was somewhat surprised to find that her mind was not in a turmoil. She felt that it should have been since, after all, what was she doing? Having a date with a married man in the full knowledge that she would never want his wife to know that she was in love with him! She reflected on her feelings about Briony, whom she had still never met, and realised that she felt a strong affection for her, and also gratitude. Gratitude to her for looking after Bruce so well all those years – probably much better than she herself would have been able to. For, despite now believing that Bruce really did love her, she <u>still</u> felt totally unworthy of him. So why did she not feel guilty about the forthcoming meeting? The answer came from something she remembered the astrologer having said to her: "When it's your Higher Self telling you to do something, you feel very calm about it."

Angela's inner calm did not prevent the initial sickness and trembling, but the meeting nevertheless went off much better than she had dared hope. Bruce rightly insisted that it should be short, but he was more relaxed than he had been the previous time, and she felt that they were completely at ease in one another's company and could have gone on talking for ever. Just before they said "Goodbye", he took her sealed envelope and said with a smile, "So this reveals all, does it?" and then kissed her, squeezing her hand affectionately. She of course felt on top of the world, but the only trouble was that her yearning for further meetings was now increased still further.

This meeting took place in early December, and a couple of weeks later what did Angela (who had always sent <u>him</u> a card) receive but her first ever Christmas card from Bruce! It was big and beautiful and it was signed "With love". She knew she was banqueting off crumbs, yet now she felt that she at long last almost had what she wanted. Rather, however, than sending a simple card in reply, complete with her usual good wishes to his family (which she now feels would have been better), she enclosed a long letter pouring out her woes and (while making it <u>very</u> clear that she could never dream of wishing to hurt Briony) saying how much she wanted him to understand how hard it was for her being single when she was so much in love with the man who she knew to be her twin soul. She forgot what the astrologer had told her about not putting him on a pedestal and somehow felt that, if he fully understood exactly what she was going through, he could somehow or other make her pain a bit more bearable – that pain shared would be pain halved. She gave no <u>real</u> thought to <u>his</u> probable pain, and the reason for that of course was her difficulty in believing that such a "wonderful man" could possibly feel really deeply for her. She also forgot that we are never given more pain than we need.

The new year came and went, and Bruce's sabbatical was due to start before the next annual Criminology conference, which might well be Angela's last. She was keen to see him again, partly because she couldn't imagine when the next natural opportunity would be, and partly because she still hadn't managed the discussion about their relationship that Malcolm had told her to aim for. So she wrote again, giving three possible dates when they might be able to meet, one of which was when there was going to be a Criminology day in Manchester. The first date passed with no reply, then came the meeting in Manchester. To Angela's disappointment most of Bruce's department turned up except for him, so she gave one of his colleagues a plaintive note asking, "What about May? It'll be my last chance of seeing you for goodness knows how long." This time, she thought, he <u>must</u> reply, but he still didn't.

She says, "Now I reacted as though I'd suddenly been thrown right back into my childhood. Bruce's silence made me feel exactly like the ignored, rejected child of so many years ago. At first I just sort of curled up into myself as though I <u>was</u> that 'good-for-nothing' child, but then the adult me pulled me out of it again, saying, 'Why <u>should</u> you be ignored? You <u>are</u> worth something. If he doesn't want to see you, he should at least have the decency to <u>tell</u> you so!' So I wrote yet again, but this time it was a very different sort of letter. This time I accused him of not treating me even with the decency he would accord to one of the worst criminals, referred to the agonies I had suffered through not knowing whether he was going to be at the Manchester meeting, and I even enclosed a stamped addressed envelope."

The reply, which came within only a few days, gave Angela much more of a shock than she had bargained for. She had always seen Bruce as the nicest, kindest, politest man she had ever met, and so she fully expected him to be truly apologetic. In fact she was still daring to hope that the reason for his silence was indecision, and even that he might finally agree to the May meeting. "What I <u>hadn't</u> anticipated was that my letter had rather pushed his buttons, and what does a normal man tend to do when a woman pushes his buttons? React very defensively." Bruce's letter (written hurriedly on the tube) began:

I am sorry I put you out so much in not replying. What I wanted to indicate – and there's no way this can be unhurtful – was that I really did not want to continue this contact which is (on your side) beyond reason.

She says, "This hurt me unbelievably because of the fact that I hadn't yet had the chance to explain to Bruce the nature of the contact that I really desired. The words "beyond reason" were the worst, as I was so, so much wanting our friendship to be <u>within</u> reason and wanted to meet him again precisely to find out what, from his point of view, would <u>be</u> within reason." But there was worse to come! The first paragraph continued: *I know you as a friend and that is all – the rest, however much <u>you</u> believe it, means nothing to me. Rather than nurture those beliefs therefore I wish to end the contact altogether. To do otherwise I am convinced would be cruel to you and in the long run cause more pain.*

The next paragraph referred to the Manchester meeting, where he made it clear that he had planned to come but had been dissuaded by colleagues at the last minute on account of the fact that he always took more than his share of the work load. From this she deduced that he really had hoped to make his excuses personally (and politely), and that this was his real reason for not having replied sooner by letter. She also thought that perhaps he had really hoped to see her that day.

So here she was again plunged back into the misery caused by being unloved (unloved <u>and</u>, she felt, unlovable). And she says that she immediately blamed herself entirely. "I told myself I'd <u>never</u> been any good at relationships with men, and now I'd gone and bungled what could have been a wonderful spiritual friendship just through my own stupidity!". She explains: "While the phrase *as a friend and that is all* cut right into the depths of my being, the words *it means nothing to me* were more or less equally painful. The philosophy of reincarnation and karma had become one of the most important things in my whole life, and he seemed to be implying that he didn't like the idea of our ever being together. So those words <u>felt</u> to me tantamount to his having said, *<u>You</u> mean nothing to me* . . . Also, his use of the word *believe* distressed me. While both of us had been brought up in a Church which taught belief and theological <u>theory</u>, I was now tired of theory and wanting <u>real information.</u> I knew that what I'd been taught about reincarnation, karma and twin souls was neither belief nor theory, but <u>fact</u> channelled from very high spiritual sources, and it was this that I had so desperately wanted to put over to him.

The third paragraph gave a genuine excuse for not being available on the May date, and the penultimate paragraph read:

But I do not want to suggest we should not meet simply because of the dates. I am saying we should not meet. I did not want to say this so sharply and categorically, but you have driven me to it. I am sorry for the hurt. I do not want you to write again.

The letter ended *I hope you accept what I am saying. Yours sincerely, Bruce.*

What happened next to Angela, after she had read the letter through three or four times, was interesting. She says, "I felt kicked in the teeth and devastated, of course, but, much to my own surprise, while the tears were still falling, I found myself detaching myself from my own emotions and observing what was going on inside from the viewpoint of a therapist who was right outside the situation.

I remembered what I'd been told so many times – that I should learn to love myself and not look to others to provide me with love – and also that I'd been told that twin souls often met in order to teach one another lessons. So now it was crystal clear: the student who had taken me out in my youth in Reading, the Methodist chaplain, Julian – even Malcolm – had failed to teach me that lesson. I had even refused to learn it from Louise Hay, much though I admired her teaching. So now, because of my own obstinacy, the only person who could teach me that lesson had taken it upon himself to do so; my twin soul, the person whose love mattered more to me than anyone else's ever could."

So now at last Angela turned to God with the greatest fervour she had ever managed. She had for some years been trying to discipline herself to meditate regularly and so, over the next few weeks of unhappiness, she says that she found herself able to turn to meditation as a real source of consolation. She realised that she had become much, much stronger than she had been when Julian had hurt her, and that "the lesson had been sent to me at exactly the right time, i.e. that even a year or two earlier I would have been completely broken by it."

Another thing struck Angela as interesting while she mulled over what had happened. She realised more and more that she had only seen Bruce as an ideal rather than as a man, that she had imagined him to be more or less perfect and incapable of exuding anything but sweetness and light all the time. Now she had had a big glimpse of another side to his character, and this made him suddenly appear a lot more human. And what was the consequence? "Well, I felt that it made me love him even more, for shouldn't true love, which must be unconditional, include love of the warts as well as of the beauty? After all, he was right: I had driven him to it. I had put him, a good Christian, upright man, with a wife whom he cared for, in an extremely difficult position. And besides, while I was surrounded with people who took my new knowledge for granted, he had no such contacts apart from me, and so it was perfectly natural that a concept such as that of twin souls should appear completely weird to him."

'Twin souls teach one another lessons.' My own lesson was clear, but what, I wondered, was the lesson that Bruce had learnt from me? Especially since he had refused to be converted to reincarnation. Well, I thought maybe I'd begun to open his mind a bit, and anyway (Malcolm said) something was bound to have got through on some level. Even if he remained impervious this time round, the information I'd given him would affect him in some way for a future incarnation. And maybe too, if the astrologer was right about Bruce's fear of 'affairs of the heart', he also needed to learn something about unconditional love – to understand that nothing he could ever do or say would in any way change my feelings for him."

After the initial shock and disappointment were over, Angela began to reflect at times less on her own hurt and more on what writing the letter would have done to Bruce. She saw it as a spur-of-the-moment, impatient act, performed when he was desperately overworked and tired and, knowing his true nature to be the soul of kindness and compassion, one which could have led him to worry subsequently about the effect it might have had on her. The last thing she wanted was for the matter to weigh on his conscience throughout his sabbatical and, since he had forbidden her to write again, she couldn't think what to do about that. One day, in meditation only a couple of weeks later, an idea came to her. She found a nice quotation about the love of God being the most important thing for anyone, copied it out and sent it to him at his College. She felt that, since she had not written a letter, he could not complain that she had gone against his expressed wishes, and she felt that receiving the card would reassure him that she had taken what he had said in good heart. She said her daily prayers for him with increased vigour (often she felt sure that he must be the most prayed for man in the whole world!), and she reminded herself that she still talked to him every night, when they met up in sleep.

Angela still had her demanding social work to keep her occupied, and now many of her evenings and weekends were taken up with study for the Crystal Healing course, which she found very enthralling. Over the next months her moods fluctuated: there were days when she scarcely gave Bruce a thought, while on others she again felt pretty miserable. She remembered her mother telling her all those years ago, when she had been going out with a student in Reading, that a girl should "play hard to get" with a man and not let him know easily if she was interested in him. Being a lover of honesty, that had gone against the grain for her, but now she occasionally wondered whether she should have taken her mother's advice seriously. "On the other hand," she told herself, "I only ever wanted Bruce to love me for myself, and if he can't love me the way I am . . ." (She meant, of course, a spiritual love, since she would never have wanted Bruce to contemplate adultery for a single moment. She admits now to a certain naivety in imagining the ease with which this can be achieved when there is sexual attraction involved.) Often she believed that he had really meant what he said about having no feelings for her, sometimes she felt he had only written it out of a sense of duty and marital fidelity, while at other times she thought perhaps he wasn't at all sure what he felt (after all he must sense the twin soul link somehow even if it didn't affect him as profoundly as it did her), and had simply acted out of a natural fear of the relationship developing in a way in which he would not be able to handle it.

A few months went by, and then Angela suddenly wondered whether there had also been some karmic cause for Bruce's reaction. So then she remembered Moira, the regressionist, and managed to get an appointment for the following week. Moira listened sympathetically to the tale about the letter and the impossibility of a meeting in the foreseeable future, counted Angela down slowly in the way to which she was by now well accustomed, and then said, "Now I want you to go to a life in which you treated Bruce badly. Can you see anything in the past which might have given him good cause for being angry with you?"

Almost immediately Angela (who was a very good hypnotherapy subject) saw herself standing over Bruce's slumped body with the carving knife dripping with blood in her hand. Then she remembered all the events leading up to it. Though she could in no way identify with the unpleasant character she saw standing there, she knew, to her horror, that this person was undoubtedly one of her former selves, and that the dead body was that of the soul she had loved from the time of their very first incarnation. Moira took her gently forward through the rest of that life and then to the point just after her own death, when she met Bruce again in the astral realms and told him how dreadfully sorry she was. Then she brought her slowly back to full consciousness, telling her to close the door on that lifetime, since the person she had been then was dead for ever and she, Angela, had now returned to her true nature as a gentle and loving human being.

On returning to full consciousness, however, despite Moira's admonitions to detach herself fully from that lifetime, Angela found herself unable to stop sobbing. "How could I have done it?" she exclaimed to Moira. "No wonder he hates me! I deserved far worse than that unfriendly letter." Moira calmed her down as best she could and continued talking her through it. Then, to cheer her up, she tried a new technique she had recently started employing just occasionally: progression. Gently she put Angela under once more and told her to go forward to a future life – one, two or even three centuries hence.

This time the result was totally different. The year 2212 flashed into Angela's mind and, though the picture was more hazy than that of the Elizabethan life, and though their sexes were reversed, she knew for certain that the happily married man she could see was herself and that his beloved wife was Bruce. Not only were they living together, but also working together, and it was very clear that they were both teachers. They were in a valley with beautiful mountains all around it, and they appeared to be joint guardians of some important mysteries, into which they were gradually initiating their students. Angela came round from the progression full of peace and joy, and on that note Moira felt that she was ready to take leave of her.

Angela had that evening to herself, and so she had plenty of time for reflection. Now she saw the whole of what had recently gone on between herself and Bruce in a very different light and – with an increasing confidence in her own potential as a therapist – she found herself able to analyse what had happened from a therapist's viewpoint. She thought hard about what must have gone on with Bruce when he had written the letter, and became aware of the three different levels of his consciousness. Firstly there was the subconscious provocation she had caused. Her being annoyed with him for not replying to her letters had triggered his subconscious memory of the dreadful murder he had once suffered at her hands. His instinctive reaction was to retaliate but, at a distance, and being the gentlemanly, upright and loving man he now was, the means of retaliation open to him were extremely limited. So he simply seized the only weapons he had to hand. The only two weapons available to him, but which also happened to be the very two which would hurt Angela the most in her present circumstances: telling her that her feelings were unrequited, and telling her that her belief (in their past and future together) meant nothing to him.

Next there was the conscious level. They had become friends over a period of several years, during which they had met only at occasional meetings and conferences. He had probably felt, at least mildly, attracted to her, and also slightly flattered by her evident very strong attraction to him. He would have been content to have left things at that, but then she had started apparently asking rather more of him. Definitely more than he felt he could reasonably handle without in some way jeopardising his relationship with his wife. So, rather than run the risk of getting himself into deep water, the natural and obvious thing to do was to cut off the relationship completely, regardless of the hurt he knew it would cause her.

Then finally there was the super-conscious level. The Higher Self, the spirit being which originally sent off two souls on their journeys all those aeons ago, keeping a permanent eye over both of them, watching what they do to one another and to other souls, supervising the work they do, and judging when they need to be together again, what they need to do to make themselves ready to be together again, and engineering their joint eventual return to spirit. This same Higher Self knew what lessons Angela and Bruce still had left to learn, it knew that Angela had to be able to stand on her own feet without Bruce's declared love, and that this was the lesson he was the soul best equipped to teach her. So, on the super-conscious level, Bruce had simply been obeying their joint Higher Self when he had implied to Angela that he did not love her.

Now that it was all clear, Angela knew that she could move forward and get on with her own life – with what she was _really_ meant to be doing. She began almost to forget the pain and to be conscious only of the closeness she felt with Bruce. Gradually she became more and more sure that the letter was no more than a minor incident which he would in due course put out of his mind and that perhaps, when (and if!) they met again, he would behave as though it had never happened. She had already given up her idle day dreams and now instead, before falling asleep at night, she took Moira's advice of talking to Bruce in her mind. She told him she forgave him for getting cross with her, even though it still hurt a bit, that she would _certainly_ never kill him again, or even be at all horrid to him, that he should appreciate her unconditional love for him, realising that it was eternal, and that they _must_ get their relationship with each other right and learn to look in exactly the same direction, since they were going to have important work to do together in the future.

Then one night Angela had a dream which she felt to be very significant. She knew that people sometimes had "past-life" dreams, but could not imagine that ever happening to her. This dream, however, quite clearly took place in an earlier century, and she was sure that in it she and Bruce were different people and yet the same (she was even calling him "Bruce", though he looked different). It was clear that they were living in a society where marriages were arranged and that consequently, though they were both "free" and in love, they were not going to be permitted to marry. The dream was full of people and it was virtually impossible for the two of them to be alone, but at one point Bruce picked up a torch and took her out of the large building they were in into the dark, on the pretext that he had lost some gloves outside and she must help him look for them. Once outside, he took her by the hand and kept walking and walking. Though there were still lots of people around, he told her of his great need to express his love, but he was doing so guiltily and apologetically. She tried to convince him that he didn't need to feel guilty and that "they" had no right to prevent them from marrying, but she woke up before reaching the end of the story. This dream reinforced Angela's feelings about Bruce's deep-seated fear of going in the tiniest way against what was expected of him.

Christmas came and that year Angela felt a joy which was for her quite unprecedented. Though she had not yet handed in her notice as a social worker, her future as a healer now seemed assured, and she was looking forward to, and confident of, being able ultimately to give help to a large number of people. Coming from such a large family, she was never short of relatives with whom to spend the festive season, and this time she took pleasure in her nephews' and nieces' excitement without her usual touch of envy of her siblings' families. Though she did not dare hope again for a card from Bruce, she felt an overwhelming desire to share her feeling of Christmas joy with him. Since she knew he was still on sabbatical, she looked up his home address in the London telephone directory and addressed her card there. Rather than "wishing" him "much JOY", she wrote "sending you and your family much JOY", hoping that he would sense that she actually was brimming over with joy herself, and therefore had a surplus of it to pass on to him.

After Christmas, however, when she knew he would have returned to work, she also sent to his office a church magazine in which she had written a little article on pain. It began, "Pain can be being in prison when one is innocent, hunger and cold in Bosnia, when a special friend gets cross and misinterprets or exaggerates in their mind what it was one was wanting or asking for (especially when one realises that it was one's own fault and that it's too late to do anything about it) . . ." She didn't enclose a covering note, because of course he had forbidden her to write, but she trusted nevertheless that he would read it and get the message.

Soon after that she had another dream, which she recognised as indicative of her spiritual progress. She recounts: "I dreamt that we were both at a conference, and when Bruce stood up I noticed that he had shrunk and was exactly the same height as I am (instead of about ten inches taller, as he must be really). I was puzzling over how this could have happened when I woke up, but of course I realised immediately that the dream was telling me that I should stop putting Bruce on a pedestal because twin souls are always exactly the same size spiritually! This helped me to stop feeling inferior to him."

A few weeks later Angela decided to go to the astrologer for another reading. What came out in this reading gave her an immense shock: she was told that Bruce was doing his utmost to put her completely out of his mind and that, though he had opened the Christmas card, he had opened neither the envelope with the quotation nor that containing the magazine. She says, "I was devastated! I had been trying so hard to make <u>him</u> feel better, but what I did was actually counter-productive. Now I thought he must be cursing me for sending letters when, if only he'd open them, he'd immediately see that they weren't letters at all and consequently soften in his attitude towards me. The sense of frustration was unbearable, since I had no control over what was happening, but on the other hand I tried very hard, too, to leave the matter entirely in the hands of God, remembering that Bruce still had karma to work out from that life in which I treated him so badly. I kept reminding myself that if one really is working for God, firstly He won't make things easy for us (or we wouldn't get stronger), and secondly that everything will turn out all right in the end."

She went to the next conference filled with apprehension, not knowing whether Bruce would even be there, since the astrologer had predicted that if she saw him it would only be "at a distance", and her worst fears were fulfilled. "In fact," she says, "he <u>was</u> there for the whole weekend, but he made absolutely no attempt to say even 'Hullo' to me! Once or twice he came near, almost as though he was expecting <u>me</u> to say 'Hullo' to <u>him</u>, but how could I when I didn't know whether I would be cold shouldered? Being ignored was bad enough, but being cold shouldered would have been even worse! Besides, he had said that I wasn't to write and that he wished to end the contact *all together.* I wasn't to know whether he also meant by that verbal contact; whether he felt that we were no longer friends at all. If he didn't mean anything so extreme, all he had to do was give me a simple greeting. In the past, when I was feeling incredibly nervous about greeting him, he was usually so good at putting me at my ease, nearly always wonderfully friendly. So I just stuck it out for the whole weekend, trying hard not to cry in public, and thinking about my own new career as a healer and how much I hoped to be able to help a lot of people.

On the first evening I got into conversation in the bar with someone whose suffering made my own pale into insignificance, and the next evening I did some baby sitting for people who wanted to be able to go to the barn dance. I suppose it was partly the fact that it was so awful that I couldn't believe it was really happening that enabled me to get through the weekend. It seemed absurd really! But tears are therapeutic, and gradually I became able to put the whole thing into perspective – to be aware that what was happening now was less than a split second out of eternity, and that anyway what was happening on the Earth's plane was totally different from the more important things going on on the higher levels. I knew that Bruce and I were working together at night, when we were out of our bodies, and that we would achieve that unity all the time once we had finished this lifetime. I also got even more confirmation of the fact that we are twin souls from the talk that he gave at that conference. Although he was using slightly different vocabulary, and although he himself would not admit that our message was the same, in fact what he was saying was identical to what I am saying through my work. It feels as though we are working together even though we are apart, and of course it's good too because at the moment we are each getting stronger on our own.

At one point during that weekend I felt that Bruce had been being deliberately callous because he was still cross with me about nagging him for a meeting, but then I realised that that wasn't in his nature. I remembered that Six Metals[4] are always leaders in relationships, and so decided that he really had expected me to take the initiative with the greeting. It seemed odd that he should imagine I'd be able to do that after having been hurt so badly, but there couldn't really have been any other reason for his deliberately coming quite near me more than once, when I was trying quite hard to avoid him. I suppose he just felt awkward, being such a kind-hearted man, and maybe he hoped that I'd behave as though nothing had happened between us. I think men must be better than women are at shutting themselves off from their feelings, and the astrologer assured me that that was what he had done. For me that would be impossible, so I found it hard to imagine, but at least I no longer believed that he had never had any feelings for me. That's one way in which I've made considerable spiritual progress! Now I can believe that I am lovable, and I know that it's not possible for twin souls not to feel some sort of attraction to one another."

Angela reflected, too, that weekend and subsequently, that perhaps the weekend might have taught Bruce a lesson. For, if she was right and he had been expecting her to greet him almost as though nothing had happened, he needed to realise that one could not hurt someone that badly and then expect them to forget it easily. She thought that, even if he had succeeding in shutting himself off from the pain, he should not expect her to be able to do so.

Though at the time Angela's pain seemed quite unbearable, now, several weeks later, she is absorbed in her work and believes that Joudry and Pressman's observations on "Twin Souls in Conflict"[1] apply to her:–

Conflict will arise over and over again; it is part of the cycle of nature, and of the growth process. With each cycle, twin-soul love is strengthened. Growth is twofold: they grow closer in oneness, and together grow upward. Gradually the conflicts become fewer, and their growth centres around their inner work, each aided by the other.

She does not know when (or even if!) she and Bruce will meet again in this lifetime, but has at last learnt that it does not matter. She knows that her most important lessons for this incarnation are loving herself, standing on her own, and patience, and that so long as she is working on herself it can only improve their spiritual relationship. Also, whereas before she believed that she would have to keep coming back to Earth until Bruce was ready to make the final return with her to spirit, now she has learnt that, once she has paid all her own debts, she will be able to wait for him in the higher astral realms (very likely serving him as a spirit guide) until he has worked out the feelings that he has justifiably had against her ever since the Elizabethan lifetime. Though she realises that she almost certainly still has a number of lifetimes to go, she is also looking forward to the in-between life periods because, as Arthur Ford explains to Ruth Montgomery in *Companions Along the Way*[5], she knows that the unity between lovers is better there than it can ever be down here.

As for Angela's professional work, it is building up gradually, and she is finding it increasingly satisfying. Besides the crystal healing and *Shiatsu*, she has learnt to dowse, which is also useful in her work. (Angela obtained all the information about Bruce's background from a combination of dowsing and feminine intuition. She points out, however, that the former is not a hundred per cent infallible, since it is easy for the subconscious mind to control the pendulum, so sometimes she asks Malcolm, as an impartial outsider, to do the dowsing for her. He confirmed in this way that the dream she had had in which they were unable to marry was in fact a real past-life dream.)

Although Angela's story is the longest of my "case histories", I feel that it is a valuable one both from the point of view of the lessons that twin souls teach one another, and also as an excellent example of what can be done in a single lifetime when a person who has had a difficult start really works hard at self-healing. Angela's is probably one example of many of someone who chose to incarnate into difficult circumstances as a learning experience both for herself and others. "For," she concludes, "had I had a much easier life, I would certainly not have become a healer!"

Notes

1. *Twin Souls: A Guide to Finding your True Spiritual Partner* by Patricia Joudry and Maurie D. Pressman, M.D., published by Element Books, Shaftesbury, Dorset.
2. *You can Heal your Life* and other books by Louise L. Hay, published by Eden Grove Editions.
3. *Life between Life* by Dr. Joel L Whitton and Joe Fisher, published by Grafton.
4. This refers to the Japanese *Nine Star Ki* system of astrology.
5. *Companions Along the Way* by Ruth Montgomery, published by Fawcett Crest, Random House, New York.

Chapter III

THE TIES CAN NEVER BE CUT
The story of Carol and Dan

It seemed too absurd to be true, and yet it <u>was</u> true. The dog had bitten Carol really badly before running off and yet, rather than showing any concern at all about her wound, her husband, Carl, was blaming <u>her</u> for the loss that the family was suffering. Carol herself had never been a great dog lover and it was for the sake of the children and her husband that she had finally been along to the RSPCA and picked up Scraggy. Scraggy was skinny from neglect as well as unkempt, but he had such an appealing look in his forlorn brown eyes that Simon (the eldest) and Joanna (the second of the six children) had fallen instantly in love with him. Things had gone quite well the first couple of weeks – Scraggy ate reasonably well and seemed gradually to be responding to all the children's affection – but then disaster had struck the first time they had let him off the lead on the Clifton Downs. A dog twice his size had come and attacked and Scraggy, in terror, had bitten wildly at Carol's leg before bolting. Simon had tried in vain to pursue him and Carol, being in intense pain and scared of infection, had taken herself straight to Casualty before informing the police of the loss. And now Carl was ignoring her huge bandage and limp and yelling at her, "The children and I all yearned for a dog for so many years. You selfishly refused for ages to accede to our desires because you felt you couldn't cope, and now you've confirmed your incompetence by allowing the poor creature to escape. If we ever get him back, <u>I'll</u> have to be the one to walk him. As though I didn't have enough on my plate already!"

Carol's marriage had been doomed to failure from the start, and it was only fear of difficulty in coping with the children on her own that had kept her in it for so long. Not that Carl ever really gave her any support in the house, but at least he had always, as a solicitor, brought in a reasonable income. In recent years she had found her vocation in a job at the Bristol Cancer Help Centre, but her salary was not big enough for seven to live on, and she was sure that if she left Carl it would be difficult, if not impossible, to get money out of him for the children.

Carl had not been Carol's first boyfriend – she was extremely attractive and always much sought after in her youth – but she made the decision to marry him

57

in a hurry, in order to escape, she <u>thought</u>, from the "suitable young man" who her tyrannical father was trying to press upon her. I have underlined the word *thought* because often through our lifetimes we get trapped in repeated patterns without being consciously aware of it. Some time <u>after</u> Carol had finally succeeded in breaking free from Carl, she discovered (from a clairvoyant reading) that he had abused her many times before. In fact in the previous lifetimes his abuse had been physical as well as verbal (as in this one), and one of her most important tasks for this lifetime has been to end the karma with him completely. This took some doing, as living for years with someone brutal weakens and exhausts even the strongest of wills. (The reason they had so many children was because of Carl's refusal to use contraception, thinking that a large family was the only way he had of binding her to him.) What finally gave Carol the strength to make the break was meeting and falling in love with Dan, her twin soul.

Dan – not surprisingly since twin souls, as we have seen, tend to have similar experiences – was also trapped in a loveless, destructive marriage and, fascinatingly, it was his wife, Diane, who was responsible for bringing them together. Joudry and Pressman[1] make the important point in their book that, though they <u>can</u> precipitate them, meetings of twin souls do not and should not <u>cause</u> marriage break-ups – that such break-ups only take place in consequence of a twin-soul meeting when a marriage was crumbling already. Well, we have already looked at Carol's karma with Carl; Dan's with Diane is exceedingly interesting.

In a fairly recent previous lifetime Dan had been a zookeeper and, Diane had, as quite a young girl, fallen into the bear pit. Dan had of course rushed to her aid and, being the conscientious zookeeper and caring person that he was, had never got over being too late to save her. He had consequently married her in this lifetime in order to do what he subconsciously felt he had failed to do in that previous one. She had had to be admitted to a mental hospital for a few months shortly after the wedding, which had made him realise his mistake, but his subconscious feeling of "karmic debt" made him persist in his commitment to her. This despite the fact that her intermittent mental illness proved to be a lesser problem for him than her jealousy and constant demands on him.

Prior to his incarnation as a zookeeper, Dan had gone through a number of incarnations in which he had failed to care for and respect himself sufficiently. The causes of this were various, but the result was that in this lifetime he had completely failed to realise his potential. Born, like Carol, into a working class family with a very dictatorial father, his innate intelligence had never been given the encouragement it needed in order for him to pursue the education of which he would have been capable. He had consequently left school at an early age and become a bricklayer like his father.

Dan's only son, to whom he was devoted, was really his only source of any joy. His wife considered herself too ill to be able to work, yet had expensive tastes, which was a constant strain on his pocket. It was therefore not at all surprising that, when he and Carol first met, he was suffering from a number of physical ailments.

After she had been working at the Bristol Centre for a while, Carol (who had been training as a nurse when she got married, and had become interested in so-called "alternative therapies" through her reading while the children were little), had discovered that she had healing power in her hands and was supplementing her income by offering the occasional massage and healing in the evenings. She had become acquainted with Diane through school, where Simon was in the same class as their son, Jonathan, and she told her about her work at home when Diane complained to her of a headache. Rather than deciding to try it herself, however, Diane sent Dan round that very evening "to see if you can relieve the tension in his neck, which is his excuse for not redecorating the lounge".

Carol felt attracted to Dan (whom she describes as <u>very</u> good looking) straight away, but she says, "At first I just didn't let myself think about it. I thought that he and Diane, whom I was quite unable to like, seemed a rather odd match, but I had no reason to think that he was unhappy in the marriage. The first treatment seemed to be beneficial and so he kept coming again, but we talked very little really. The empathy between us just seemed to grow gradually – it was as though we didn't need words to communicate – and it so happened that the evening I suddenly found myself in Dan's arms was the very one when Carl had gone out to search for the dog after haranguing me for losing it. I needed a sympathetic ear, so I just poured it all out, and when he'd listened consolingly, he told me a bit about his own problems. How Diane had refused to sleep with him for years, though he would have liked more children, and how the tension at home must be what was making him ill, but that he'd promised himself early on in the marriage always to care for her because she was so helpless."

Then Carol added, "It seemed <u>so</u> frustrating! Here we were in each other's arms as though we belonged to one another, each desperately unhappy in our own marriage and aware that we <u>could</u> find happiness together. But just as soon as we'd begun to admit that, Dan was filled with instant remorse and said that he'd better not come for any more treatments. I was devastated, but my resolve was firm. I told my husband the very next day that I was leaving him. The dog incident was sufficient for me not to have to mention Dan, and anyway I wasn't at all hopeful that he would also make the decision to end his marriage. Carl was <u>furious</u> and the rows over the next weeks were very upsetting for the children, but they supported me a hundred per cent and a good friend helped me to find a house to rent. I took a day off work to move out, so that Carl couldn't prevent me from doing so physically, and the local vicar was also very helpful. Carl – amazingly! – does go to church, but the vicar is intelligent enough to see that I was in the right and not to believe the lies my husband told him. I had been unhappy all my married life, but I'm not sure that I would ever have had the guts to leave him if I hadn't met Dan. I knew I was jumping into a void, but it was the realisation (in Dan's arms!) of what a man-woman relationship should really be like that helped me finally to free myself. I found out later that Carl had abused me several times in the past – often with violence and even worse than this time – and I had kept on failing to learn that lesson."

This is one of the many reasons why learning about reincarnation is so valuable. For it is difficult to learn the lessons we have come to learn until we have become aware of what they are! In life after life Carol had subconsciously recognised Carl's good looks and superficial charm, but forgotten where they had led her. Now finally, thanks to the love of and for Dan, who alone could enable her to be fully herself, she became able to break free from Carl and cut the karmic links with him for good. And now that she has done that, she is open to and available for Dan, and whether or not their physical union can be accomplished this time round or in a future incarnation is comparatively immaterial.

Their meeting for Dan's treatment of course triggered in both of them many subconscious memories of previous happy times spent together, which is why they fell in love so quickly. Dan is an old soul, who incarnated for the first time in Lemuria, while Carol remained in higher realms and acted as his spirit guide. There was at that time no feeling of separation for them, since the Lemurians never became fully disconnected from their spiritual essence, and so Dan was constantly aware of Carol's presence, which enabled him always to feel complete. The same happiness was felt by all the first Lemurians who were involved in working closely with the Creator, for they sensed that they were at the beginning of a very wonderful adventure. It was only very, very many years later that the realisation began to dawn on these souls of the extent to which they had become trapped in the new environment, and of what an immense and lengthy struggle it was going to be finally to return to the Source.

Dan subsequently had a large number of incarnations in which Carol still remained discarnate and served him as a guide. In many of these he retained his close connection both with Carol and with his Higher Self, in others less so. (The same is no doubt true for most of us.) In addition there were several occasions on which they incarnated together, one of which was in Ancient Egypt, where they were priest and priestess in the Temple of Rameses III.

Although Carol feels that she is the masculine energy of their pair, in this incarnation as in their present one, she was the woman and Dan the man. They were both from well-to-do families and were put into the temple by their parents at about the same time, at the tender age of twelve or thirteen. This was not unusual in that civilisation, where fourteen or fifteen was the normal age at which to marry.

The role of many of the Egyptian priests was that of healers. While Dan had a talent for administration and rose fairly rapidly to a high position in the Temple, Carol was singled out quite early on for special training as a healer – a talent which has manifested itself again in her present lifetime. (It may be remembered that Edgar Cayce's past-life readings helped many people to find themselves a suitable career.) The educated section of that society was still very much aware of its Atlantean inheritance, and the Temple of Rameses III was known as one of the Colour Temples, colour being one of the main methods of healing used there. Carol had always had an acute eye for colour, and so she took rapidly to the Atlantean-style training in that area. Soon people were coming from far and wide to benefit from her colour treatment, and she pioneered some new ideas as well as making use of what she learnt about the Atlantean methods.

Since, too, this temple was situated within fairly easy reach of the Gizeh plateau, both Carol and Dan were able to benefit from the energies of the great pyramids, and learn much of what their Atlantean refugee ancestors who built them had been aiming for. On occasion they went there together, and Carol remembered vividly for the whole of that lifetime the day on which she had first noticed Dan's beauty, his dark skin contrasting so strikingly with the dazzling white walls of the Great Pyramid. It was on that day also that they studied together the prophecies it contained, and Carol suddenly found herself thinking about her eternal nature and wondering whether they would again be together in the distant future when some of these prophecies came true.

While most of the Egyptian priests were celibate, a minority were not and Carol, being an attractive and sensual young woman, never felt any desire to commit herself to celibacy. Dan, on the other hand, was so spiritual in nature that the possibility of marriage or a close relationship with a woman did not enter his head during those years of training in the temple. While never making a formal commitment to celibacy, he saw himself initially as remaining unmarried during that lifetime.

The Egyptians, as Joan Grant has conveyed so beautifully in some of her "far memory" books[2], were among those ancient peoples who developed the art of remembering what they did at night when out of their bodies. Since it is only the physical body that needs rest, not the soul, they knew (as do many advanced souls today) that the work which they did at night was at least as important as that which they did by day. Carol and Dan were both given rigorous training in remembering their nightly "sorties" (i.e. in becoming what the Australian clairvoyant Edmund Harold calls "Adepts" – the first stage towards becoming a Master), and their main task at night was going to the help of souls who were passing from their earthly bodies to the other side.

Remembering this work that they did together at night filled Carol with the desire to be more closely linked with Dan during the day too, and she tried at first to seduce him by paying even more attention to her appearance. When this failed, the answer came to her in meditation: since the link between them was a spiritual one, it was to his spirit that she should be appealing, not to his body. She therefore began to increase her reading of spiritual literature, sometimes memorising extracts from Pta-Hotep, with which she would regale him at appropriate moments. Dan had a very fine mind and was well versed in the nation's literature, and gradually he began to view Carol more and more as his most treasured companion.

So in due course they married and, while Carol knew her joy to be unbounded, Dan wondered how it was that he could have failed for so long to notice his twin soul's beauty and to see that his life of celibacy had been anything less than perfect. As their conjugal life began they found, as twin souls who are ready for each other always do, that everything each undertook was enriched by the other's energy, and so respect for them both from those around them grew ever stronger, everyone sensing their combined energy as something from which strength could be drawn by those in need. Towards the end of their life Dan, sensing that his end was near, gave Carol the most beautiful piece of lapus lazuli, saying, "Keep this for ever as a symbol of our eternal love." When she died just a few months later, she took measures to ensure that the stone would be buried with her, and now in her present life, having relived this scene in a regression, she is searching for a duplicate of it. Carol currently feels that this Egyptian lifetime has much bearing on their present one, but that Dan has to a large extent cut himself off from the "true self" that he was then, and that part of her task in their present incarnation has been to try to steer him back to it.

Many centuries later Carol and Dan were again man and wife, this time in black Africa, where she was the village shaman. Colour healing was not practised in that society, but she was a very skilled herbalist. Dan was the village chief and, while not having himself very much knowledge of her art, he was in a good position to protect her both from neighbouring tribes people, who sometimes wanted to attack her through jealousy, and from the white colonials who were trying to stamp out shamanism in favour of the Western medicine which they ignorantly regarded as superior. Working with Carol in that African lifetime was Simon, her eldest son in her current incarnation. He is a very old soul and, though only a teenager, has been an extraordinary support to her through her marriage break-up and subsequent trials.

So, returning now to the present, Carol's subconscious memories of previous happy times spent with Dan, together with the momentary glimpse of "total bliss" that she had that one evening in his arms, were the incentive she needed to make the decision which (for very understandable, very common reasons) she had not had the courage to make years earlier. The same was alas, however, not true for Dan. Guilt and confusion are feelings experienced almost inevitably by twin souls who meet when they are already committed to somebody else. (We saw this very clearly in Bruce in the last chapter, and it is also the title of Chapter VI.) The guilt that his commitment to his wife immediately aroused in Dan was genuine, but, since Diane had actually refused for years to be a proper wife to him, these feelings of guilt were not really justified, and there was actually more to it than that.

Carol and Dan, when they met in their present lifetime – on account of negative experiences since the African incarnation they shared – were neither of them as ready as they had been at that time not to be dependent on the other for their sense of self. Dan in particular (since Carol had had a number of boyfriends who had appreciated her before finally settling for the wrong one) had never been given the love that he deserved. That is why, although he responded initially when Carol saw in him the "ideal other half" that she had kept locked in her heart over the aeons, and although it gave him too his first profound sense of true joy, his lack of <u>self</u> love prevented him from allowing himself to feel worthy of <u>her</u> love. So, feeling unworthy, he immediately rejected this love. He rejected it that first evening by telling her that he had better not come for any more treatments because of his wife, and he rejected it many times subsequently by very cold behaviour towards her if they happened to bump into one another in the street or at the school if he was having to pick up Jonathan because Diane was ill. This rejection was of course excruciatingly painful for Carol who – particularly since Carl had undermined her self-esteem for so many years – took it personally rather than being able to see it as <u>his</u> problem.

We need not go into the lengthy story of Carol's separation from Carl, the intense difficulties she went through in setting up house on her own with six children, and with the arrangements about access when each meeting with Carl caused upheaval and distress amongst them all. Suffice it to say that these years were an intense learning experience for Carol, through which she has undoubtedly worked out a vast amount of negative karma, and the result of which has been firstly to make her very much stronger and secondly to cut all the ties that the seven of them had with Carl. (He has now moved away from Bristol and has lost his job, which gives him an excuse for not sending her any money. Her financial difficulties have been immense, but her trust in God's care for them all has also increased enormously. Meetings with Carl are now very rare, and the children are all happier when they do not see him.)

So often do we find in life that difficulties and pain act as triggers for our spiritual growth. This has certainly been the case with Carol and, thanks both to the contacts she had through her work and to her wide reading, her knowledge of spiritual matters and of healing have grown apace. From a fairly humble beginning as a member of the nursing staff at the Cancer Help Centre, she has regained the interest and skill which she had in Ancient Egypt as a colour healer and she now has a nation-wide reputation in that field, often being invited by other hospitals in the country to go and give talks and advice[3]. The financial remuneration she began to receive from this enabled her to employ a child minder, and Simon was in any case now maturing more and more rapidly and able to take increasing responsibility as the eldest of the six children.

The fact that Carol had no karmic debt to her ex-husband, since the fault had been on his side, made cutting the ties with him fairly easy as well as desirable. He of course still has an immense debt to her, but that is his problem entirely. Forgiveness is always difficult when one has been abused, but Carol (who realises too that <u>she</u> had things to learn from the relationship) has been working on it determinedly and, since she does not want ever to have any further links with him, she has set Carl free from her for ever. That does not mean that his debt is wiped out – no one can ever do that for another person – but he will now have to work out that particular debt in a future life by being good to somebody else. (If we always had to come back to enable our debtors to pay their debts to us personally, final escape from *samsara* might never be achieved!)

When, however, it comes to ties with twin souls, we have another question entirely. Having seen the difference that cutting the ties with Carl made to the happiness of the whole family, and still feeling the most intense pain whenever she set eyes on Dan, Carol took it into her head to try a tie-cutting exercise with him as well. She felt this to be necessary firstly because of an increasing ambivalence in her relationship with Dan, and secondly because of a realisation that there was no reason why, if he was refusing either to free himself from Diane or to catch her up spiritually, she should not now be available for another man. The pain of her love for Dan was so unbearable that she wanted some distraction from it, and in any case she needed love and support as much as the children needed a father.

While Carol's work was developing and giving her increasing satisfaction, Dan's was doing exactly the opposite. With the recession there was less and less demand for bricklaying, and in any case he knew deep down that he was capable of even more important types of building (building up people, for instance). He did not know how to go about finding his true vocation, but because of their strong spiritual link, Carol's progress inevitably affected him, and seeing her growth filled him with envy, admiration and an ever-increasing sense of his own failure. For her growing self-confidence enabled her when they met gradually not to let him get away with his coldness. Sometimes she chided him on looking "so miserable", and occasionally her cheeriness forced him to ask questions about what she was up to. She recounts:–

"It angered me so, seeing him wasting his life and, being now so much more in control of my own than I had been when I was under Carl's thumb, I resolved to help him realise some of his own potential. Sometimes the barrier he put up was impenetrable, but at other times he looked genuinely pleased to see me and it was on one of these latter occasions that I managed to get him to admit that, following his realisation of having fallen in love, he had shut his feelings away into a box and cut himself off from them. I then pointed out to him that it wasn't only his own feelings that he'd shut away but mine too, and I tried to get over to him how much unnecessary suffering this had caused me. This made him express the extent to which he felt unworthy of my love, and I realised that his feelings of unworthiness made it difficult for him to appreciate the extent of my pain. But once I'd made it clear to him, he was filled with genuine remorse, which I found extraordinarily touching."

Here, once more, we can see a parallel with Angela and Bruce in the previous chapter. Angela, who felt so unworthy of Bruce, could not imagine that he could feel pain on account of her, but no doubt eventually (in a future lifetime if not in this one), he will realise exactly what he did and feel a need to make amends. For, as Joudry and Pressman say, *Emotional conflict is hard for anyone to bear; for twin souls it is unendurable. Being so much a part of each other, they feel the other's hurt ever more keenly. One heart breaks for the other. They must end the other's pain in order to heal it for themselves.* Dan's recognition of Carol's pain and his finally admitting to having cut himself off from his own, represented a major turning point in his spiritual development. For, as Sogyal Rinpoche explains so beautifully, we cannot have compassion for others until we allow ourselves fully to feel <u>our own</u> pain:–

If you keep your heart open through everything, your pain can become your greatest ally in your life's search for love and wisdom. And don't we know, only too well, that protection from pain doesn't work, and that when we try to defend ourselves from suffering, we only suffer more and don't learn what we can from the experience? As Rilke wrote, the protected heart that is "never exposed to loss, innocent and secure, cannot know tenderness; only the won-back heart can ever be satisfied: free, through all it has given up, to rejoice in its mastery."[4]

Like Angela and Bruce, however, and unlike several of the couples whom we shall be looking at in some of our ensuing chapters, Carol and Dan are not yet quite ready for one another. Or rather, while she is rapidly approaching the point of complete readiness, he still has jagged edges which need smoothing. As an analogy, let us imagine the spirit (the Higher Self) as a circle:–

In the beginning, and again when the final reunion is achieved, the two souls which represent the masculine and feminine energies fit as snugly into that circle as do the two halves of a yin/yang symbol. The "eye" in each half of course represents the seed of the other, permanently embedded within its partner:–

In between, however, because of spending sometimes centuries at a time separated on Earth from its other half, and getting battered by the trials and tribulations of difficult lifetimes on the planet, and sometimes trapped in materialism, selfishness and other vices, the smooth outline of each soul often becomes jagged:–

and therefore, when they meet, it is impossible for the fit to be perfect. Sometimes the jagged edges are so great that there is no way for the two halves even to recognise each other, but when the edges are almost smooth each partner will realise that they ought to fit:–

and then the thorny bits of each will dig deep into the flesh of the other, and the consequent pain is greater than any that can be felt through an ordinary heartbreak.

So, being now quite spiritually aware and realising that coping with the pain caused by Dan's thorns was taking energy both from her work and from her children, Carol performed a tie-cutting exercise. There are various ways of performing such an exercise, some of which are described by Phyllis Kristal in her well-known book *Cutting the Ties that Bind*[5]. Carol found the effect of this extraordinarily profound and, while bringing up floods of tears, the exercise left her temporarily with an almost ecstatic sense of freedom. The next time that she and Dan met at the school she sensed that it had affected him profoundly also. (Remember that, the links between them being spiritual, twin souls do not need to be together physically in order for the actions of one to affect the other.) Dan's look of pain was more acute than ever, yet at the same time Carol read in his face a sense of resignation, acceptance and distance.

Now Carol felt ready to welcome into her life, should he appear, a companion soulmate who would cherish her and give her support with the children. Partnerships between twin souls are still comparatively rare. In fact the number of people in the world who even know who their twin soul is, is quite small, and the fact that I was able to find enough subjects for this book is evidence for me of it having been guided by spirit. Indeed "find" is not really the right word at all. With each chapter the people I needed quite literally landed in my lap (or were sent by God or by my or their spirit guides) at the precise moment when I was ready to write about them!

So, marriages and partnerships between twin souls having throughout the ages been rare, many of the best partnerships have always been – and will no doubt continue to be for a long time – between companion soulmates. Joudry and Pressman explain very well that we all belong to "soul groups" in addition to being halves of a pair, and they say that each group will have to make the final return to the Source together. In order to facilitate the return, we raise each other up through loving relationships, and of course the more people we can help to evolve, and the more people who can be added to our group through love, the more quickly we can all be reabsorbed into God, which is the aim and destiny of humanity.

As explained in the Introduction, "companion soulmates" are people with whom we have a strong affinity on account of past-life connections, and it can happen that love for a companion soulmate is more comfortable than love for a twin soul. Returning for a moment to the yin/yang analogy: one can visualise two members of two separate pairs having become distorted in such a way that there are many similarities between them:–

The fit between such pairs will never be perfect, but then life on Earth is never perfect. It is up to us always to make the best of what is available to us, and companion-soulmate partnerships are always of benefit to the world as well as to the individuals concerned, who can blossom and grow through their love for one another.

So, when Robert came into Carol's life, firstly she gradually recognised him as a companion soulmate, and secondly, though the pain over Dan was still great, she genuinely believed that she had cut the ties with him and was therefore completely free and available for somebody else. Of course for anyone who is acquainted with their twin soul it is normally (there are exceptions to every rule, as will be seen in later chapters) very difficult to view anyone else of the opposite sex as attractive, but in the case of Robert his genuine caring and his selflessness gradually won Carol's heart (or at least a little bit of it!), and she found his companionship very pleasant. Also, of course, his availability was another strong point in his favour!

Robert is older than Carol, a widower with grown-up children of his own and, having taken early retirement with quite a reasonable income, he made it clear to her quite early on that, if she wanted a "wife" on account of her career and the children, he would be more than happy to take on that role. He has a great love of children and, though Joanna, the eldest girl, had still not processed the problems over her father and found it difficult to accept the idea of any other man coming into her mother's life, Robert began gently to endear himself to all of them. Carol found that they had much in common, he took an interest in her work, and was eager to learn more about healing.

Ever since the evening when Carol and Dan had declared their love for one another, relations between Carol and Diane, which had never been easy, became intolerable. Dan did not say a word to Diane, but his feelings of guilt were intensified by a conviction that she knew intuitively what had happened and, while still treating him abominably, she became even more dependent and demanding. Occasional meetings between the two women were made inevitable by Simon's friendship with Jonathan and, while Carol made every effort to be friendly and helpful, she found Diane's hostility difficult to cope with. Before Robert appeared on the scene, Dan occasionally confided his troubles briefly to Carol, and a few weeks _after_ the tie-cutting exercise, he began to open up to her more readily. This made Carol realise that in fact cutting the ties with him was impossible. Dan's troubles involved not only his difficulties with his wife, but also his diminishing work and, though he <u>listened</u> to Carol when she told him repeatedly that he was capable of greater things, and told her that her appreciation meant more than anything in the world to him, he showed no inclination to follow up her suggestions as to how he could set about realising his potential. Also, on his darkest days when, she says, "He looked simply dreadful, he would make out that everything was fine, and that was hardest of all for me to cope with because then the barriers he put up were impenetrable."

Although, as we have said, Joudry and Pressman say in their book that twin soul acquaintanceships should not normally cause marriage break-ups, they also make the important point that sometimes a partner can be an impediment. At such times progress on the spiritual path can only be made by severance. In the case of Dan and Diane, they had long since admitted to each other that the relationship was an empty one and that they were each holding the other back, but Diane was quite simply terrified of being alone and also considered herself incapable of supporting herself financially. Joudry and Pressman's words are so appropriate here that another quotation seems useful:

This becomes a particularly difficult problem when the limited partner is one who is given to neurotic illness. (That is certainly the case with Diane.) _Then the caretaking partner is nurturing the sick aspect of the other, to the detriment of both. It is necessary in these cases to confront the limited partner with the difficulty, even at the threat of dissolving the marriage . . . The strong partner_

will not always find it easy to distinguish between care-giving and self-sacrificing
. . . Unenlightened self-sacrifice impedes the advance of both personality and
soul. The self is not ours to sacrifice: it is God's.

While Dan did not have the self-confidence or trust to see that this was what was going on with him, Carol was able to see it very clearly, and (having established with the help of a clairvoyant that he was indeed her twin soul, and feeling in consequence a strong sense of responsibility for him), she set out to help him understand the situation. It is important here to point out that her motives were not selfish ones. Much though she yearned for a sexual relationship with Dan, she knew that that was by no means the most important aspect of the link between them. In fact she knew that their link was a spiritual and eternal one, and that expressing it sexually would only be of use to either of them if it helped them along the spiritual path.

Though she has been given little opportunity in her life so far to make use of it, Carol has always had an innate talent for writing, and so she began to make a habit of putting her thoughts about Dan down on to paper. This she found cathartic for herself, particularly when she was feeling at her most low, and she also felt sure that what she was saying was what Dan needed to hear – that it was things which only his twin soul was able to teach him. Meetings at the school gates were sufficiently frequent for Carol to be able to hand over her letters to Dan. Some of them were quite brutal, but they were always full of love too, and often Dan's face would light up expectantly when he saw her approaching. At other times, however, he would look truly downcast and say, "Oh no, not another letter!" but Carol's self-assurance about the rightness of what she was doing was growing and he never attempted to dispute her insistence that he read her latest letter very carefully.

Now Carol's moods would fluctuate along with Dan's. At times he appeared to be making real moves along the spiritual path and she would feel quite elated and optimistic, but at other times he would seem to be all gloom and doom and that would make her feel very depressed and weary. (Despite having a child minder, the combination of her work and the children's demands on her were taxing her health and she was never able to get sufficient rest.) It was on one of these days of "gloom and doom" that Robert, with whom her friendship had gradually been deepening, put a marriage proposal to her very seriously. She says:–

"I was desperately torn. I had told Robert early on about my love for Dan and the exact nature of our spiritual relationship, he had been incredibly understanding, but I thought he might weary of me. He isn't yet all that spiritually aware, but he is very eager to learn. He said he quite understood if I was more attracted to someone nearer me in age, but I assured him that age had nothing to do with it. Spiritual age is the only thing that really matters in relationships and, although he is a bit less evolved than Dan, Robert is such a thoroughly good and loving person and there is genuine understanding between us which no doubt comes from previous shared incarnations. I felt confident that

I could be reasonably happy with Robert, and that we would be good for each other, but there was always the nagging thought in the back of my mind, 'Supposing Diane died – she's ill so often – or supposing Dan did pull himself together sufficiently to be able to leave her?' So I told Robert that I did really care for him, but that he must give me a bit of time to think about it. I also told him that I would have to talk with Dan about it, and he was amazingly understanding."

Dan was of course not unaware of Robert's existence – Carol would not dream of keeping such a thing from him – and Diane, having seen them together, had become rather more friendly. Though it clearly pained him to do so, Dan had actually encouraged Carol to deepen the relationship if Robert wished it – "Since you're free and I'm not" – but she had said initially that she could not possibly care for anyone other than him really deeply. Now that Robert had convinced her of the seriousness of his intentions, logic told her that she should say "Yes", but she says:–

"Each night after I thought I'd really made up my mind to settle with Robert, whom I couldn't bear to hurt, I would have a really vivid dream about Dan, and then in the morning my mind would again be in a turmoil. This went on for days, and eventually I poured it all out in another letter. I thought perhaps that the reality of Robert's proposal might just give Dan the kick up the backside that he was really needing, but alas I was wrong. Although he has quite given up his attempts at denying the love bond between us, the next time that we met Dan told me that he was keen to meet Robert – almost as though he wanted to give his approval. Well, since Diane was now being quite friendly to me, I decided to take the plunge and invite them both round for a meal. I told Diane when I issued the invitation that Robert had proposed to me, and she accepted with apparent delight, congratulating me on "finding a new father for all the children". I told her that I hadn't yet quite made up my mind – especially since Joanna was still finding Robert difficult to accept – but she more or less ignored that. Well, the evening was a rather extraordinary experience. Simon, who now knows all about the fact that Dan is my twin soul and actually prefers him to Robert, kept introducing spiritual subjects into the conversation. Both Dan and Robert (who got on very well and each told me afterwards that he really liked the other) responded with questions, and the four of us got into quite an interesting and deep discussion. I didn't want Diane to feel left out, and I tried a few times to draw her into the conversation, but she just sat in a corner growing visibly angrier and angrier, and then found an excuse to leave in order to pick up Jonathan from Scouts. As soon as she had left the house the atmosphere lifted almost visibly. My clairvoyant friend had warned me that there was a lot of darkness in Diane, which I would find it difficult to penetrate, and suddenly the full truth of that really dawned on me. When Dan finally got up to leave too, it was a visible effort. My heart ached for him more than I can describe, but at the same time I felt that he had given Robert and me his blessing."

The next day Carol decided that she needed to repeat the tie-cutting exercise. So she went into meditation and asked to be shown which ties with Dan had been restored and which needed to be cut again. She was not all surprised to be shown that they had <u>all</u> been restored, and she felt that it was necessary to deal with every one except that linking their hearts. This time she pulled them out by the roots, which caused visible (and painful!) wounds, but then Dan appeared in her vision and bathed the sores for her. After that she felt better, but she accepts the fact that she may need to repeat the exercise at regular intervals.

So now Carol is settled into a worthwhile life with Robert, whose support is a boon both for her work and with the children. She can never put Dan completely out of her mind, and when they meet he sometimes comments on points she made to him in her letters. So she knows that their heart tie will never be severed, and that their meeting when they did was part of the Divine Plan and has helped to prepare them both for being together in a future incarnation.

Notes

1. *Twin Souls: A Guide to Finding your True Spiritual Partner* by Patricia Joudry and Maurie D. Pressman, M.D., published by Element Books, Shaftesbury, Dorset.
2. All Joan Grant's books are published by Ariel Press, U.S.A.
3. I need to point out here that this is not factual. A certain amount of disguise is necessary for the characters in this book, and therefore some of the jobs I have given people are fictitious. The <u>essence</u> of Carol's work, however, has been captured.
4. *The Tibetan Book of Living and Dying* by Sogyal Rinpoche, published by Rider.
5. *Cutting the Ties that Bind* by Phyllis Kristal, published by Samuel Weiser, U.S.A.

Chapter IV

TWIN SOULS ARE OFTEN VERY TELEPATHIC
The story of Ellen and Fred

They were in the early years of their married life, and Fred was in the Navy. Ellen, who ran a florist's shop, always warned her assistants if she was in a bad mood, giving the reason for it. One morning, however, she simply did not know what was wrong, so she didn't say anything. She had been restless from the moment she got up, and as the morning wore on she became more and more anxious. Eventually one of the girls said to her, "Look, what's wrong? There's something worrying you, isn't there?" She replied, "Yes, you're right, but I don't <u>know</u> what's wrong. Perhaps I'd better phone Fred's superior and ask whether he's OK."

Fred's superior promised to make enquiries and phone her back in a couple of hours. The two hours seemed more like two days. Eventually the phone rang. "Fred's been having a bit of ulcer trouble and has been poorly for a few days. He didn't want you to know about it because he didn't want you to worry, but he's going into hospital for an operation. I'll phone again as soon as I have any more news."

Ellen's anxiety mounted. "Are you telling me the whole truth?"

"Well, that's what Fred asked me to tell you."

"That's not the whole story, is it?"

"Well, as a matter of fact, the ulcer has turned out to be worse than we thought. But please don't worry. I'll phone you again the moment I have any more news."

The next phone call informed Ellen that Fred was extremely ill following the operation and had only a fifty per cent chance of surviving. This confirmation of her premonition naturally made Ellen quite frantic with worry. Fred's superior, too, was now unable to hide his own deep concern. He could see that she was the only person who could possibly give Fred the will to live, and urged her to send a telegram. Ellen of course lost no time in getting the telegram off to her beloved husband. She longed to be able to visit him. Just two days later, however, wonderful news came. Fred was up and about, had made an amazing recovery, and before long – to his colleagues' complete astonishment – he was back at work as normal.

Ellen and Fred are reminiscent of Raki and Piyanah in Joan Grant's *Scarlet Feather*[1]. Like Raki and Piyanah, they are first cousins, and also like them (who, it may be remembered, were suckled together by Piyanah's mother following the death of Raki's mother), it is probably true to say that in this lifetime they have never not been in love. Fred was born in Birmingham in 1940 and Ellen, who is five years older, in Stratford-upon-Avon, and their mothers were sisters. Because of the bombs in Birmingham during the War, Fred's family were evacuated to Stratford when Fred was under a year old and, owing to shortage of space in Ellen's parents' home, he was put into her bed. Now Ellen says jokingly, "And he's been trying to get out of it ever since!" (They have seven children!) Fred did get engaged to someone else at one point in his youth, but it didn't last long. Ellen says, "One of the first things he did was to bring her to meet me. She was very nice! And all through the years when we were apart – though we were never apart for that long because of course our families kept very much in touch after the War was over and Fred's family were able to move back to their own home – his mother always made a point of coming and telling me what he was up to." (No doubt Ellen's aunt realised, at least subconsciously, that they were twin souls. She was the seventh daughter of a seventh child, and it is a well-known fact that such people tend to have special psychic talents.[2])

Fred was in the Navy for seventeen years, and the time when he was so ill was only one of many quite dramatic instances of telepathy between them. On another occasion Ellen recalls having gone into a shop to buy something she needed and found herself also picking up a packet of turquoise pen refills. As she paid for them, she commented to the assistant, "I don't know why I'm buying these!" but then, when she got home, she found a letter just arrived from Fred in which he had asked her to send him some turquoise pen refills – a colour she never used herself!

During those seventeen years, despite being so busy with her florist's shop and the care of their children, Ellen wrote fifteen pages a day to Fred. He wrote to her three times a week, and all his letters were illustrated. They have kept all the letters and often have fun nowadays looking through them together. I felt privileged at being granted an interview for this book, as they once turned down an offer of £18,000 from a magazine that wanted to publish their love story in a three-part series! Besides that, two other people have expressed a desire to write their biography. (Ellen says, "I could write a book about all the people I've known in my life. My mother always had an open house for everybody, and Judi Dench says that she'd like to write the Preface to my book!)

Ellen and Fred are, however, a very spiritual couple and have no interest in money. For the past year and a bit they have been running the Lifeways Health Centre in Stratford, and, because they both work all the time, it is there that our meeting took place. Lifeways, which was founded by my friend Heather Burton and her deceased husband, is an exceptionally attractive centre with a large garden and orchard, and it contains many quite beautiful therapy rooms which are used by a wide variety of practitioners. Fred, who has a long history of healing (thirty-five years in this life, but we shall mention previous ones shortly!), runs twelve-week courses for the Healer Practitioners' Association International, and he had to leave the office before we had finished talking, as a healing group was scheduled for that morning. This did not matter, however, since Ellen was still available and had plenty more to tell me.

If working together is seen as both the primary purpose of and the ideal for twin souls, then Ellen and Fred are undoubtedly a prime example. In Ancient Greece Fred, who was at that time a lot older than Ellen, was a healer-priest in a small temple dedicated to Asclepios (the Greek God of medicine). They met after Ellen and her mother had been stricken with the plague and journeyed a long way to the temple for healing. Fred failed to save Ellen's mother's life, but Ellen recovered eventually after he had nursed her for some time. Then, having no family to return to, she remained in the temple while thinking about what to do next. The decision was made for her, however, as he taught her all his healing arts, she became his assistant and then also a priestess, and for the rest of that incarnation they remained bound together through love. It was during a time of great civil unrest in Greece, and so they practised their skills together to heal those wounded in battle.

Several centuries later, during the Middle Ages, Ellen and Fred were again involved together in helping people through a time of war. In that incarnation Ellen was married at first to another man, who got wounded in battle. Fred, who was Ellen's husband's comrade, brought him back to her, and the husband told her on his death-bed that he was entrusting her to Fred's care and protection. Fred consequently stayed on to fulfil his best friend's wishes, and in due course the couple fell in love and married. They held combined lands – Fred's own and those left to Ellen by her husband – and they ruled jointly over these lands benevolently, making use both of spiritual philosophy and of herbal remedies and other healing arts in which she was then expert.

Though Fred has had rather more incarnations than Ellen has – frequently with twin souls, one stays behind in spirit to serve the other as a guide, or if he/she is not acting as the other's guide, they often work together at night – they have been together on the planet many times. And when they have not actually been living together, they have often been acquainted – residing, for instance, in the same village. They have undoubtedly returned this time as helpers in a time of crisis and, though Fred himself feels that this is his last incarnation as he has already "done everything", Edwin Courtenay believes that there is still much work for him to do here. As for Ellen, she says that she has never had time to think about what her future might be after this lifetime!

My own research has led me to the view that advanced souls frequently have either conscious past-life memories or occasional flashbacks to previous lives. Fred's "age" viewed in this light was confirmed by a little story he had of being out with Ellen for a walk in a part of the country they had never visited before. He suddenly said to her, "I'm <u>sure</u> there's a church somewhere around here." So they hunted and hunted and eventually came across a sign saying, "To the church". On arrival at the church, Fred said, "It felt very familiar."

Fred's decision to be of service to the planet yet again was demonstrated not only when, as a young man, he was given only a fifty per cent chance of survival from an operation, but also, much earlier, by a determination to be born! His parents' marriage had been one of convenience and, his mother never having been happy, he, as the youngest, was the result of an extra-marital affair. Hoping to keep the affair secret, his mother decided to have an abortion, but it turned out that she had conceived twins and only Fred's twin was aborted. Fred did not find out about this until well after he was grown-up, but he says, "I was conscious all through my childhood both of feeling different and of missing someone, of being incomplete. Later of course, when we got together, Ellen filled the gap. I feel complete with her. But also, after I'd found out the truth about my parenthood, I remembered my elder brother commenting, 'Why is it that <u>you</u> are always the subject of our parents' rows?' So then <u>everything</u> made sense. My mother really loved my natural father, and we got to know him towards the end of his life and kept up with him till the end."

When Ellen and Fred told me their story it was just at the time when a woman who had aborted one of two twins was much in the news in England. Hundreds of abortions take place without comment day after day, yet this one caused a national outcry. The reason seemed to be twofold: firstly, the question in everyone's mind, "How could one decide which baby to keep?" and secondly, reflection on the feelings of the surviving baby when it found out later on what had happened – that it had only had a fifty/fifty chance of not being murdered. No doubt that child, too, will all its life be conscious of missing someone. Apparently there has only been a handful of cases the whole world over of one twin surviving an abortion.

Ellen and Fred, as we have said, are very spiritual, and in both cases this side of their character was nurtured from an early age. Both their mothers were Christian Scientists, but they did not force their beliefs on to their families. Both did the rounds of all the churches from an early age. Fred's mother did healing, which probably explains why he started that so young. He describes his father as a "real Christian, but who never went to church, believing himself to be closer to God in his garden. (He was a professional gardener.)" Fred became an Anglican through his own choice and was at one time a candidate for ordination. He gave it up when he found that he couldn't go along with the dogma. Ellen's grandfather was a Quaker and she was brought up to regard that as a little "odd", but recently they have both begun to feel at home in the Quakers, and she is about to join their ranks officially.

Their backgrounds were conducive to their healing work as well as their innate spiritual natures. The grandfather that they shared was a healer and herbalist, and their grandmother was clairvoyant as well as Fred's mother. Both of them have always seen auras and – like all the other people I have heard of with auric sight – did not realise for some time that there was anything unusual in this. Both of them see "ghosts", and they say that they attract "ghosts", often having shared residences with them. Here I put the word "ghosts" in inverted commas as I feel that a more accurate epithet would be "friendly spirit". The definition of the word "ghost" to which I adhere is that used by, for instance, Lance Trendall, in his book *Dead Happy*[3]. These are spirits who are trapped on the Earth's plane on account of the simple fact that they do not know that they are dead. As Trendall explains in detail, it is important to help such spirits, and this is easily done even by people who are unable to see them. All that is necessary is to explain to them that they are dead (and that that is why everyone has been ignoring them!), and that all they need to do to move on is to think of someone they loved who they know to be dead too and then that person will immediately come to their rescue. Since Ellen and Fred and their family enjoy the company of their "ghosts", it seems clear to me that that is not what they actually are.

While Ellen and Fred both clearly have psychic gifts, she is the more strongly psychic of the two. She is the one who has experienced all the really dramatic instances of telepathy between them, and she often knows exactly what he is thinking. She has received messages all her life, and part of her work nowadays (for which she does not charge) consists of giving people such things as Tarot readings. She has a habit of holding conversations with photographs, and one of the most dramatic incidents of their life involved an old lady they had befriended and nicknamed "Annabel".

Following his seventeen years in the Navy, Fred joined the probation service, and for twelve years he ran a hostel for ex-offenders in Rugby. (He was very successful in this work, partly on account of the spiritual guidance he was able to give them. He used to take them to a different church each Sunday.) When the eldest of their children were already grown-up, someone once made the comment that what they were really doing with the hostel was running a hotel, and this gave them the idea of switching to a career in that domain. "Annabel", who, while living in Rugby had spoken often and affectionately of Newark where she had been born and brought up, was dead by this time. Ellen and Fred had found what they thought was the perfect hotel to buy, and were all set to move when the purchase fell through at the last minute. After reading through brochure after brochure about hotels all over the country, most of which were much too expensive, they were near to despair, when Ellen spoke to Annabel's photograph and heard her voice say, "Don't worry, my dear. I'll sort it out." The next day – unusually – just one envelope arrived through the post and it was advertising a hotel in Newark.

Neither of them knew Newark and it was not a place that they would ever have thought of but, sure enough, the hotel proved to be an ideal purchase for them.

Ellen's artistic bent helped them to do it up beautifully, and they opened a restaurant for a hundred and twenty, which Fred ran single-handedly. The hotel was always full and the restaurant rapidly became known as the best in the area. Often when they asked clients, "How did you hear of us?" they replied, "A little old lady told us." So they are firmly convinced that "Annabel" was still helping them! In due course some of Ellen and Fred's children joined them in the business, and after a while they felt redundant and moved elsewhere.

Ellen and Fred decided to give up the hotel business and return to Stratford when the wife of one of their sons left him and their three children. The job running the Lifeways Centre cropped up before they had had time to worry about finding work, and it is obviously the perfect position for them. Their only concern at the moment is that Ellen, who is employed part-time on a voluntary basis, now really needs to find paid work in order to help their financial situation. Fred cannot conceive of managing without her.

This is fully to be expected with a pair of twin souls. As the two halves of one being, twin souls always complement one another totally. In Ellen and Fred's case, though Fred has artistic talent (demonstrated in the illustrations and poems he used to include in his letters to her from the Navy), she is in the main the artistic one and he the scientific. (Besides her talent as a florist, Ellen is an accomplished writer and regularly publishes stories in magazines under a pseudonym. He, however, often gives a hand by reading her drafts and editing them.) Fred says, "Ellen has an extraordinarily quick mind and she's always one step ahead of me. So that I often say, 'How did you know I wanted that?' Despite the Swords of Honour I was awarded in the Navy, I'm not really a businessman. She has a business brain. On the other hand, if someone comes wanting figures and contracts, I deal with that, whereas if there's someone wanting to unload their problems, I hand them over to Ellen." And Ellen added, "Then I pass them back to Fred when I've sorted them out!"

Fred has exceptional energy and, as we have said, he works all the time. Ellen says, "He has to have two secretaries because just one gets a nervous breakdown. When he was running the hostel and I wasn't actually working with him, he had an excellent secretary, but if something cropped up when he was out, she always used to phone and ask my advice about whether to bleep him. We don't really know how he'll cope when I leave Lifeways. I'd love to stay, but we just can't afford for me to carry on working voluntarily. He's unsettled when we're apart. One of his hobbies is metal detecting, but as I never go with him, he doesn't go very often."

They complement one another, too, in that she loves décor and he can execute everything that she wants. When their children were young, they shared all the work of caring for them. She has always cooked a lot, "but he cooks the things I don't know how to do." They have the same taste in books, similar tastes in music ("though I like Chopin, whereas he prefers Beethoven") and, while she tends to get bored in museums, he, who is very interested in Roman history, picks out the things that she likes. She is less interested in history than he is, but they both love genealogy.

So, of the three pairs we have looked at so far, Ellen and Fred display the characteristics most typical of a twin soul couple. We shall, however, be meeting more such "perfect matches", and in any case – unless Angela achieves her desire not to return! – both Angela and Bruce and Carol and Dan should be able to live similar lifetimes to this before very long. What is clear is that Ellen and Fred have <u>merited</u> their happiness together this time round from previous lifetimes of service. Angela and Carol are aware of that fact, and aware that we come to Earth primarily to learn rather than to seek happiness. They know that, before they can be <u>completely</u> ready for full union with their twin, they need to be (as Joudry and Pressman say), sufficiently secure not to be dependent on the other for their *sense of self*[4]. Angela and Carol are both working hard on that and feel that they are drawing ever nearer to it. Bruce (who has in any case cut himself right off from Angela and is certainly not at all dependent on her for his sense of self) and Dan will also be learning it later if not sooner. Ellen and Fred, having already reached this point, are among the teachers that our planet so badly needs, and I have no doubt that they will go on leading the way for a long time yet – whether again on the Earth's plane or (as Fred himself hopes and feels) in spirit.

Notes
1. *Scarlet Feather* by Joan Grant, published by Ariel Press.
2. See *The Miracle of Colour Healing* by Vicky Wall and *Dreams that come True* by Barbara Garwell, both published by Thorsons.
3. *Dead Happy* by Lance Trendall, published by Lance Trendall Press.
4. *Twin Souls – A Guide to Finding your True Spiritual Partner* by Patricia Joudry and Maurie D. Pressman, M.D., published by Element Books, Shaftesbury, Dorset.

Chapter V

TWIN SOULS OFTEN FIND THAT THEY DO
SIMILAR THINGS AT THE SAME TIME
The story of Graham and Helen

"It was on the fifth day that I told Helen that I had had a dream about the frog ring I was wearing. In this dream she had asked me for the ring. I therefore suggested that she wear it the following night and 'see what happens'. So she did, and that was it! That was the beginning. At that point we realised that there was something between us. On the final day of the week we were inseparable, but that was the day she had to go back to Germany and so I was very sad."

Our next couple feel neither need nor desire to be anonymous, and the woman's real name is Elfi, but, not wanting to upset our alphabet, I am calling her Helen. Graham is the well-known clairvoyant healer Edwin Courtenay's elder brother; Helen, who is German, acts as Edwin's organiser and translator for the many workshops and readings he does in Germany. Needless to say, it was through Edwin that they met, and it was Edwin too who first told them that they were twin souls.

Edwin Courtenay was the chief clairvoyant advisor for my first (autobiographical) book, and he receives many mentions in that, both in the account of my present life and in previous ones in which we knew one another also (when he prophesied my future work on karma). I was fortunate in being introduced to Edwin when he was at the very beginning of his career and consequently had quite a lot of time to give to me. Since that book's completion he has become so well known that he is now very difficult to get hold of – even for five minutes on the telephone. Graham, who is nine years older than Edwin, has consequently inevitably suffered to some extent from being regularly introduced to people simply as "Edwin's brother" rather than as an interesting person in his own right. Their voices are very similar, and now, in order to avoid the sound of disappointment at the other end of the phone when someone who has been chasing Edwin for a while thinks that they have at last got him, Graham always answers the phone by giving his own name.

The Courtenays are a very happy and united family, and in between the two brothers there is a sister, who now has her own family. The first eleven years of

Graham's life were spent in Middlesex, but then the family suddenly moved to Yorkshire because Mrs. Courtenay heard of a house that was being sold. ("She's impulsive, is my mother!" he says. "She just does things like that.") Graham has few memories of his years prior to the move – "only silly little things like playing in a paddling pool with a spotted ball, treading on a bee and getting stung. I remember the garden of the house near London, which was nice, and long; and I remember firework parties and being chased up a ladder by a Jumping Jack firework. I don't think that I'm suppressing any traumatic memories, though I do think that moving at the age of eleven was probably quite a wrench for me."

Edwin's psychic gifts became apparent at an exceedingly young age, as he started seeing his spirit guides when he was only four, and by the age of fourteen or fifteen was already leading meditation groups and giving advice to people on spiritual matters. Graham says that the clairvoyance was accepted as quite natural by their family, and his father in particular also had much interest in such things. Now that he has met his twin soul and is moving into his own power, Graham himself is also beginning to display a certain amount of clairvoyant ability, sometimes seeing his own spirit guides when he is in meditation. He has attended many workshops in which Edwin has done guided meditations, and these have enabled him to find out a good deal about his previous lives, and so he has not needed readings from his brother for information about his past.

Graham left school at sixteen and went to College for a four-year course in Graphic Design, but two months before the end of his studies he realised that he didn't want to be a graphic designer but an illustrator. He failed the "big test" at the end of the course, and following that spent a number of years "searching". He embarked on a number of other courses – in cartooning for instance – did various little jobs, but was never happy. The family, as we have said, are very close and supportive of one another. Edwin also has artistic talent, and while he was in his teens and Graham in his twenties, Graham gave him advice and encouragement in his art. Edwin, however, in due course went to College to study Drama, soon abandoning that as recognition of his clairvoyant powers grew to such an extent as to render his more-than-full-time career seemingly inevitable. This was hard for Graham, as his younger brother seemed to him to find life much less difficult than he did.

Another cause of Graham's unhappiness during these years was the need he felt for a satisfactory relationship. He was twenty-eight when he got his first girlfriend, and after that he says that he had a series of relationships, all of which were very short-lived. It is my belief that, just like Angela in Chapter Two, Graham incarnated this time not only with a determination to find his twin soul, but also that he had subconscious knowledge even of her appearance, for he says, "The girlfriends I had were all very similar. I realise now that I must have had a pre-fixed idea in my head of what 'she' was going to look like eventually. Because they all had dark hair, bobbed haircuts . . . Very similar to Helen in looks in fact. Some of them were spiritual . . . There was always something there – something of what Helen has – that I would latch on to. It was as though I was always on one big search for my soul partner. I think it must have been subconscious, because I didn't realise what it was that I was looking for." Joudry and Pressman say, like Moshab, that each one of us carries the image of our twin soul deep within: *The image may be blurred, but it is there. For this reason, everyone who comes on earth has a vague hope that he will meet somewhere a soul who will be everything he needs, and that with this soul he will find indescribable harmony and perfect fusion.*[1]

Helen's family are less close than Graham's, and she left home at the age of nineteen after studying pottery for three years. At twenty-one she came to England as an *au pair* in order to learn the language (little knowing at that point quite how useful it would be to her in later life!). She moved away from her parents and elder brother because she wanted to be free and independent. On her return, she worked again as a potter in different workshops both in Germany and Austria. When she was twenty-four she decided to go back to College for two years in order to become a "Master of Pottery", and after that she started up her own pottery workshop. Two years later she met her first husband, but they separated after nine years, when their daughter was only two years old.

The years of bringing up her daughter on her own, having to earn a living for the two of them with her pottery workshop, were far from easy. The fact, however, that she had already taken courses in "Esoteric Psychology" given by Thorwald Dethlefsen in Munich, and also started to read spiritual books before her daughter was born, gave her a great deal of help in understanding life from a different perspective. For this had given her the knowledge that there are no accidents, and that she had to take responsibility for the circumstances of her own life.

At the end of 1988, after a few years of being almost totally tied to her home and workshop while her daughter was very young, Helen attended a New Age conference. There she met Janet McClure, a famous American channel, and that proved to be the real beginning of her spiritual life. In 1990 she started to organise programmes with different spiritual teachers. Most of these came from America, and so she resumed her studies of English in order to improve her powers of communication. After about two years her English had improved so much that she was able to translate "readings" for people, and it was only a year or so after this that she began to act as translator for Edwin's weekend workshops.

Helen was always told by the channels whose visits she organised that there would be a man in her future, but that she needed to be patient. And so the years went by, her daughter grew to be a teenager, life's problems continued, but she threw herself more and more into her spiritual work and, what with her pottery as well, she had little time for anything else.

At the age of thirty-one, when he was still searching and feeling somewhat frustrated with life, Graham, too, went back to College to try to regain his illustration skills. "I began then to get interested in Sculpture, and I was back at the same College as I'd been when I was sixteen. Being taught by some

81

of the same tutors as I'd had at sixteen, but, as a mature student, I was also older than some of the tutors, which was very strange. I felt something of a fish out of water among all the teenagers and sometimes, when they heard that I'd been at the College before, they would think, 'He's over thirty and been here before, so he must know what he's talking about.' So they would come and ask me things. But I didn't know any different. I was in the same boat as them, having just started again." Having decided on studying Sculpture, Graham in due course got accepted for a degree course, which he was due to start in September 1995.

The earlier part of the summer of 1995, however, had seen the end of yet another relationship for Graham – a relationship which had lasted longer than most of the previous ones. He was consequently feeling exceedingly depressed, and Edwin, in order to get him out of himself "and out of Mexborough where all the sadness was", offered him a free place on a week's guided tour of the Sacred Sites of Cornwall in which he was leading a group of Germans. Graham (who had by now decided that he had finished with relationships for ever and was going to give up looking), said at first that he would go, but then changed his mind at the last minute. In the end his younger brother's insistence won but, not knowing the other participants on the tour and not speaking any German, Graham did not enjoy the trip at all until the fifth day.

It was on that day, as Graham explains at the beginning of the chapter, that it all began. Now Helen, who had not been in a serious relationship for eleven years, had been told not only by Edwin, but also by other clairvoyants, that she would in due course be meeting her twin soul, and she had also been told less than three months previously that it would be within three months. So, unlike Graham, she was prepared for the meeting and recognised him more or less instantly. Graham felt sure straight away that this new relationship was "different from all the others, very special", but at the same time his past negative experiences naturally made him very cautious. He says, "It was a bit scary at first because you never know what might happen, and in any case I didn't at this stage know very much at all about twin souls and soulmates, but now I feel much more secure about it."

So the last three days of that Cornwall trip must have been pretty amazing for Graham and Helen. In meditation, both on those three days and on a subsequent tour a few months later, they began to have visions of previous lifetimes they had shared and, interestingly, they found very strong connections with the South West of England. The earliest lifetime they have glimpsed was in Egypt, where they were seated side by side on a throne, but no more details of that have as yet been forthcoming. Little, too, has been seen of the details of the Arthurian lifetime in which they were both Knights of the Outer Round Table, but after being killed during that period, they returned very quickly into a post-Arthurian incarnation which Graham feels has much bearing on the present.

Graham lived during the first part of that lifetime in Cornwall, where there was a group of people who were trying to stamp out the local religion. Very important to this religion were the energies in certain rocks, and while Graham and Edwin were with the Germans on the above-mentioned tour, they meditated around a rock engraved with two spirals, and obviously a third spiral missing. In his meditation – to his disbelief – Graham saw himself actually removing the section of the rock which held the third spiral. It was terrifying, because he was surrounded by armed men who he knew were intent on killing him, but he also knew that it was vital for him and for the fellow light workers of his religion that he preserve this spiral. So he fled, thus leaving the remaining two spirals and the temple safe, because the enemy were now more interested in catching him than in wreaking further destruction at the site. The day after Graham had seen this scene in meditation, a local person told Edwin that there was a theory that someone had forced the third spiral off the rock face!

From then on Graham found that the rest of the tour formed a continuous story in this post-Arthurian lifetime of his. "I saw myself running. And there's a place called 'The Cheese Wring', where there's a big rock-pile. I remember hiding there at night time, being scared, knowing full well that I could get killed at any second. Eventually I went to Glastonbury Tor, which was an island then, there was water all round it – I was walking all the way, so it must have taken months I think – and at Glastonbury Tor I met Helen, who was a high priestess, and also two other people, a man (who was a knight just as I was) and a woman, both of whom I know now. The four of us went inside a kind of chapel on the Tor and there we broke the slab of rock that I had brought with me into four. It broke into four equal parts, and we each took a piece. I went with Helen to hide our pieces, while the other two went off together somewhere else and I don't know what happened to them.

Helen and I obviously formed a relationship very quickly then too, and we took these pieces of rock all the way back to Cornwall (still walking!), where we slung them into Dewsmary Pool, which is where Arthur's sword Excalibur was supposedly thrown into. I've tried to work out the journey and it seemed to be all over the place. When I went to Dewsmary Pool on this first Cornwall trip, I had an overwhelming feeling of sadness and I couldn't work out why. Eventually I was told that it stemmed not from the visit there that I had made with Helen when we were carrying the pieces of rock, but from previous lifetimes when we'd been knights together. We'd had many battles there, and I'd probably died in some of these battles. It could well have been a sadness from many lifetimes that I was feeling then."

Graham had to wait for the next year, when he went back to do a second Cornwall trip, to get the end of his story. He says, "It was very strange. It was a completely different energy this time, and I couldn't understand what I was there for, because I wasn't getting any more bits of the story. But then we went to Avebury Stone Circle, and I was drawn to a really big stone at the end. I kept looking at it and asking myself, 'Why am I here?' and I couldn't walk away from it. So in the end I just put my back to it, closed my eyes and meditated, and

I was shocked because I saw my own death. I had this tremendous pain in my solar plexus, which must have been where the sword went through. Helen told me later that near Avebury there was a sanctuary – a place where the energies were such that you couldn't get harmed – so we've come to the conclusion that that's where we were going to. In that lifetime, as in some others that I've found out about, I sacrificed myself to save Helen. I knew that people were chasing us and that they were catching up, and so I told Helen and whoever else may have been with us to go on, and that I would stay there to try and keep the enemy off and then try and get back to them. But I remember one knight in black chain mail, who came up to me on horseback. I was fighting him, but his lance just went straight through my armour and through my solar plexus, and that's where I died. I died at that stone. So that was why I had to go to Avebury, because we didn't go to Avebury on the first tour."

Graham explains that this post-Arthurian lifetime is the most relevant to his and Helen's present situation "because it's that that actually brought us together, and we're still working with that energy and we know for a fact that we have to return to that area and take the energy that we find back to this place. We're going to keep working with the spirals. One day I'm going to write about it – it's so interesting!"

Another particularly interesting thing about the karma from that lifetime is that the man who killed him at Avebury is someone known to Graham now! They get on well, and Graham does not feel that there is any debt outstanding, but he discussed with Edwin whether to tell the person and decided that he should. "At first he just didn't know whether or not to believe it, and it worried him much more than it worried me, but now it's OK." (Most of us have probably taken other people's lives at some time in our past, and knowing that should make us less quick to condemn those whose actions now horrify us.)

Graham has as yet only ever found one life in which he was female, and that was not one of those he shared with Helen. She, however, knows of several lifetimes in which she was male, and besides the Arthurian period in which they were Grail knights together, Graham and Helen have found another life in which they were both male. In this incarnation they were Tibetan Buddhist monks, at the time that they were being slaughtered. Graham says, "I remember how there were people breaking into the temple, and I was shot at point blank range in the solar plexus (again!). As I lay dying on the floor Helen came up to me to try and stop the bleeding. I just looked up and saw this man put a gun to her head and shoot her (or rather him). So we died together that time."

I was interested to know whether, as two males, Graham had been aware of the twin soul bond to a similar extent as in incarnations in which they had been opposite sexes, and he replied, "Yes, I think so. Because there were other monks dying all around, but it was me she was really distraught about. We were obviously very close friends, though I have no idea whether we knew that we were twin souls."

In the Introduction to my first book, I have listed a large number of ways of finding out about previous lives, but only four of these come into this book. "Far memory" such as was held by Joan Grant (and also the character who I am calling "Xavier") is extremely rare. The other three we are covering are much the most common methods. Obtaining a reading of the Akashic Records from a clairvoyant (such as was done by Carol, Fred and Ellen, Iris, Kenneth and Lucinda, Mary, Oliver and Polly, Rosie, and Susie) is popular; regression through hypnotherapy (used by Angela) is also a common practice. Regression through meditation (used also by Carol as well as by Graham and Helen, and in Carol's case she found that her meditation confirmed a reading she had already been given) differs from hypnotherapy in that with the latter the subject who goes into a deep trance does not normally remember anything of the regression after coming out of it. Hypnotherapists therefore tend to use tape recorders. (See *Jesus and the Essenes* and other books by Dolores Cannon[2].)

Regression through meditation is a skill I personally am only just beginning to develop, but now that I am training as a past-life regressionist therapist I expect to increase my powers in that direction. Such skills sometimes develop slowly, and while I was writing my first book I needed to meditate a great deal on each previous life before I wrote about it, and it felt more to me like imagination than reality. It was only afterwards that clairvoyants confirmed the information I thought I had imagined to be genuine subconscious memory. I therefore found it quite fascinating talking to Graham, who has really relived his past lives in his meditations. Whereas I have always needed to make a conscious effort to get into a past life, and have found that it only worked for one that I already knew about, with Graham (as with some of the people I am now practising on) it just happens of its own accord. Sceptics could no doubt argue here too that this is also "imagination", but I cannot accept that. Why should Graham suddenly see himself being killed at Avebury when his conscious mind would surely want the story to end happily? After all, he had sent his twin soul and his companions on ahead in order to protect them, and so would clearly be desperately anxious to rejoin them. Similarly, it was only the day after Graham's meditation in Cornwall that Edwin was told about the theory of the spiral having been removed from that stone. It seems most unlikely that the vision of himself doing such a thing could have come simply from Graham's imagination.

Another point that is worth noting is the fact that on two occasions Graham has seen himself being killed in a past life through the solar plexus. It is well known that we carry the scars of wounds with us through from body to body; sometimes people are born with birthmarks which are the scars of wounds received in a previous lifetime[3]. Well, Graham has found that he has a blockage now in his solar plexus. When he was in the meditation at Avebury, he felt intense pain in the solar plexus as he saw the lance go through it, but there had already been previous times as well when the pain in that area had been very severe while he was meditating. Finding the karmic cause of this pain has made some improvement, but it is still something he needs to work on. Edwin has suggested to Graham the following method – a method which anyone could perhaps find useful: imagine the past-life scene which you know to have been the cause of the problem, but then change the ending. Instead of seeing the lance piercing your solar plexus, visualise yourself escaping just in time and carrying on with that lifetime instead of dying.

Graham and Helen have also found lifetimes in which they were North American Indians together. One was at the time when they were being massacred by white men. In his meditation Graham saw himself and others running to get away, and he was able to recognise other people besides Helen whom he knows now. These include his sister and her deceased boyfriend (who was very close to Graham in this lifetime). Helen was his wife in this scene, and they had a son, and his sister and her boyfriend were also obviously husband and wife. He can remember seeing people getting shot and falling, but his group managed to run into a cave. They realised, however, that the white men would not give up until they were dead, so all the men decided to save the women and children by leaving the cave themselves and making a lot of noise so that they would be followed. In this meditation Graham did not see their deaths, but he knows that he and the other men were killed in the knowledge that their wives and children were safe.

Graham has retained from his North American Indian lifetimes a great interest in things shamanic. In fact he at present likes to describe himself as a "Shaman in training". He feels that he is at present making up for a lifetime in which he was accidentally killed as a little boy called Snake Dancer, just as the elderly Shaman of his tribe was about to pass on his powers to him. The Shaman lay dying, but before he could perform the transferring ceremony, Snake Dancer was mistakenly shot in the neck by the arrow of some children who were playing outside the tent.

A few years ago Graham started making wands for healing, which he sold at Edwin's workshops, and now he is adding other shamanic instruments to his range, such as feather fans (for cleaning the aura), burners for herbs to cleanse the room, "prayer sticks" (for people to insert their prayers and leave on trees), rattles for use in meditation as well as for cleansing and healing, and "dream catchers" (which the American Indians hung over their beds to catch nightmares before they could reach the sleeper!).

When Graham got home after that first August week in Cornwall with the German group, he was in a real quandary about what to do. He had a place at College, his family and friends were all expecting him to start the course more or less immediately, but he found that he simply did not want to. His thoughts were continually with Helen, and he knew that he couldn't be happy if he was committed to a course which would keep him away from her. On the other hand, he kept thinking to himself, it seemed absurd! They had only just met, had only had two or three days together, and the memories of his previous relationships, which had ended so disastrously, were still fresh in his mind. He asked himself, "Does it really make sense to throw up the chance of training for a good career when relationships are such a gamble? Besides, she lives in Germany, which is quite different from everything I'm used to, and I don't even know the language!" Yet underneath all these doubts and fears in his mind was a little voice which kept trying to assure him that this time it was different, that often if one was to do the right thing in one's life one should follow one's heart rather than one's reason. So, ignoring what anyone else around him said (and even Helen's worries about him abandoning the course), and realising that it was time that his spiritual life began once again to come into play, he renounced his place at the College.

As for Helen, she felt quite confused in the beginning. There was such a deep feeling of love and longing, for she knew that she had just found a part of herself which she had always been searching for, yet having only just found it, here they were being immediately separated again! Also, although she had been prepared for the meeting by clairvoyant acquaintances, she knew that one should never rely completely on outside sources (however accurate they proved to be). She therefore decided also to listen to her <u>own</u> inner voice and obtain confirmation from <u>that</u> about their future together. Perhaps for that reason – painful though it was – the enforced separation was an equally important part of the divine plan. As they communicated by phone and by letter, the "Yes" from Helen's own inner voice grew ever stronger, but this did not stop the difficult decision which needed to be made from troubling her immensely: should Graham take up his place at the university and not see her again for the next four months, or should he just cancel the course and come to Germany four weeks later with his brother? She knew that the decision was made even harder by the fact that, in the latter case, Graham would lose the dole as well as his grant and consequently have no money at all! They discussed it several times on the phone, but Helen felt that Graham must make the decision entirely by himself. She was obviously overjoyed when, against everyone else's doubts and fears, convinced that the decision was the right one, he decided for Helen, for Germany, and for his spiritual path. For they both felt sure that Graham's spiritual path lay with Helen, neither of them wanted to wait any longer, and they felt confident that, if he was really doing the right thing, minor worries such as financial ones would be taken care of! (This, in the Joudry and Pressman book, is the *jump off the bridge*, the *necessary leap of faith* of Johanna's dream, which, *entrusting herself wholly into the other*, enables her to come *into possession of herself*[1].)

The information about the fact of Graham and Helen being twin souls came through a couple of weeks after their meeting – initially in a reading that Edwin did for Helen, in which he channelled the Archangel Michael. Normally Edwin can identify twin souls straight away from the similarities in their auras, but he explains that sometimes such information is withheld until the time is right. Graham will have known *subconsciously* right at the beginning that this lovely German girl he had fallen for was his soul partner, but he needed to do a little bit of sorting out on the conscious level before he could be ready fully to absorb the implications of the wonderful thing that had happened to him. Similarly Helen, although she had been promised that the meeting was going to happen and so was at least half expecting it, needed to prepare herself gradually for making a big commitment after being completely on her own with her daughter for a whole eleven years.

One factor that appeared to Helen initially to be an obstacle is the fact that she is about fourteen years older than Graham. This, however, does not bother him in the slightest (he says, "She looks younger than me anyway!"), and now they both feel that society's disapproval of such an age gap is irrelevant to them as well as being nonsense. They realise too that in spiritual terms twin souls are always the same age anyway.

Once back in Yorkshire Graham was desperately anxious to go to Germany to see Helen again, but he had, of course, no money. Helen is at present tied to her home by her work, and the only way Graham could visit Germany was by borrowing the money for his fare from her, which, though she of course did not mind at all, he was unhappy about. He was also unhappy about the idea of flying for the first time, but Edwin persuaded him that he would be fine, and in due course it was agreed that he should accompany his brother on the next trip to Germany, already arranged for a few weeks later. They agreed that he could take some of his wands to sell at the workshops, as well as some attractive sets of Rune stones that he had been making, and that this would help his financial situation.

The weeks of waiting were really mind blowing for Graham. He and Helen were in constant contact by letter, cards and phone, and it was very difficult for either of them to believe that they had met only so briefly. They seemed continually to be tuned into one another's moods, and even whereabouts. If Graham went out, he would ask his mother on his return, "Has Helen phoned?" She would reply, "No" and then sometimes the phone would ring more or less instantly. He might say, "I've been worried about you. Are you feeling OK?" to which she would reply, "I'm OK now that I've got you on the phone, but I've had quite a bad day." Besides the correspondence and almost daily phone calls, they meditated "together" at the same time each day.

Even more amazing, they found on numerous occasions during those weeks of waiting that they bought almost identical picture postcards to send one another. One day they both bought each other cards of seagulls. Another time Graham did the writing on his postcard in the shape of a spiral, and it actually crossed with one from Helen which she had also written in the shape of a spiral! It felt to them almost as though they were the same person, divided in two by the English Channel. But then, after all, that's exactly what twin souls are.

Graham, as we have said, found it scary at first – it seemed too good to be true that he had at last found the woman he had spent so long looking for – but, now that he is sure about it, he looks back on his previous relationships and sees that this one is right because, unlike the previous ones, it is a relationship of total equality. He says, "In the past it was always me that was giving and them who were receiving, but with Helen and me it's very balanced. We both give and we both receive all the time, and it's very relaxed and nice."

So Graham's first trip to Germany went very well. He overcame his fear of flying and, whereas he had previously felt very much an outsider at the workshops he had attended, now he was much more involved. His artefacts sold well, and in due course he was able to repay Helen for his fare. As for their relationship, they soon felt as though they had always been together. Graham was still cautious nevertheless, realising that part of his trouble in the past had been a tendency to move too fast, and this (combined with Helen's own caution) is the reason they are still not living together all the time. "We've both got a lot of adjusting to do, especially since Helen has been on her own for eleven years. We've got to get used to each other slowly and to move into each other's energies and learn to balance them gradually. I know that she needs her own space every now and again, and I'm learning as I get to know her more when to move away and let her have that. When she's working I just vanish into the front room, because I've got this annoying habit of talking a lot, which stops her concentrating."

Graham also of course had to make a relationship with Helen's daughter, who was not used to having a man in the house. He says, "At first I was very nervous about meeting her, but now it's fine." Someone told him that he would have to be a stepfather, but Graham disagreed with that "since the child has a father whom she sees regularly". He wants to be Verena's friend and Helen's partner, and he feels that this is being achieved gradually. He says that she is a "typical teenager and fun to be with", but that he does not feel that it is his right to discipline her.

Graham says that when he and Helen first met "she was way ahead spiritually". He had taken an interest in spiritual things several years previously but, with his difficulties both in relationships and in finding himself the right career, all his books and other things were simply gathering dust on the shelf. Now, however, though she is still much more knowledgeable than he is (having attended so many workshops and also read a great deal), Graham is, with her help, catching up fast. For twin souls – as we shall see in a later chapter under that heading – always eventually catch one another up spiritually.

Another way in which Graham started to change rapidly was in his eating habits. Helen is both very healthy and health-conscious and strongly disapproves of the Courtenay family's high-sugar diet. Graham had had a skin problem for some time, which she persuaded him could be cured by a homoeopath. So on his second trip to Germany he found that she had made him an appointment. The result has been a remarkable improvement in his health in a very short time, greatly helped by Graham's obedience in sticking rigidly to the prescribed diet (even over Christmas!).

During those first trips, whenever Helen had any time to spare from the work of organising Edwin's workshops, she and Graham began working together. He says that to start with she had all the creativity, having been involved with her pottery for so long while he had not been in that energy for a very long time, but they quickly found that she was feeding her creativity to him. While she was busy with her pottery he would be making healing wands, but she would often come over to him and give him different ideas for ways of doing the wands. After a short time of working on the wands together, Graham started sometimes to say, "What do you think of this idea?" to which she would reply, "That's exactly what I was thinking . . ." They found in fact that they were more or less reading each other's minds on the different ways of making the wands.

Twin souls working together tend to find that they gain one another's talents, but this can of course sometimes take time, and they also often feel the need of one another's physical presence. Graham says that when he was in Germany initially, Helen's own creativity for her pottery was somewhat diminished while she was feeding it to him for the wands. Then, more recently, following a seven-week trip there, he found for a whole three weeks that, without Helen by his side, he was completely unable to work. He said to her on the phone, "I've left my creativity behind with you." By the fourth week he had managed to make himself settle down to work again, but he says that "in Germany I could feel the wands talking to me, telling me how they wanted to be created. At times I would actually see a design or a symbol on a stick, so I would pick it up and make it into a wand." As we saw in the previous chapter, twin souls who have grown accustomed to being together and working together, feel incomplete and a trifle lost when they are separated. (Ellen, it may be remembered, described Fred as "restless" without her.)

Graham feels that they still need to work on balancing all their energies, not simply the creative ones. An odd thing that happened is that, while at home Graham normally never remembers his dreams whereas Helen dreams a great deal, when he went to Germany he dreamt a lot and she stopped dreaming. They had a joke between them that he was stealing her dreams. After returning home, however, he again stopped dreaming and she started once more. Curious!

When I interviewed Graham he had recently returned from this seven-week trip and was greatly looking forward to another, two-month one. This is much longer than his previous stays in Germany, and he said that he felt a bit homesick at first, as seven weeks was a really long time for him to be away from home, but that he had rapidly adjusted, and that the real problems only arose after his return. In fact he now realises more and more that for all of the first part of his life he didn't feel whole and was seeking Helen precisely for that reason.

Since normally when twin souls are brought together it is not primarily for their own happiness, but rather in order to bring more light into the world, the forces of evil sometimes attempt to exert a divisive influence almost at the last moment. Joudry and Presssman explain this by using the symbolism of scaling the sunlit side of a pyramid (which is of course quite a good image, since our return to spirit entails an arduous climb over countless lifetimes). They say that *the pure light of consciousness, free of duality* lies above the apex of the pyramid, but *just at the tip, where we are closest to the light, we are also closest to the dark*[1] (i.e. the side of the pyramid which is in shadow). They say too that we should not be afraid of admitting to the reality of evil because recognising it makes us better equipped to protect ourselves from it.

In Graham and Helen's case the evil manifested itself in the form of negative feelings being aroused first in him (about himself and his abilities) and then, once he had fought his way through that, in her, by giving Helen herself doubts about the direction in which she wanted her work to go, as well as great worry about not being able to make enough money for the three of them. Talking the whole thing through with Edwin, they came to realise what was going on and that the fact that evil forces appeared to be working against them meant that they had important work for good to do together. This of course increased their resolve to overcome the difficulties.

Now that they have overcome these initial setbacks, Graham and Helen are ready to think ahead and begin to make plans regarding their future work as a couple once they have made the permanent commitment to each other which they desire. Ultimately they hope to be running workshops of their own, though for the moment there is much to be done with the organisation of Edwin's German workshops. It is Helen's responsibility to write and send out all the letters of invitation, and in this Graham can be very useful with the boring part (which he says he actually enjoys) such as putting things into envelopes and sticking on the stamps. Another, quite different, way in which he feels he supports Helen is by "bringing the child back into her life, helping her not to take things so seriously and to laugh in a way that she was not always used to. Now, after speaking to my Mum on the phone, she imitates her Cockney accent, which is really funny. She's more and more fun to be with now."

Graham is working hard at learning German and making good progress, and he says that he would be quite happy to go and live over there. Helen has, however, been told by clairvoyants that she will ultimately move to England to work, and she fancies somewhere in the South West such as Glastonbury or Cornwall. They would both like to live in a rural area rather than a big town. Helen's work interest is at present turning from straightforward pottery towards models incorporating crystals, a few of which she has already sold at various workshops.

With regard to future workshops of their own, Helen has already given a few "devic workshops", where she has taken people into woods and found power places, and this is something she would like to develop further. They have talked about doing workshops using clay and symbolism, and Graham feels that while Helen will be a teacher as well as a healer, his own work will lie more in the field of healing – an ability he discovered in himself some time ago, though he left it dormant for quite a while. He does, however, feel that he could teach children, and they both like the idea of running spiritual workshops for children using both painting and clay. Graham says, "Making use of play is a good way of teaching spirituality to children."

Besides having healing ability, Graham is good at chakra balancing, and he knows too that he will be working with symbols. "I know that the energy that I use will be very Earth-centred. I've been told by my guides and others that everything I need to know is within me, and that all that I need to do is find it and understand. It's a matter of having confidence in myself and, when I do find things in meditation, having the confidence to believe in them. The other day, for instance, I made a wand that was more like a rattle. When I showed it to Edwin I said, 'I just made it. I don't know what it's for,' and he said, 'Oh, it's a Celtic silver stick!' and explained about it to me. I was amazed, but obviously I'm finding things in my subconscious that I've known about before in previous lives and now they can be brought into play. It's fascinating!"

So at the moment Graham and Helen are simply taking one step at a time, both in the development of their relationship and with regard to their future work together, and trusting that, since their union represents the fulfilment of a divine plan, where they must go and what they must do will all be taken care of. They realise – as twin souls must – that they have a oneness of purpose and that they have been brought together for a reason. The reason, as Joudry and Pressman say, *may unfold gradually, but it will unfold as a result of their focused attention, for they are aware in their depths that life is nothing if not the fulfilment of divine purpose . . . they will dedicate themselves, as one, to the chosen service for which they are destined.*[1]

Edwin, who says that he and his brother have not incarnated together many times before, has found Graham (despite his spiritual interests and creative and healing talents) to be a young soul and reckons that he still has many lifetimes to come. Graham says that that suits him fine "so long as I can keep coming back with Helen. Before I knew her I didn't enjoy life so much, but now that I've found her, and feel more whole and happy, I think it's pretty good!" So long as they do not stray far from the right path, there is no reason why twin souls should not keep coming back together over and over. In future chapters we shall see instances of couples who, like Fred and Ellen, have already done this. As for Graham and Helen, they clearly have an exciting future ahead of them.

Notes

1. *Twin Souls – A Guide to Finding your True Spiritual Partner* by Patricia Joudry and Maurie D. Pressman, M.D., published by Element Books, Shaftesbury, Dorset.
2. *Jesus and The Essenes* and other books by Dolores Cannon, published by Gateway Books.
3. See *Reincarnation* by Roy Stemman, published by Piatkus in May 1997.

Chapter VI

SOMETIMES THE STRONG ATTRACTION CAN CAUSE
FEELINGS OF GUILT AND CONFUSION
The story of Iris and Joe

Arnold was greatly loved in the little Costa Blanca town in which he and his beloved wife, Veronica, had retired a few years previously. Unlike many of his compatriots, he really loved the Spanish and never had anything but a good word for anybody. He was still grieving intensely over the death of his wife ("For me the only woman that there ever was or ever could be." Twin souls? Possibly, but not necessarily. Companion soulmates maybe, but no matter – they are not the subject of our story.), but this had not put an end to his appreciation of his relaxed life in the sun, his care for others in the apartment block, and his independence.

It was eleven o'clock in the morning and Iris was busy in the restaurant. Joe had his Indian menu completely under control, but she had tables to lay, wine to order, linen to sort through, the accounts to complete before Martin passed by to collect his rent. She glanced out through the door just for a moment and saw Arnold walking past. She was concerned. She knew he hadn't been too well lately, and this morning he looked worse than she had ever seen him. His face was almost grey, his shirt was hanging out, and he looked so old and tired. She thought for a moment that he might be dropping in for a coffee and a chat as he so often did, but instead he walked on and sat down on a bench at the end of the street. "Never mind," Iris said to herself, "I'll be through with the most urgent tasks shortly. Then I'll go out and have a word with him." Barely half an hour had passed before Iris decided she could free herself for a few minutes, but when she went out to the bench Arnold was nowhere to be seen. A few moments later Madge burst in to the restaurant. "Have you heard the news? Arnold died at six o'clock this morning!" (Note that this was a full five hours before Iris had last seen him.)

Iris has always known that she had psychic abilities, but has never wanted to develop them. As a young child she found that she could open drawers simply by looking at them. This frightened her, so she shut the ability off. This may sound odd, or even incredible, but in a recent article in the magazine

93

Kindred Spirit, in which John Chambers interviewed Dr. Michael Grosso, there is a reference to research done by Kenneth Batcheldor into "psychokinetic energy". It is stated that a group of four people, after several sessions of working together, achieved total levitation of a table. In reply to the question, *Why does it work best in a group setting rather than individually?* Grosso says, *Batcheldor suggests that in a group setting you lose what he calls "owner inhibition". You don't have the feeling that you are doing it – there's something "out there" that is doing it. The group is doing it. That seems to liberate the psychokinetic potential. It can be very threatening to think that, just by thinking, you personally could cause some physical event to take place in the outside world. The findings indicate that when the person involved in these experiments becomes conscious of himself or herself causing the event, it freaks them out. And that can stop the effect. Even to be too astonished at the result can inhibit it.*[1]

Iris had a younger brother with whom she was very close – in age as well as in other ways. Their mother is far from being an easy person, the three children had had a difficult childhood, and Frank, as we shall call him, had become a heroin addict. This was quite a few years after Iris had switched off her psychokinetic powers, when she was in her early twenties. She and Frank lived quite near each other and generally saw one another fairly regularly, but they had not met for a week or two and he was on Iris' mind. That night she had a dream which was not like any ordinary dream; it seems much more likely that it was a real out-of-body experience, which she remembered in fairly minute detail. (We shall be stating more than once in this book that nightly out-of-body activity can be remembered, and that the Ancient Egyptians are not the only people who trained themselves to do this[2].) In this dream Iris and Frank were sitting together above the world, looking down at it (the picture is still quite clear in her mind, years later) and Frank was saying to her, "I've really botched it this time." The following morning Iris' mother phoned to tell her that Frank had died in the night from a heroin overdose.

The death of her much loved brother is only one of many very difficult things with which Iris has coped in her present lifetime. Edwin Courtenay told her in her reading that part of the reason for this is that she is approaching the end of her necessary incarnations, that she only *has the last cluster of two or three before she's complete.* Consequently she decided to *cram a lot of experience into this lifetime, to carry out a great deal of releasing and absolving of karma.* Besides a long and difficult birth and a bad relationship with her mother, she has suffered many things, including rape, five miscarriages, three births by Caesarean section, and two failed marriages. Yet none of this has left Iris with any bitterness. On the contrary, she always appears joyful and cheerful and is ever ready to give a helping hand. Clearly, in fact, an old soul who has earned the final reunion with her twin.

The reunion with Joe has, however, been far from straightforward. Though she is now on excellent terms with her first husband and regards him as a good friend, that marriage ended when Iris found herself pregnant within a year of giving birth to their daughter. Iris herself was overjoyed at the thought of having another child so quickly, but "Donald" was horrified, and Iris simply could not cope with his negative reaction. Her losing that baby did not redeem the marriage relationship.

It was when Iris' daughter, Crystal, was a couple of years old that she fell in love with "Ivor" (who was also divorced, though he had no children). They both came from the same part of the south of England (Sussex) and had in fact been at school together, but had not met again during the intervening years. Iris had not been brought up with any clear-cut religion but had always been a spiritual seeker, and at the time of her marriage to Ivor she was very interested in Spiritualism. Ivor's parents were strict Anglicans, his father being a vicar, and they disapproved strongly of Iris' religious inclinations. They also regarded her as a "wicked sinner" in view of the failure of her first marriage – the fact that their own son was also divorced was apparently much less grave a sin! – and the relationship was consequently difficult from the start. (In fact the very first time that Ivor took Iris to his parents' home, when they had just got engaged, Ivor's mother put on the video of their son's previous wedding!)

The karmic relationship between Iris and her second husband is more or less identical to that of Carol and Carl in Chapter III, i.e. a history of her having been subjected to violence from him and getting trapped – as we all so often do through our lifetimes – into a repeated pattern. In a late Victorian lifetime the two of them had married very young and he used to beat her. This was an exceedingly torturous lifetime for Iris, as it was all kept quiet and she had no one in whom she could confide. Ivor beat her too when they were man and wife in the Wild West, and that time, though it was not suppressed, no one dared to do anything about it as Ivor was a very formidable character. In the latter lifetime, however, Iris was rescued by Joe, her twin soul, with whom she fell in love. Since she was white and Joe was black, they had to run away together.

So one of Iris' tasks for this lifetime, though she only found it out recently, some time after freeing herself once and for all from Ivor, was to break that pattern of subjection. Here we see a repeat of the story of Carol and Carl, and it is interesting because it shows how our subconscious mind so often seems to be ahead of our conscious one. Both Carol and Iris came in to their present incarnations having resolved firstly to break a certain pattern and secondly to find their twin soul; both married and then divorced the person with whom they needed to end a particular karmic pattern, and both learnt subsequently that that was what they had succeeded in doing. Also, both were enabled to do that by meeting their twin soul.

When Iris married Ivor, however, a second divorce was far from her mind. In fact she was quite determined to make a go of the relationship despite the unwelcoming and unchristian treatment she received from her "Christian" parents-in-law. In spite of further miscarriages and difficult pregnancies and births, she presented Ivor with two beautiful sons. She had been mother to all three of these children on previous occasions, and she had created karma for herself in the relationships by a feeling of having failed to look after them properly. This, however, had never been her own fault – for instance in an earlier Victorian life (that is earlier than the lifetime in which Ivor had been such a violent husband to her), she had been a single parent, very poor, and the children had consequently had to live off the streets – but in this lifetime she is nevertheless punishing herself for what she sees as her "failure".

So Iris was determined this time to provide a really good home for these three children. Ivor had expressed willingness to accept Crystal and treat her well, and in any case in this lifetime he has fortunately not continued his former habit of physical violence. He ran a business in Sussex to support the family, and all seemed to go well initially. As the children had got a little bit older, Iris, who had never given herself the opportunity of realising her academic potential, enrolled for a degree in Psychology and Sociology, which she was thoroughly enjoying.

Before, however, Iris had come anywhere near to completing her course, Ivor, who had tired of the business in England, took it into his head to take the whole family off to Spain and start a business there. Being the dutiful wife that she was, Iris made no attempt to argue with him. So they let their house in Sussex, took out a mortgage on a flat in the little Costa Blanca town for which they both fell, and then looked around for work there. Before long a restaurant became available to rent and, in view of the large number of English tourists who frequent that particular resort, they decided that between them they could manage to offer "Roast Beef and Yorkshire Pudding", "Fish and Chips" and other such delicacies always in demand by a certain section of the English residents and visitors. It was hard work and not at all easy to make ends meet, but they managed to establish themselves and soon became well known and popular among their compatriots, not to mention also a few of the Spanish, who now and again welcomed a change from their own traditional menus. Though Iris still had regrets about having had to give up her course, and though the two older children did not settle well in the Spanish school, she soon fell in love both with the climate and with the way of life on the Costa Blanca, and anyway, as she says, "Our family unity and security was my priority, and Ivor and I seemed to be working quite well together running the business. He developed talents as a cook that I would never have suspected he had in him, and I found that I was really quite good at keeping the accounts and so on in order. As for things like laying and clearing tables and washing up, of course they were already second nature to me."

Running an English restaurant on the Costa Blanca is, however, far from easy. For a start, there is invariably a lot of competition. Iris and Ivor were

96

doing quite well, were run off their feet in the summer, but in the winter business tended to be slack, and the rent of course had to be paid twelve months of the year. Ivor had discovered before leaving England that he had healing power in his hands, and he had also taken an interest in and taught himself (from books) to perform Acupressure. Iris had had a recurrent illness for some years, and they found that he was able to do much to relieve her symptoms. He therefore decided to develop this ability, and word soon got around the little town that Ivor was offering healing during the hours when the restaurant was closed. He did not charge very much, not being professionally qualified, but the few extra pesetas that came in in this way brought some relief to their slightly precarious financial position.

Now let us turn to Joe. Joe in his present lifetime incarnated in India into a Sikh family. The custom in that culture is of course for marriages to be arranged by the parents, and Joe did not set eyes on his wife until the day of their wedding. The two of them took an instant dislike to each other. He says, "She was tiny and looked so frail that I was afraid she would break if I touched her. In fact we didn't consummate the marriage for a whole month, but then an aunt of mine accused me of 'not being a man', so I proved her wrong by engendering two daughters." Being a conscientious man and a devoted father, Joe stayed with his family for a number of years, despite the fact that the marriage was totally unsatisfactory for both parties. Then, when he felt his daughters were old enough to leave, he decided to come to Europe. Joudry and Pressman say: *Twin souls can live on opposite sides of the world and continue in oneness of being. The two rings can stretch infinitely without breaking.* In Iris and Joe's case, however, the stretching did not need to go on infinitely, since their coming together had been pre-ordained.

If twin souls are destined to meet in a particular lifetime, being born in different continents will not prevent it. Joe went first to Amsterdam, where he had a brother, and where he obtained a job in a restaurant. There was at one point a strong chance of Iris meeting him there because Donald, her first husband, and his new partner went to Amsterdam on holiday, and Iris had agreed to join them there briefly but was prevented from doing so at the last minute by illness. Donald, however, had a meal in the restaurant where Joe was employed and got into conversation with him!

But destiny will not be forestalled either by illness or anything else. Since Iris had failed to make it to Amsterdam, Joe's spirit guides or guardian angel (or both!) whispered into his subconscious that he must go and find her in Spain, and at the same time they had him made redundant in Amsterdam. It may seem extraordinary, but as we are saying over and over again, in life there are no coincidences. The Costa Blanca resort where Iris and Ivor settled has a vast number of restaurants, and in the very same street, in fact right opposite theirs, was an Indian restaurant. And it was there, believe it or not, that Joe landed his next job. It was not, however, Iris who first made friends with him, but Ivor.

Now Ivor, as we have said, was at this point supplementing their income by giving occasional healing and Acupressure sessions. Iris, who was <u>always</u> busy, was very happy about this and simply left him to get on with it. During one of these sessions, however, she had cause to pop into their flat for something she needed, and walked quietly into the bedroom where Ivor was "treating" a nineteen-year-old English tourist whom we shall call Caroline. Ivor was so absorbed in what he was doing that he did not notice her come in, and Iris says, "I was <u>horrified</u>! There's only one word for this so-called 'treatment' and that is that it was quite simply erotic. I went back to the restaurant as quickly as I could, and for the rest of that day I was too upset to say anything. After that it rapidly became apparent that Ivor had started having an affair with this girl and, would you believe it, he borrowed Joe's flat for his carryings on!"

Joe is certainly not a man who would normally approve of adultery, but Ivor spun him such a convincing yarn about how he just <u>had</u> to escape from his nagging wife's tyranny and hen-pecking, that his kind heart was touched. Then, before long, when she had found out where Ivor was, Iris herself confirmed the picture drawn of her by coming round to Joe's flat and yelling and screaming that Ivor should be looking after his children! Iris said to me, "You tell me that a first meeting between twin souls is normally a memorable event? Well, I was slapping him around the face and screaming at him to send my husband back!"

Well, Caroline's holiday came to an end and Ivor did come back. Not only did he come back but, realising that he had made a complete fool of himself, he told Iris that he was genuinely sorry. Iris forgave him and they started anew, but it was not to last very long. A few months passed and then Ivor decided that he had had enough of Spain and restaurants and that he wanted to go back to England and think again. Iris, however, had no inclination to give up her new life, and anyway she could see no future for the family "back home", where they had long since given up their business. So she decided to let Ivor go off and stay with his parents, waiting patiently while he made a decision about his future, and trusting that he would return to her.

In order to break the pattern into which she had become trapped and bring a final end to the karma between them, Iris in this lifetime needed to stand up to Ivor and not surrender to him or allow him to oppress her. This she did to a large extent initially by not putting up with his adulterous behaviour which was so damaging to the children. She still, however, felt a very strong bond with him, and that was why it was again necessary for Joe to come to her rescue (just as he had as a black man, when she had been a battered wife in the Wild West of America). The fascinating thing about the story is that this time it was Ivor who was instrumental in the rescue. For he did have <u>some</u> conscience about leaving her in the lurch with the children and the restaurant, and so, before he departed, he asked his friend, Joe (who he knew was badly underpaid in the Indian restaurant) to step in and give Iris a hand whenever he had any time off. In doing this he was no doubt to some extent paying off the karmic debt that he had to Iris.

Iris' fidelity to Ivor, combined with her initial dislike of the man who had aided and abetted her husband in his unfaithfulness to her, inevitably delayed to some extent the making of the twin soul connection. And we must also remember that Joe had been given a very inaccurate and jaundiced view of Iris by her unfaithful husband! So, for a few months, while anxiously awaiting Ivor's decision about his future, and desperately hoping that he would return, she simply put up with Joe's frequent presence by her side, knowing that she could not run the restaurant single-handedly.

Then it happened! Firstly Ivor announced that he had decided that he wanted to obtain some qualification and was consequently becoming a student. (This entailed of course a further announcement that he would have no money to send Iris for the maintenance of the children. His parents, happy to have their darling son home again, were willing to support him and seemed to have no qualms about his abandoning all responsibility for his children.) And secondly, Iris and Joe experienced a sudden mutual recognition of the deep spiritual bond between them.

One of the truly fascinating aspects of this case is that, besides having been born in different continents, Iris and Joe have virtually no common language. She of course has never had cause to learn Gujarati, and he speaks extremely little English. But twin soul connections are completely above such Earthly things as language! Gradually they found both that they were working extraordinarily well as a team and that they were able to communicate by telepathy. At first Iris suppressed her feelings of attraction for Joe. Ivor had made no hint that he desired a divorce, even though he had made it clear that he did not intend to return to Spain, and she was still determined to make a go of the relationship mainly for the children's sake, but also because she still felt in some strange way bound to Ivor.

As we have said, however, destiny will always take its course come what may, and where the joining of twin souls is concerned, what is right on the spiritual level will override Earthly restrictions. Joudry and Pressman put it succinctly thus:– *If twin souls meet and one or both are already married, then there could be a conflict between the man-made law of marriage and the spiritual law of soul attraction. But while laws made by man take little account of the heavenly, the spiritual laws have regard for the earthly. The divine agency that directs the movement of souls is not likely to bring twin souls together in such circumstance as to break any true moral code.* Well, Iris had remained faithful to Ivor, but where was his moral code in abandoning her doubly: firstly through adultery and secondly by returning to England after himself having made the decision that they should settle in Spain!

Iris and Joe, as we have said, communicate very largely by telepathy. She recounts: "One day we were standing opposite each other and I just looked at him. I found myself looking deep into his eyes and I was overcome by this incredible feeling of 'I know you'. It's impossible to describe, but there was a sort of timelessness about it. It was as though we were looking straight at each other's souls with a sense of having known one another for ages and ages, aeons and aeons. Neither of us said anything. Time just stood still for I don't know how long. Eventually we came back to reality and the present day and realised that we were just standing there in the kitchen, but it was a really strange experience and I know he felt it too."

After that events had to take their course; the twin soul connection had to express itself sexually. Joe's marriage had never existed in any real sense, and in any case his divorce was long since history, but he was nevertheless not ready to give up his flat and move in with a married woman. As for Iris, she was beset with feelings of guilt and confusion. She genuinely thought that she still loved Ivor in a way, and she felt it important for the children not to lose touch with their father (the boys, that is; Crystal, when she went to England, normally stayed with her own father). Ivor, however, was in the meantime becoming increasingly unco-operative and, while still not sending her any money, his letters were full of requests for things that she should send him or do for him. So she, not unnaturally, felt used, and she began to sense that her love for him was wearing thin. Here again we can see a parallel with the case of Carol and Carl. It is, however, only too easy simply to label both Ivor and Carl as the "baddies". It must always be remembered that we all have lessons to learn, and that the broad outlines of our incarnations are planned before we come in. Both Carol and Iris, though apparently the "innocent parties", needed their experience of very unsatisfactory marriages for their own learning and spiritual development, and it can therefore be said that in a sense both Carl and Ivor were acting partly as teachers.

Iris and Joe have a whole history of their love being frowned upon by society. In Ancient Greece she was the wife of a senator, he a slave; they fell in love and she absconded with him. There have been other lifetimes in which their match was an interracial one, and racial prejudice has been one of this world's major scourges for aeons. In Spain the owner of the Indian restaurant who employed Joe was an extraordinarily unpleasant person. He had treated Joe badly all along, and as soon as he learnt of his liaison with Iris, he gave him the sack. This of course made Joe even more dependent on his work with Iris, and she also appreciated the increased number of hours that he was now able to give to helping her.

The first time that I, the author, met Iris was when I was on holiday in Spain. I had no desire for an English meal, but I did fancy an Acupressure treatment, and so I made an appointment with Ivor through her. On that occasion I had more conversation with him than I did with her and, as an "older woman", I did not find myself the victim of anything at all erotic. The next year I went

100

on holiday again to the same place and was surprised to find that Ivor had departed. Iris then told me her tale of woe and we became good friends, also discovering that we had similar spiritual interests. On this occasion Joe was very much in the background, and I was simply left hoping that Ivor would decide to return to Iris.

Several months passed before we met again, and by the time we did, Iris' divorce had just taken place. On that occasion I had gone to Spain not on holiday but in order to work uninterruptedly on this book, and so I told Iris when she asked something about it. Though, as we have said, she is an evolved soul and very spiritually aware, the concept of twin souls was new to her. This meeting and discussion was clearly part of the Plan for her life, for, as soon as I explained twinsoulship to her, it rang deep bells and she knew in the depths of her being that reunion with her own twin soul was her destiny for this lifetime. She completely ignored me when I said, "Maybe your twin soul isn't incarnate, or maybe you've never met him!" (I hasten to add that at this point I had still not really made the acquaintance of Joe, or even seen them together properly.)

By good fortune for both Iris and Joe, the Indian restaurant owner had been unable to carry on making a go of it after sacking Joe, and had been forced to close down a few months later. This left them free to convert Iris' English restaurant into an Indian one, thus completely annihilating the previous competition. (Joe is a very accomplished Indian chef and Iris, who loved his food anyway, was happy to hand over that department to him entirely. In any case the rest of the work involved was more than enough for one person.) "When twin souls are together it increases their strength" is actually the subject of our next chapter, but in Iris and Joe's case it has clearly happened too. Now their restaurant is doing so well that they are able (and need!) to employ some junior staff under them.

So on the trip that I made to Spain to work on this book, I was somewhat surprised to find Iris' restaurant converted to an Indian one, but (especially since their prices were much more reasonable than had been those across the road!), I was keen to try it. It was the winter, so business was fairly slack, which gave Iris plenty of opportunity to tell me the rest of her story while serving me with Joe's delicious food. She explained that the divorce had been a really hard decision, and that Ivor had given her the opportunity to back out even at the very last minute, "but I couldn't in conscience carry on the relationship with Joe while I was still officially married to Ivor. He'd completely ended his affair with Caroline – even though they did see each other again after his return to England – and I told him I wanted him back and that the children wanted him back, and I also told him that I was prepared to sacrifice my relationship with Joe for the sake of our family unity, but he just seemed so indecisive and weak. He didn't even seem to care that much about seeing the children. It's really terrible when you're torn between two men! I felt bound to Ivor in so many ways, yet Joe was so much more caring. Besides he was here and Ivor wasn't, and so he was actually being a much better father to my children than Ivor was. Someone had to make a decision, so in the end I just did what I felt I was being led to do. The divorce was only last month, and to start with I felt tremendous relief and freedom, but now I keep getting qualms about whether it was the right thing. You see I'm happy living in Spain, and I'm really happy with Joe and we work together perfectly, but the Spanish school is <u>dreadful</u> and Crystal and Jim absolutely hate it. The little one's fine – he's learnt Spanish well and has got quite integrated in the nursery – but I think Crystal and Jim may just <u>have</u> to go back to England for the sake of their education. They could live with Ivor's parents and go to school in Sussex, but then I'd only see them in the holidays. And then another problem is Crystal and Donald. If she went back to England, she'd really rather live with her own father than with Ivor, and he'd be quite happy to have her, but firstly she doesn't get on very well with her stepmother, and secondly that would mean that all three children would be separated from each other as well as from me. So sometimes I think we should all go back together. But it would mean I'd have nowhere to live because, even if we got rid of the tenants in our house, it's right next door to Ivor's parents and I couldn't bear to be in such close proximity to them . . ."

I empathised so much with Iris' dilemma as we talked and, after I had explained the concept of twin souls and she had read the first chapter of this book, which I happened to have with me, we had another discussion. "How can I find out who my twin soul is?" she asked. "I'd really like to know whether it's Ivor or Joe." So I offered to get a reading for her from Edwin Courtenay, and she was delighted at the suggestion. Edwin is so busy these days that he has had to give up doing postal readings but, since this book was originally his idea and since it was obvious that Iris would be a suitable subject for one of the chapters, he agreed to let me go and see him for her. After I had sent Iris the tape, her joy was immense and we spoke on the phone: "<u>Now</u> I know where I am! Now I know for sure that I'm really meant to be with Joe. Ivor's being quite useless as a father, and I really want to cut the ties with him for ever."

My next visit to Spain was a brief holiday with my husband and our younger son. Iris and I had talked before of having a *paella* together one evening when her own restaurant was closed, and since I needed to discuss this chapter with her in the light of the new knowledge, and since she and Joe (like other twin soul couples I have come across) are both workaholics, this seemed an obvious opportunity. It was the school holidays and all Iris' children were in England, which left them both free to come out for the evening. I asked my husband and son to sit at a separate table with Joe to leave Iris and me greater freedom to talk, and this they all kindly agreed to. My husband took an instant liking to Joe, but they found conversation extremely difficult in view of the latter's limited English. When, however, we were ready for the dessert, I suggested that we all sit together as by that time Iris and I were through with our more intimate discussion.

102

Though my husband is much better at following my work than I am at following his (Mathematics!), he had not up until that point fully grasped the concept of twinsoulship or taken any real interest in it. (We are happy together and, like many, if not most, companion soulmates, he has never been able to envisage a good relationship with any woman other than myself.) When, however, he saw the sudden change in Joe the moment they moved to our table, he suddenly understood the nature of the spiritual concept about which I was writing. He exclaimed to me afterwards, "They're like one person!" and he was also amazed at how communication, which had been so difficult when they were at different tables, suddenly became easy as soon as Iris and Joe were together.

We talked a bit about this book, and we talked about reincarnation in general, and Joe had a fascinating tale of his own to tell about the latter. (It will be appreciated that my quotations of Joe's were either "translated" on the spot or relayed at second hand to me by Iris.) He recounted, "When my grandfather was dying at home in India, he told us that he would come back soon. After he was dead, his body was left for a while in its resting place on a sandy floor. Shortly before the funeral, although no children had come anywhere near, we noticed a baby's footprints in the sand right by the body, and so we took it as a sign my grandfather was giving us of his immediate return. One of my cousins had just got pregnant, and so in my family we all believe that her son is the reincarnation of our grandfather."

So Iris and Joe share their spiritual interests, and he too found immediately that the concept of twinsoulship resonated deeply within him. They are now doing more or less everything together, and the restaurant, as I said, is really flourishing under their joint management. They work most of the time, but when they do have any leisure they like to do the same things: to read, to visit other parts of Spain, and to enjoy being with the children. For Joe has an excellent relationship with Iris' children. Though he has never been their father, he has positive karmic links with all three of them. In the past the situation has been similar to their present one, in that they have come into his family through another man. They have always previously been younger than him, which helps them this time round readily to accept and respect him as a father figure.

Besides the fact that they narrowly missed meeting in Amsterdam, Iris has noticed other "coincidences". They both have daughters born in 1984; to both their youngest brother was special, and these two have the same birthday. In addition, she says, "I first came to the Costa Blanca on 1 April 1994, and on that very day he left for Andorra. But he came back here just before my troubles with Ivor began, so that was obviously in preparation for rescuing me. Then, before we'd got emotionally involved or had any inkling of the way things were going to develop between us, he got offered a really good job in a restaurant in Alcoy, which is quite a way from here and he would have had to move.

In fact he was all set to move, but then he suddenly said to me, 'I don't think I should go,' and I, without knowing why, said, 'No, I don't think you should either,' even though it would have been much better for him financially."

So in this case it is crystal clear how destiny was literally forcing the couple together. One of the principal themes of this book, however, is the fact that the getting together of twin souls is by no means always easy. At the time of my last meeting with them, Iris and Joe had two major problems with which to deal. Firstly, they want to get married. That might not sound difficult since both are divorced, but it must be remembered that Joe is Indian. In Spain the law is applied in a racist way just as it is in England, and Joe's continued residence there is far from secure. Since I (the author) speak Spanish, I accompanied Iris to see her solicitor, who explained that it would take a long time for Joe to qualify for a civil wedding and that the simplest solution would be for them to become Catholics and be married in church. They were willing to do this in order to escape the risk of Joe being deported but, since he is a Sikh and Iris' spirituality is hardly in line with traditional Catholicism, that idea seemed a trifle farcical. (I also spoke to the priest for them, who – as would have been expected – said that they would first have to undergo a course of instruction, and since they know little Spanish and the priest knows no English . . . !)

Their second problem was the future of the two older children. Iris was happy neither at the thought of their returning to the Spanish school, nor at being separated from them for so much of the time. She recounted, "The other week Joe's brother and family came down to the Costa Brava on holiday and we went up there to meet them. We had a wonderful time, with an all-night party, and at one point Joe and I were just standing together at the top of a cliff and he said to me, 'Why don't we just jump? We know we're going to be together now for ever and ever, so whether we're together on this plane or another wouldn't make any real difference.' Well, I knew what he meant and for a moment I felt really tempted, but then I thought of the children."

Despite these difficulties, Iris and Joe are confident deep down that they will be taken care of, and that together they will overcome all obstacles to their permanent union. They are happy for the time being in Spain, but Joe wants at some point to return to India for a while at least. He is concerned for the welfare of his daughters and would like to start a dairy farm to support them. Iris, too, would love to visit India and would love to help him in this task, but of course the immediate obstacle is again her children. Edwin Courtenay believes, however, that they will achieve this ambition at some point, and that the children will be able to accompany them for at least part of the time. Also, he says that, since twin soul unions always have a spiritual purpose, *In this lifetime they've got something to do together – some sort of business or teaching partnership. There is something that they can only bring forward to the Earth together; something for which their combined energy is needed, and it will be something other than the restaurant in Spain – something spiritual.*

Another thing that Iris and Joe need to sort out is their future as a family. Being so much in love, and his own daughters living so far away, Joe would love Iris to give him another child. She, however, has reservations about this – not least on account of her difficult gynaecological history. So much of their future is at present uncertain. What is certain is that the "guilt and confusion" with which we entitled this chapter has now been resolved and ended, and that Iris and Joe, whether or not they have a Catholic wedding, will stay together and perform the work that they are destined to perform and which they alone, as a twin soul couple, can perform. As for Ivor, we have sadly to leave him alone with his karmic debts, but they are his own concern and no one else's.

Notes
1. *At the Frontiers of Reality*, an article which appeared in the Autumn 1996 issue of *Kindred Spirit*, Volume 3, No. 12.
2. See Joan Grant's Egyptian "far memory" books, published by Ariel Press.
3. *Twin Souls – A Guide to Finding your True Spiritual Partner* by Patricia Joudry and Maurie D. Pressman, M.D., published by Element Books, Shaftesbury, Dorset.

Chapter VII

WHEN TWIN SOULS ARE TOGETHER
IT INCREASES THEIR STRENGTH
*The stories of Kenneth and Lucinda
and Mary and Norman*

Apart from an interest in the spiritual, and from gaining strength from being together, the two couples whose stories make up this chapter have only about one thing in common, and that is that they both only know of one previous lifetime they have shared, and that was at the time of Christ.

THE STORY OF KENNETH AND LUCINDA

Anyone who knows Kenneth now in his present incarnation would be highly amused, and also not surprised, to hear that he had been told in a past-life reading that Jesus had nicknamed him his *Tower of Babel* and also called him his *Constant Challenge*, on account of his habit of coming up with philosophical and metaphysical debate to disprove who Jesus was. For Ken loves to pose as the eternal sceptic or Devil's advocate. But, just as the friends he has nowadays rapidly become accustomed to his cynicism and recognise that it masks a deep commitment to things spiritual and care for other people, so Jesus knew full well that in the depths of his heart Kenneth really did believe in him.

Kenneth first met Jesus just at the time when he was earnestly beginning his work of bringing the message of God to those who were open to hear it, and he followed him right up until the crucifixion. Jesus tended to give him a "ringside seat" when he performed his miracles and, though Kenneth would always be convinced at the time, by a couple of weeks later he would have figured out a way in which it could have been nothing but a trick. Hence the nicknames, but Jesus found it amusing and a source of joy rather than frustrating, and he said that with Kenneth as his friend he could never be defeated by his enemies because it made him stronger and prepared him for the final trials that lay ahead.

At the crucifixion, however, Kenneth stood at the foot of the cross saying, "If you're the Son of God, then free yourself! Remove the shackles! Show these people your power!" and he was saying it not from cynicism but from desperation, because he knew that he was losing this incredible friend and master, and he believed that he would be unable to cope without him. Afterwards he became very disheartened, took to alcohol, and sank into a state of self-absorption. While Kenneth was still in this depression, Jesus appeared to him in a dream and told him that he could in fact have saved himself as Kenneth had suggested, but that it would not have been any proof to the people present. Christ said to him then, "Had I come down from the cross, it would have been no sacrifice. My mission is now accomplished, and the proof of my holiness is that in generations to come my Word will be on the lips of everyone."

Jesus then assured Kenneth that this was not a drunken dream, but a true prophecy, and also that he was giving Kenneth the gift of his "trickery" – that from that point on he would have healing gifts himself. Kenneth was bemused and confused by this, but gradually he began to experiment and found that he really had acquired healing power. Though he continued constantly to doubt himself, he lived to a ripe old age, working with Lucinda, his twin soul, who had actually grown up in the same village as Jesus.

Lucinda had been a few years older than Jesus was, and Mary his mother sometimes asked her to watch over him. She consequently noticed from early on the extent to which Jesus was unusual and "different", and she experienced healing from him when he was still very young. It was a very dramatic healing, for she nearly died from an allergy to a certain herb with which some bread that she ate had been dusted, and it caused her to decide to keep a very close eye on Jesus from henceforth. She was consequently there to greet him when he returned from his early travels to such places as India[1], and when he came back to his own village he had Kenneth with him.

Though Lucinda found Kenneth unusual and realised that there was something special about him, she was not in that lifetime particularly attracted to him. It is important to appreciate that, even when twin souls are of opposite sexes and meet in an incarnation, they do not inevitably fall in love. In some lifetimes our inclinations are much more spiritual than sexual. It depends upon what we have come each time to do, and Kenneth and Lucinda's task at that time was to carry on with Jesus' work. Lucinda was also present at the crucifixion, and a link was formed between her and Kenneth because they were both despondent, feeling that they had somehow betrayed Christ.

Jesus had told Lucinda on his return from his early travels that while he had been away he had been informed by angels of his origin and of what his ministry was to be. She had warned him to be wary of talking about it – partly because she was not initially convinced of the truth of it – and so she had become a disciple on the pretext of watching over him. She rapidly became convinced, but her doubts resurfaced when the crucifixion appeared imminent. Christ told her at that point that she simply must believe, since she was to be one of the people to continue spreading his Word. After being beset by dreams, she linked up with Kenneth and, while he was doing his healing work, she prophesied and taught for the remainder of what proved to be for

107

both of them a long incarnation. (One of the lacunae in the New Testament is any account of the work of the female early disciples – or even any acknowledgement of the fact that there <u>were</u> women among them – and it is for this reason, as well as for many others, that I strongly recommend the books of Anne and Daniel Meurois-Givaudan[(2)].)

People such as Edwin Courtenay who have auric sight find that those who had lives around figures like the Buddha or Christ exhibit violet in their aura, and that a large amount of violet is a sign of having also received healing from the Master in question. Lucinda is possibly unusual in that, besides having been a follower of Christ, she was one of the first disciples of the Buddha. He taught her to go to a place of stillness inside herself and he healed her from the inside out, but then he sent her away to give out his knowledge. This was painful for her, just as was the later separation from Christ at the crucifixion.

Some centuries later Lucinda had an Arthurian incarnation, in which Merlin singled her out as his apprentice and assistant. These *heavy duty incarnations around powerful, highly spiritual, beings* have given her the potential both of sight and of healing ability, but also (she was told in her past-life reading) a lack of grounding in her physical body. It is perhaps this lack of grounding, combined with the fact that, while Ken has had a large number of incarnations, she has spent more time in spirit serving him as a guide, that gives Lucinda her somewhat "ethereal" look! Although twin souls tend to develop at the same pace, and although the ideal is for them to work together, their joint work does not necessarily have to be on the Earth's plane. Quality of incarnations is more important than quantity, and it may be remembered that Carol too has had many incarnations in which she served Dan as a spirit guide. Lucinda's long blonde hair also contributes to her rather angelic appearance, while Ken, on the other hand, tends to appear quite "Earthy", and he is also something of an eccentric – a characteristic that Edwin Courtenay has frequently observed among people who are nearing the end of their incarnations. He has a great zest for life, which he believes is meant primarily to be enjoyed, yet there seems at the same time sometimes to be something of "I've had enough of this!" or "I really can't be bothered" in his manner – perhaps the hallmark of someone who feels that he has done it all before.

Yet Edwin Courtenay finds when he gives past-life readings that people who came into contact with Jesus were profoundly influenced by him at the level of perception and healing, because of his immensely strong energy, and that that is something that they rarely lose in subsequent incarnations. Ken clearly still possesses the sensitivity to people's pain that contact with Christ gave him, and he has returned this time to continue that particular mission. Ken was described in his reading as a *prophet and awakener, with the ability to show people the miracle of seeing God within themselves, in other people, and in the natural environment.* Edwin also noticed blue in Ken's aura which he said was indicative of both clairaudience and clairsentience (profound wisdom).

The chief way in which Kenneth has chosen to carry out this mission is by teaching meditation, and it is also through this that he met Lucinda. It will be remembered that first meetings between twin souls tend to be "memorable events". Well, Lucinda says: "I remember the very first time I saw Ken. I was with my boyfriend for a meditation talk that he gave, and I thought to myself, 'This guy's got something I want.' I remember his very strong eyes. The other, woman, teacher seemed quite all right, but I didn't feel she had what I wanted."

As for Ken, he is a trifle reluctant to admit to a feeling of instant recognition or attraction because, by the time that Lucinda's existence really registered with him, she had enrolled for a full meditation course and had come to him for a "check". He says, however, "I have a very clear memory of her walking up the stairs in front of me wearing a very short, blue skirt, and I said to myself, 'Hey, you're supposed to be checking this girl's meditation, not fancying her as she's walking up the stairs!' So I put it aside. But then, after the checking, we talked for about an hour or an hour and a half, which I don't normally do, and I was surprised to find myself saying all these things, some of which I didn't know that I knew, to this person that I'd never really spoken to much before. It so happened that I had recently had a Tarot prediction about meeting a young, blonde woman, and consequently it crossed my mind that it might be her, but then I said to myself, 'No. She's too young to be interested in me, and anyway she's going out with this other guy. Besides, she irritates me because she always wants to wear my sunglasses, and I can't stand people who do that.' Some time later though, when I was dropping off to sleep, I had this vision and I knew it was Lucinda, and in it, it was very much like the heart expanding, almost painfully in a way, and a sort of feeling of spiritual orgasm. But I still ignored it, because I thought I was too old for her, and because she wasn't free."

For Ken is, at a guess, twenty years older than Lucinda. I say "at a guess" because he never tells anyone his age as he feels that it makes them "pin one down". But, as we have seen already, physical age is always completely immaterial to twin souls, since they will inevitably be the same age spiritually. Now that they have been together for several years, Ken and Lucinda say that they simply never think about the age gap between them and that they don't see it in photographs. Ken said that, when they were first together, "Lucinda would sometimes do something and I would think, 'Hey what's she doing?' and then I would realise, 'Of course, she's twenty-four. She's doing what twenty-four-year-olds do,' but now I don't even think that." And he feels that from Lucinda he gets a reflection of youthfulness, "which is quite nice!" and that it stops him from "thinking old".

As for Lucinda, she says, "There are a lot of advantages in going out with someone older. Ken's filled me in on a lot of stuff that could have taken me years to sort out. He's saved me a lot of time. When I was twenty-three I was still very much in the younger people's world and thought that anyone over thirty was "totally sussed", and I was a bit shy. But now, knowing Ken's older friends, I've realised that age is totally irrelevant and I can relate to people of any age. Lots of men my age think it's weird for a woman to go out with someone much older, but that's their problem!"

There are both similarities and differences in Ken and Lucinda's backgrounds. Ken had what he describes as an "untroubled, fairly idyllic" childhood, with no real religious upbringing, his parents having turned from being nominally C of E to agnostic. He says that he is grateful for that, as it left him free to explore. He had an elder brother and, nine years later, a younger sister. He was close to his brother, who is four years his senior, until he was about ten, but then they "split off". Much of his childhood was consequently relatively solitary, but not, he says, lonely. He cycled a lot, read a lot, and was altogether "pretty self-sufficient". Every now and again his parents would ask, "Are you all right?" to which he would reply, "Fine." His relationship with his parents was "pretty good", though in retrospect he feels it would have been better if they had been more open and loving – "rather than this kind of English middle class nonsense!" Ken had no real problems with his mother, but was closer to his father.

Lucinda, on the other hand, when she was very young, spent a lot of time in hospital, having hip operations from the age of eighteen months. This meant that she received a great deal of attention from both her parents and grandparents, and her Dad always told her that she was "tough and strong". (In fact, when one gets to know her, one rapidly appreciates that her Dad was right, and that the ethereal, almost "walking on air", impression conveyed at a first meeting masks something of a gentle Amazon!) Lucinda says that she has always been aware of being the favourite in her family, "which wasn't that good for me". So the two have in common a closeness with their fathers.

Like Ken, Lucinda had no religious upbringing at all, and she says that her parents "never pushed anything on to us". Interestingly, however, she says that when she was very young – perhaps not more than about five – she went occasionally to Sunday school, and, although she knew full well that she had no desire to be involved in the church in any way, she had a strong inner feeling of knowing Jesus personally. Normally past-life memories tend to remain completely buried, but one finds now and again that little (or in this case big!) things push their way through into our conscious mind. This feeling of knowing Jesus personally is not something that Lucinda ever felt inclined to talk about, but when she had her past-life reading, the account of that particular lifetime came as no great surprise to her. Her intimate knowledge of Jesus perhaps explains also her lack of desire to belong to any Church, thinking that the Churches have moved a long way from the original message[3].

Ever since leaving university Kenneth has mainly been teaching meditation in various contexts, but a few years ago he started doing counselling courses, and so he now does a bit of counselling as well. He is at present taking an advanced counselling course. Initially his family weren't too pleased when he left university, as they had anticipated that he would have a conventional career like his brother and sister, but now they seem to have accepted it and in fact, he says, "They criticise my brother and sister more although they do 'all the right things'. Perhaps it's because they've given up on me!". During the years prior to meeting his twin soul Ken had a number of relationships, none of which was entirely satisfactory, and at the time when Lucinda first came into his life he was completely free.

Lucinda acquired a boyfriend when she was fifteen, and moved out to live with him when she was only sixteen. She learnt secretarial skills and book-keeping, did a youth training scheme after a short period on the dole, and then took a book-keeping job "on the other side of the Bridge". (She is referring to the Humber Bridge, which links Hull, where she and Ken now both live, with Lincolnshire.) She says that her childhood before the divorce was very quiet, part of the problem with her parents being that they never argued. ("My Dad did as he was told unless it was very important!") She says that she was very intense as a child, always wanted to do the opposite of what everyone else wanted, and was "the member of the family who turned everything upside down".

Lucinda still saw her father regularly after the separation, and in fact he became more rather than less involved with her, and when she was seventeen she started working for him. She still has good relationships with both her parents and their new partners, as well as with her half-brothers and sisters.

We have already made it clear that an initial impediment to Ken and Lucinda's forming of their relationship was the fact that she was living with a boyfriend. We have also, however, said in previous chapters that – since twin-soul connections are high, spiritual ones – they will not override other relationships unless these were crumbling already. Well, besides enrolling for the meditation course, Lucinda had joined a *Universal Principle Support Group*[4], which she says was giving her much more purpose and direction in her life. She had tried in vain to involve Lewis, her boyfriend, in her new interests, and so it is hardly surprising that the relationship had become rather shaky.

Soon after the above-mentioned meditation course, Lucinda went with the local group, of which she and Ken were both members, to her first *Universal Principle Support* seminar, which she enjoyed immensely. She had, however, a bit of a block about hugging people she hardly knew, and she confided this difficulty to Ken. He replied that she could start by hugging him, and she says, "Yes, it did feel very natural. I felt more connected to him than to anyone else there, though I never imagined at that point that we would have a relationship. It felt loving but not sexual."

Ken says, "People talk about 'just ending up in bed together', but with us it really did 'just happen' and we were both taken completely by surprise, and both thought that it was a one-off." Since Lucinda was still living with Lewis at the time, they both suffered the proverbial pangs of guilt. She says that when it happened "the whole thing took me completely by surprise. I had been in a wrong relationship for eight years, yet had no thought that it was going to end." She thought initially that she would not tell Lewis, but then decided that she should. "He went crazy and said, 'That's it!' but then he changed his mind about ten times." Being, however, part of the Divine Plan, when twin soul connections are made it is <u>always</u> for an important purpose.

When Lucinda moved back to Hull, it was not because of what had happened with Ken, but because she realised that she needed to end her relationship, and also because she wanted to give up her job. She felt some guilt about leaving Lewis, but "not as bad as it could have been because I knew it was meant to be. Life with him had been about smoking dope basically, and that whole scene, and I just wanted out of it. I didn't know whether anything would happen with Ken. Learning to meditate and the support group were both a great help to me. I knew that the universe had given me the opportunity to move."

Lucinda got a flat on her own, aware that she needed to learn to be independent. Ken was worried that he had been instrumental in breaking up her relationship, but he says that it was not clear to him initially that she had really left Lewis for good, and so he did not really think that they would get together. Gradually, however, they began seeing one another more and more frequently, and the full relationship began about fourteen months after they had first met. One of the things that drew them together was the fact that neither of them has the slightest desire ever to have children. This was a relief to Ken, who had found that to be a factor when his previous relationships had ended.

Ken and Lucinda differ from most "couples" – in that they have never felt that they wanted to make a total commitment to one another in the form of marriage or anything equivalent. For that reason, even though they now, to all intents and purposes, live together and feel totally committed to each other, Ken has still kept his own flat. He says that, despite being committed to Lucinda, he doesn't like the idea of giving up his freedom, and so he likes to feel that the flat is there even though he doesn't use it very much. So one can say that they take to its extreme the notion of the *pillars of the temple standing apart*[5]!

Indeed, they have gone further still, for this "freedom" that they have agreed upon even includes sexual freedom. Lucinda explains that she has never been able to "buy the idea that if you're in one relationship and you have another loving relationship with someone else, it should have to stop at sex.". Ken, too, says, "I wouldn't want to be restricted myself, so why should I restrict Lucinda? When we go to parties we hardly see each other." For Lucinda, who is the only one so far to have taken advantage of this agreement, it's about "becoming bigger and open to more love. It's like expanding myself so that I can have loving relationships with more than one person." And also, she says, "Because of Ken having had a lot more lovers than me, there's a bit of me that wants to sleep with loads of people because I haven't, and try all these different and delicious spices of men and of life." Before, when she felt restricted to a single relationship, she blamed it on the other person ("I can't do it because he wouldn't let me."), but now she says she has come to see that it was to do with herself – "about my own blocks about allowing that much abundance into my life. It's about how much unconditional love you can have in your life – intimate loving relationships – and sex is part of that." Perhaps, too, since Ken has had a large number of incarnations and she only a few, she now feels a desire to pack as much as possible into this lifetime.

Ken and Lucinda admit to having been a bit naive when they first thought about allowing each other this sexual freedom, and Ken says that he is beginning to have second thoughts: "When it happens initially we are more in alignment with each other, but then the whole thing falls to pieces and we get into real difficulties." Lucinda, however, who still feels that she wants to understand why most people feel that sexual relationships should be restricted to a single partner, believes that, though at the moment there is stuff in her that's blocking her, "When we're in sufficient alignment, we'll be able to do it successfully." She says that over the last few months she has become clearer that it is Ken who is her basic support, and she knows that, before she can manage other relationships successfully, she needs to be quite sure "that we're in total support of one another. Before I do it again, we must both feel okay about it and okay with each other. I know that Ken's an important part of that."

I sensed something of an ambivalence when Kenneth explained that with hindsight part of it for him was a way of not being really committed. "Not that I think that having relationships outside the relationship means that you're not committed. I think you can only do it successfully if you are committed, but not in the normal sense of the word. Maybe I didn't want to be totally tied." I wondered whether Ken had had a fear of being hurt, but he replied, "No, it was more a fear of not being free on some level."

There have so far only been two affairs outside Ken and Lucinda's relationship, and in both cases she says that it was "real karmic stuff". Whereas with Ken it has always been "very peaceful and natural – like coming home", in both the other instances Lucinda experienced a "really strong feeling when they walked into the room", and it made her shaky. She feels that she has learnt a lot from these experiences, and that in both cases the affair served the purpose of resolving something karmic. For, Ken explained, "At the point when things were getting outrageous, we did some regressions," and Lucinda added, "These regressions revealed several lifetimes in which these people had been involved, and when we ran through the lifetimes and the recent incidents, it took a lot of desperation out of the feelings." She says she feels clearer with the first affair that the regression resolved what was necessary, though the second one also revealed a very heavy influence, involving magic. "The second experience was more crazy and irrational as I've nothing in common with him. I knew it wasn't very healthy, but it was still a very strong pull. I certainly had something karmic to resolve . . . Yes, I've no doubt that they were both *karmic soulmates*."

Looking back now on the two affairs, Lucinda feels also that they confirmed her in the relationship with Kenneth. She says, "I can see it wasn't right with them because there was nothing really deep there. With Ken there's a real strength and togetherness that I've never felt with anyone else. When life has got difficult in the past I've changed things on the outside – moved house or changed my relationship – rather than changing things on the inside. Now, with Ken's support, I'm realising that the relationship with him is really deeply right and strong, that it's worth totally committing myself. I'm not working so much at the relationship as at myself. Really it's about me. The universe has kept on directing me that my relationship with Ken is the most supportive thing for me – it's what enables me to work through my stuff. Even if we do have other people outside our relationship, my primary best friend and companion will always be Ken." And then she added, "Originally I saw it as a question of either freedom or commitment, but now I've realised that real commitment for me isn't what everybody else calls commitment. It's a sort of really deep intention. It's not that we plan our lives till the day we die to be together. It's a moment to moment commitment, a really deep feeling. I'm beginning to feel that commitment and freedom are on the same side as each other rather than opposing each other. That you can only really have them together. How most people relate and have relationships is not what I want. Now I feel I've got to really sort myself, get my relationship with Ken really sorted and then trust the universe. I'm not planning immediately to steam out there and plunge into loads more relationships."

For Ken the mutual agreement about sexual freedom has so far had a different result. This is partly, he says, "because I had a lot of chance earlier on in my life to experiment with different relationships in a very easy, non-problematic way, so now I don't feel a need to go and have sex with a lot of people. Though I'm not saying I would never do that under any circumstances, because I don't want a completely incestuous, jealous relationship. But now, when I feel sexually attracted to someone, it seems like it's all too much trouble – ("Oh God, not that again!") – and the reason it's too much trouble is very largely the other people. They can't handle having an open relationship such as Lucinda and I have in mind. I enjoy the flirting and infatuation, and the heart connection, but I haven't so far felt the need to take it any further than that. If I developed anything more than a smiling, flirty relationship with a girl, it would get so complicated and difficult. I just enjoy it where it is. I like the excitement of new relationships, but you can have that without getting into bed."

There was, however, though it never really came to anything, one person that Ken became interested in, and Lucinda says that she found that more threatening than anything else has been because "it was more spiritual than sexual". She said, "It was worse because he really loved her. My actual relationship was more threatened because of the fact that she was more like us than are the other girls he flirts with, or either of the people that I got involved with." So my personal feeling is that, besides carrying on the mission entrusted to them by Christ, Kenneth and Lucinda are here also partly to work on, and gain in understanding of, their own relationship. But then – apart from those really evolved souls who have chosen to come back simply to be of help – are we not all on Earth partly or mainly to sort ourselves out?

We have seen that it is common for twin souls to be telepathic – at least to some extent – and Kenneth and Lucinda are no exception to that. They say that they often pick up on each other's thoughts and feelings; they often find that they had been thinking the same thing. Their health is also quite linked, and they say that they support each other's good health. Lucinda virtually never has even so much as a cold and only goes to the homoeopath for spots. Ken says that he used to be less healthy, getting 'flu a lot, but since going to the homoeopath, his health has also been very good.

Although Lucinda "isn't interested in stereos", they feel that they share every interest that is really important. "We're both Scorpios, and – as is natural for Scorpios – we're both interested in spirituality and sexuality. And we're also both interested in the meaning of life."

Besides having shared interests, however, they are a good example of the way in which twin souls always complement each other. Lucinda is more physical – "likes walking across fields in wellingtons" – but that complements Ken, who "thinks up the things to do",while she does them. ("And sometimes I even go with her!") Ken says, too, that Lucinda was brought up a bit tomboyish and her father treated her more like a son, "while I've got certain female qualities. It's she who puts up the shelves, whereas I arrange the flowers. I'd think about doing the shelves for years, but she just gets on and does it!" This is rather interesting, since Lucinda "looks very much the part" as a female, while Ken certainly looks very masculine, with a bushy beard, but they both feel that underlying the external appearances, Lucinda's masculine side is very well developed, as is Ken's female one. This is important for the full bonding of a couple, where – to quote Joudry and Pressman again – *their gender characteristics are shared, flowing in harmonious exchange. For a truly strong woman is strong and happy in her femininity, and comfortable in her secondary masculine character; a fully masculine man exhibits all the best of his yang qualities along with yin sensitivities in high degree.*[6]

This complementarity extends also to their work. Since Ken is very good at thinking things up but not so good at carrying them out, it is Lucinda who "does all the practical stuff of getting courses off the ground". Here of course her secretarial and book-keeping skills are useful. She is also now taking an interest in counselling and has embarked on a course in it, which she says she would never have done if it hadn't been for Ken.

Having separate flats gives them the liberty to have time apart if they want it, which is important to both of them. Also, Lucinda says that there has always been a bit of her that wondered whether she would be able to live on her own,

115

but Ken's encouraging her independence has made her feel more secure – that she would be okay on her own. Being so much younger, she feels that she has needed to learn about being on her own, but of course – as we are seeing time and time again – the ability to stand alone is an essential ingredient of the readiness for union with our twin. And even after the union on this plane has been achieved, it is still important for each partner to have periods of solitude or separation, for partnerships of co-dependence are never successful. At the moment Lucinda is trying to save up for a trip to America for a course in Tantric sex, in which she has become very interested. (One is drawn to what one needs, and Edwin Courtenay explained to Lucinda in her reading that, because of her lack of grounding, she needed her base centre energy to rise – hence the attraction for her of Tantric sex.)

Now Lucinda feels that she may well one day become a teacher in this field, while Ken is "less interested in Tantra than in meditation". She sees this, however, as "the perfect yin/yang", since meditation is the male aspect, Tantra the female. "So, while at the moment I'm supporting him in the teaching of meditation, later maybe I'll be a sexuality teacher and he'll support me. Meditation and sexuality – and getting to the bottom of sexuality – are ultimate things to becoming enlightened, I guess. They tie in with the Veda, which is the oldest of philosophies, and one to which I am very drawn."

In his reading, Edwin told Kenneth that his abilities as *prophet and awakener*, clairsentience and so on were *at present all mixed up together*, giving him *intermittent blasts*, and that they *needed to be channelled and controlled*. Since two and a half years had elapsed, and since, if a past-life reading is to be really worthwhile having, one needs to digest it over a long period, to take time to "make it one's own". I asked Ken what he felt was the impact of the reading on his life now. He replied that he felt it had had the subtle effect of awakening him to his own inner wisdom. Though he has not yet fully been able to take on board Edwin's description of him as a *prophet*, part of his recent development has been that he has found himself accurately prophesying things in his personal life. As for being an *awakener*, obviously this ties in very much with his teaching, since meditation is all about listening to the God within.

Lucinda, too, says that her reading was a tremendous lot to take on board and that now she is "still working with it", perhaps believing it on one level while another part of her retains a sceptical attitude. My own recent reading of Anne and Daniel Meurois-Givaudan and Dolores Cannon[7] have given me a real fascination with the Essenes, who appear to have been as near as one can get on this Earth to an ideal community, and so I wondered whether Lucinda, who clearly must have been one of them, felt the impact of this. Like me, she very much liked the idea of being able to live without money[8], which she regards as "only energy – something one will always have enough of if one TRUSTS", and she said that the whole notion of a community such as the Essenes appear to have been was attractive to her.

As to the more distant future, Ken says that he has "no particular reason for giving up the game. I'd like to come back to have fun, and to help others to have more fun. Because I feel that that's what life is really about. It's also about unlearning. We all have so much to unlearn!" Lucinda, on the other hand, says that she hopes to "become enlightened this time round. It's not impossible, I've still got another fifty odd years to live – at least! Perhaps I wouldn't mind coming back just one more time, but once more will be my limit!"

THE STORY OF MARY AND NORMAN

Mary and Norman are a much more conventional couple than Kenneth and Lucinda, being married with two daughters, and she being a Roman Catholic. Their lifetime at the time of Christ was also very different to that of Ken and Lucinda. Mary, however, in her present incarnation is very much influenced by that lifetime, just as Ken and Lucinda are, and Norman is currently performing to perfection the duty he incurred at that time to repay a karmic debt to her.

For at the time of Christ, Mary and Norman were married as they are now, but, while she became a disciple, he did not wish to jeopardise his career as a Roman General and consequently threw her out on account of her allegiance. Loving Norman as she does now, and being in what appears to be to all intents and purposes as near as is humanly possible a "perfect relationship", Mary finds it hard to imagine how in a previous existence she could have abandoned her beloved husband even for such a wonderful person as Jesus Christ. This past life that they shared is, however, indicative of two things: firstly the fact that, in order to attain perfection, our desire to seek and spread the truth, and our allegiance to God, must always be put above any human relationship; and secondly our oft-repeated statement, that true twin soul unions can only be achieved when both partners have achieved a high level of spiritual evolution and are truly ready for and deserving of each other. In any case, sometimes the purpose of twin soul encounters is for one to challenge the other with the aim of strengthening them and raising them to a higher level (remember the case of Merlin and Morgan le Fay mentioned in our History chapter?), and it could well be that Mary and Norman had made an agreement at soul level before coming into that incarnation that he would test her Love in that way. (I put "Love" with a capital to distinguish it from the very specific love between man and woman which is also so much a subject of this book. For in accepting the challenge and forsaking her love for a higher Love, Mary was also in that lifetime teaching Norman a very important lesson about priorities and essentials.)

We have seen, for instance in the case of Iris and Joe, that, even when twin souls are quite evolved and ready for each other, their union in an incarnation does not always come early or easily. Mary chose particularly difficult circumstances in which to be born this time round, had already broken off two engagements and quite given up hope of matrimony before she met Norman, and was in her mid thirties when they were wed. Norman, though

117

his childhood was less difficult and painful than hers, is of a shy and retiring disposition and would probably never have succeeded in making the bond with Mary had it not been that a high spiritual force was driving him to meet his destiny. For Mary recounts:–

"We had become quite friendly during a holiday in Austria, though it was a little difficult for us to get together because I had a female friend with me. After that we met regularly at chamber concerts and always had a word in the interval, until I began to feel that it was maybe time that he asked me out. I had resigned myself to the idea that it would never happen, when we both attended a slide-showing reunion in Scarborough of the group who had gone on the tour to Salzburg. My car had broken down, and so I went there by train and Norman gave me a lift back to York. I felt so at ease with him when he gave me this lift, and able to be my true self in a way that I had never felt able to be with anyone else, that I began to feel sure that he was the man for me, and that, failing him, I would almost certainly never marry. To my immense disappointment, however, he still didn't pluck up the courage to ask me out.

It was some weeks later, on a Saturday morning when I was in the middle of giving a piano lesson at home, that suddenly there was a surprise phone call. It was Norman asking me whether I would like to accompany him to a performance that very evening of *The Dream of Gerontius*. By good fortune I happened to be free, and he told me some time later that, had I refused that invitation, he would never have tried again!" So clearly divine forces were at work here, forcing the connection.

Mary has read, and been impressed by, Joudry and Pressman's book[6], and she sees in her and Norman's case a parallel with that of Johanna and Philip recounted in their first chapter. She says that "like Johanna and Philip we were *both loners with a few close friends and had a haunting sense of inadequacy on that account*", and also that, while they were both successful in their careers, Norman's self-control, like Philip's, *had deep roots* and, while presenting a *strong front to the world, inwardly he suffered from feelings of inferiority, which made him defer to others less gifted.* So Mary and Norman needed to connect with each other in order to be able to connect with their own true selves. Again like Johanna and Philip, *both had stood apart from the social mix where conversation too often seemed empty and meaningless*, and both had *longed for authentic communication.* And so, once that was established, Norman's confidence was increased, and Mary was pleasantly surprised that it was only about four months until he asked her to marry him. For, besides music (which is Mary's profession), they rapidly found that they had other interests in common, such as Art and Architecture. (She says, "We both spent the greater part of our youth sitting in the front room of our respective homes reading. I spent a lot of time reading books on Art and Architecture, and I discovered early on in our courtship that he was knowledgeable on both, and that our tastes in both were also very similar.")

Sometimes we punish ourselves karmically for past deeds which were not really our fault. (Remember how Iris has committed herself in this lifetime to the children whom she feels that she failed to care for adequately in previous incarnations?) Well, Mary as a young child in an earlier incarnation accidentally poisoned "his" younger sister by giving her some berries that she had asked "him" for. She consequently chose this same younger sister as her mother this time round, and the punishment she has received for this accidental death seems somewhat excessive, and she is only now – in her late fifties – beginning to recover from it.

For Mary's mother was a single parent, her father having left her as soon as Mary was born, and Mary has only met him twice (at the ages of about four and six), and her memories of him are consequently extremely hazy. Her mother was always very harsh with her when she was young, and she told her that her father hadn't wanted children and consequently didn't love her. This inevitably gave her a tremendous sense of inadequacy, which she feels she has only quite recently begun to conquer. As a child she always felt different from her classmates, who all seemed to her to have two, very caring and supportive parents.

Twin souls so often share experiences prior to their meeting, and in this lifetime Norman too has suffered from being fatherless. In his case, however, his father died (from tuberculosis) when he was eight, and not only was his mother very loving and sensible, he also had two elder sisters who were and are extremely fond of him.

Mary's mother had something of a chip on her shoulder on account of not having a profession, and consequently having to support the two of them through work such as cleaning people's houses. This made her determined that Mary should do better and, since she herself would have liked to be a dancing teacher, this was the profession she decided on for her daughter (thinking that ultimately she would help her in it!). This idea failed, however, since Mary, despite being sent to dancing lessons at the age of only two or three, showed no aptitude at all for this particular skill. She did, however, show an aptitude for music – she had a very strong sense of rhythm from an early age – and so her mother consequently decided on a musical profession for Mary as the next best thing to teaching dancing.

So obsessed was Mary's mother with her daughter's future career, that her school work was made to suffer for her piano. She regularly sent letters to the school saying that Mary had been unable to do her homework on account of her practice, and she also missed a lot of schooling through being made to travel to numerous music festivals all over the country. Mary says that she fell down particularly in Maths because of this, whereas she thinks that she would have been able to cope if she had done the homework; but her mother said that school "wasn't important", that the only thing that was important was playing the piano. Mary was very interested in Biology at school, and she also had a tremendous love of small children and babies. The very first desire that she ever expressed was to be a midwife, but her mother simply said, "No. That definitely isn't for you."

So, as a result of her mother's will, Mary went, on leaving school, to the Royal Academy, where she was very successful. On completing her studies she became the last thing she really wanted to be – a music teacher in a school. Having an interest in accompanying, she had done an accompanying course with the hope of becoming a professional accompanist, but this did not materialise. She has, however, always performed as an accompanist in an amateur capacity, and is well known in York as an extremely accomplished accompanist!

The only practical alternative open to Mary on completing her studies was the work she is mainly doing now – giving piano lessons at home – but this, she says, although she enjoys it, firstly would not have been sufficiently lucrative when she was single, and secondly would have kept her in every night and not allowed her to have any social life, "which I don't have now, but I don't mind so much now that I'm married; but it wouldn't have been any good at all in those days, when I was very young." So, until she married at the age of thirty-five, Mary taught music in a number of schools, which she feels is largely responsible for her current minor health problems. (School teaching is a very difficult job even for those who love it, and the high level of stress it induces is an inevitable cause of ill health in many people!)

Mary, as we have said, still practises the Christian faith which led to Norman's rejection of her two thousand years ago. Oddly enough, this is thanks to her mother, who was a Christian – initially an Anglican who practised on and off and latterly a Salvationist – but who decided that her daughter should be a Catholic while she was at school, even though she herself didn't like Catholics! The reason for this was that she wanted Mary to be educated by nuns, and was under the illusion that this necessitated her being a Catholic. She put Mary into the convent school when she was five, telling the nuns that Mary would become a Catholic, which she did at the age of eight. Mary was not at all happy about this to start with, as all her uncles, aunts and cousins were Methodists, and they were horrified at her becoming a Catholic. When, however, she left school, while her mother thought that it was time for her to give up Catholicism, Mary herself was by then firmly "hooked", and is now still a practising Catholic nearly forty years later.

Norman, on the other hand, was brought up Methodist, attending Sunday school with his sisters, and, though he still has a firm belief in God, he gave up practising his religion fairly early on, as he feels that the Church is unnecessary and that all the rules are man-made rather than coming from God. Now that she has become more spiritually aware, Mary totally shares this point of view, but she agrees with Edgar Cayce (and Sai Baba[9]) that we should "stay in our own churches and build on".

120

In fact Sai Baba is nowadays one of the most important influences in Mary's life, and Norman, while being less sure than she is of his divinity, shares her interest and her view that he is undoubtedly extremely special. So great is Mary's enthusiasm that she has recently succeeded in overcoming her natural reserve and the feeling of being lacking in leadership qualities sufficiently to found the first Sai Baba group in York, and at the time of writing this group is developing rapidly and going from strength to strength. This could certainly not have happened had Mary not been married to Norman, and so it is another obvious example of twin souls coming together in order to bring more light into our needy world.

When, in the first century A.D., Mary had failed to convert Norman to Christ's teachings and had consequently gone off with the other disciples and without him, Jesus encouraged her to work as a healer, which she did for the rest of that lifetime, developing skills which became well recognised. She and Norman did meet again, but were never reconciled, and so she only had her love of Christ to sustain her. Recently Mary has read a few books which have convinced her of the fact that Jesus did not actually die on the cross[1], and she has also found out that she was among the few who learnt this at the time. It therefore seems likely that it is her subconscious memory which has made her able to accept something the suggestion of which most Roman Catholics would regard as "scandalous".

But Mary's rather unorthodox Catholicism did not begin with her recent discovery of Sai Baba and her change of view about the resurrection. During the early years of her marriage she started to take an interest in spiritual things normally spurned by Catholicism, and this was partly because her mother firstly had often had dreams which had come true, and secondly took to visiting mediums. All this triggered Mary's interest and she then became captivated by the books of the well-known medium Doris Stokes[10]. Doris Stokes was open to the idea of reincarnation, though not completely convinced, and it was several years later that Mary began to read books on that subject which finally convinced her. And curiously, one of the people who were most instrumental in this was a member of her own parish!

As a (Roman Catholic) Christian myself, I find it a little frustrating that, in all the current debate re Christianity versus New Age, it is never suggested that the two are not incompatible, or that there are practising Christians within the New Age movement. Unless they become willing to take such realities as reincarnation on board, the Churches may die sooner rather than later, and the former can probably not happen until all the "closet Christian reincarnationists" gain the courage to do what Edgar Cayce did and come out into the open.

This Mary's friend, Eleanor, has started to do, and it is partly Mary's support that has enabled her to do so. For their real friendship began when they discovered a mutual interest in healing, and that happened thanks to an article which Eleanor put into her parish magazine, of which she was the editor. In the article she advertised an *Aura Soma*[11] workshop that her sister was giving and (though one of the priests in the parish threatened to preach an entire sermon against it!) through Mary and Norman's attendance at the workshop, they discovered their shared belief in reincarnation. After that, to their mutual delight, Mary and Eleanor started to lend one another book after book and to become strong supports for one another. A support which Eleanor appreciated more than ever when, after she had had the courage to write something in which she hinted at reincarnation being an explanation for the suffering in the world, the parish priest not only refused to distribute that particular issue, but also told her that he was going to discontinue the whole magazine! Eleanor was extremely hurt by this (having put a great deal of work into the magazine for a number of years and never received any thanks for it) but, like Mary, she realises that such trials are sent to strengthen us and increase our resolve in the pursuit of Truth.

Mary realises now that without the difficult and painful childhood given her by her mother, she would probably not have been led to her wonderful discovery of Sai Baba. For it is through overcoming difficulties that we grow, and Sai Baba only makes himself known to those who are ready for his message.

Though, as we have said, Mary quite enjoys her piano teaching and is greatly sought after by potential pupils, she feels that her mother pushed her into a career that was not of her own choosing, and now, having attended a number of related workshops and also acquired *Reiki* healing, she would very much like to return to the sort of work that she did when she was one of the early disciples. At present it is mainly the financial requirements of seeing their daughters through university that is preventing her from giving up her piano teaching in favour of pursuing courses in sound and colour healing. On the other hand, in recent months she has been sent a number of pupils with "special needs", and she feels that helping them is another way in which she can practise her healing gifts.

Norman, though he gave her no support in it two thousand years ago, now shares Mary's healing interests fully. From the twin-soul point of view there are two aspects to this point. Firstly the one we have previously mentioned: that by throwing her out he encouraged her to stand on her own and develop her skills without his support, thus making her a stronger person. Secondly (the subject of our next chapter) the fact that twin souls always catch one another up spiritually, and so the work which she did all that time ago, initially under Jesus' guidance and direction, has now rebounded on to Norman and also raised his vibrations further in service to humanity. The likelihood is that, when he has reached retirement age in his profession as a university teacher, they will work together as a pair in the spiritual field, quite possibly offering both sound and colour healing.

As two halves of a single being, twin souls, as we have seen, invariably complement one another. When one is artistic, the other will be scientific, though this never means that there will not also be a great overlap of interests. In Mary and Norman's case (it can by now no doubt be guessed!), it is he who is the scientist. Norman's brilliant brain was apparent from an early age, and his widowed mother gave him all the encouragement he needed to get to university. His love of books and his pursuit of learning were more important features than his shyness, and were also what drew Mary instantly to him. Even though his life has most obviously been enriched both by the support of his family and the support which he gives them, it is very easy to imagine him as a contented bachelor totally wrapped up in his academic pursuits. It is clearly this lack of need for a partner that made him ready for, and deserving of, the joy that living with his twin soul gives him.

Of their relationship, Mary says, "Besides loving music as much as I do, and being also extremely knowledgeable on the subject, he supports me by being always there to listen when I'm talking about my pupils. And I support him by listening to what he tells me about his scientific discoveries. He manages to tell me in such a way that I can understand it; and I think that's probably a help to him, because he knows that if I understand it, then other people that he talks to will be able to understand it as well." Now this last point is a very interesting one, and is again the subject of a later chapter. For it may be remembered that Mary claims to be "completely unscientific", and to have suffered in that area in school on account of her mother pushing her in her study of the piano. One would not expect that someone like Mary, who did not even do Maths and Science to 'O' Level, would be able to follow the scientific discoveries of a university teacher, yet she is able to do so! My research has shown that when twin souls are together they tend to gain one another's talents in addition to their own, though not, as Joudry and Pressman also point out, becoming more alike, but rather becoming each one stronger in their individuality (*they adopt each other's strengths and apply these in turn to their own self-unfolding – thus continually opening new facets of the one soul*[6]).

Although Mary's mother has been, as it were, the "bane of her life", it is actually indirectly thanks to her that she and Norman first became acquainted. (Rarely in life is every evil nothing but evil, and so often do our most positive experiences stem from within our most negative ones!) It happened because at one point Mary's mother and one of Norman's elder sisters were working in the same shop, and Norman's sister asked Mary's mother to visit her own mother as she was a bit lonely. Although Norman's mother found Mary's mother distinctly odd, she appreciated having someone to whom to chat (Norman being always so wrapped up in his books and his scientific research!), and so the visits became a regular occurrence. On one occasion, Mary having just acquired a car, she volunteered to pick her mother up from the house, where she was introduced to Norman and they had a bit of a chat. She recounts, "I can't really say that I felt the proverbial 'instant recognition', but I did immediately think that he was very nice, and when, a few weeks later, after my mother had told me that he was going to be attending a concert in which I was playing, I was bitterly disappointed that he didn't come up and talk to me in the interval." (It was of course only his shyness that prevented Norman from doing that.)

After that, three or four years elapsed before their next meeting. The first meeting was obviously, however, also a "memorable event" for Norman, because, when he was preparing to attend an introductory meeting of the group which were to do the Austrian tour previously mentioned, he knew inside himself – even though he had barely given her a thought during the three to four-year interval – that Mary would be there too. For Mary it was an immensely pleasant surprise when he came and said "Hullo" and sat down next to her. In fact it was not until a few years after they were married that Norman told her about this piece of precognition.

For Mary the only "imperfection" in their married life is that she would very much like to have had more children. She had a number of miscarriages, and the four-year age gap in between their two daughters is consequently a bigger one than she would have chosen. Norman, however, has strong views that "two are enough", so Mary says jokingly that she will have to marry someone else next time round so that she can have more children.

On a more serious note, however, Mary and Norman both feel that they simply cannot imagine being married to anyone else, "because we're so well suited". They rarely have disagreements but, when they do, Mary says that they always resolve them quickly, never permitting the attitude to (in Joudry and Pressman's words) *Let him suffer*[6]. They are also a good example of people who are (to quote Joudry and Pressman again) less likely to be *swept away by passion* than *those who are more earthbound*, not constantly feeling *a driving need for physical intimacy*. Since they are both caught up in their respective professions, and since their "extra-curricular activities" are largely artistic and spiritual, *their intimacy is of the spirit, their passion directed toward fulfilling the will of God*[6]. Mary feels this latter point more fully than ever since she founded her Sai Baba group, and, although Norman does not actually participate in the meetings, she feels too that they are both *evolving at the same pace*. Again, she likes the way in which Joudry and Pressman put it: *They move forward in step, though not in military step. One progresses in one area, the other in a different one, and each draws the other forward . . .*[6]

Though not without the "teenage problems" which no parents (no caring parents anyway!) can possibly escape, Mary and Norman's family life appears to work as near perfectly as any family can hope to. The four of them share a great love of animals (always keeping at least a couple of cats, not to mention smaller household pets), and they are all vegetarian.

As far as the general running of the home goes, they have always maintained a fairly conventional man/woman division of labour, but both are quite content with that. Norman, who has never changed a nappy (though Mary is now hoping that he might learn to do this when they have grandchildren ("in preparation for a larger family next time round!"), did not take a great deal of interest in his daughters until he was able to communicate with them on an intellectual level, but Mary's real passion for babies complemented that. Also, she says, "He's a good bit more down to earth than I am. He has a grounding effect on me and is definitely more practical. I'm not practical at all!" And then she adds, "We help and support each other in all ways. Besides telling me about his scientific discoveries, he knows who all my pupils are, and if I can't get into town, he goes and buys the music for me and that sort of thing." (He is also one of those people who are more or less incapable of going into a bookshop without buying something, and as often as not his purchases include a new spiritual book which he knows will greatly interest Mary. She says, too, that he sometimes consults her on religious/spiritual matters prior to giving a lecture.)

Mary's mother only died a couple of years ago and – although she has always presented to the outside world a strong front as a "balanced, normal person" – she feels that she is only now beginning to recover from her mother's domineering and to find her true self. (This was helped very recently, when she performed, with the help of a "Sai Baba friend", a tie-cutting exercise using Phyllis Kristal's method[12].) It is no doubt Norman's support that has enabled her always to present this front. They always maintained a very dutiful relationship with Mary's mother, despite the frustrations it entailed; Norman, with his exceptionally tolerant nature, turning a blind eye to all the criticism. When, after many years of matrimony, Mary felt that she had had more than she could take and so wrote her mother a letter telling her that it had to stop, the criticism was transferred to the two granddaughters! (This was of course very difficult for both girls, but they were fortunate in receiving good support from their parents.)

So now Mary is seeing a homoeopath and working hard on her health problems, on forgiving her mother,and on developing her own personality and gifts to their full potential. In all of this she is conscious of the support both of her husband and of Sai Baba. She feels that she and Norman probably still have some way to go before being ready for the final fusion – "because I'm sure I've got loads of things still to work out. And also, although we're in alignment over most things, there are still one or two major differences. For instance, he tends to worry about money and about saving it, while I have a bad habit of spending it on the rare occasions when I have any. I think he still needs to learn to trust more about the future being taken care of, while I perhaps ought to think a bit about saving for the future." At the moment, however, her ambition is to save up for a trip to India to see Sai Baba! This will no doubt become possible as soon as their younger daughter has gone through university, and in the meantime Mary and Norman's completing will go on being *a continuous activity which has been a long time gathering and will strengthen throughout life*[6].

Notes

1. See: *Jesus Lived in India* by Holger Kersten, published by Element.
   The Way of the Essenes by Anne and Daniel Meurois-Givaudan, published in English by Destiny Books and in the original French by Editions Amrita.
   Sai Baba, the Embodiment of Love by Peggy Mason and Ron Laing, published by Gateway Books.
   The Holy Blood, The Holy Grail by Michael Baigent, Richard Leigh and Henry Lincoln, published by Corgi.
2. Anne and Daniel have written three books about their lives as Essene disciples, of which so far only the first has been translated into English.
3. Holger Kersten, the author of *Jesus Lived in India*, has founded a society called *The Nazarenes*, for people who are interested in returning to what he considers to be the true intentions of Jesus.
4. See *You Can Have It All* by Arnold Patent, published by Money Mastery Publishing, Piermont, New York.
5. *The Prophet* by Kahlil Gibran, published by Mandarin.
6. *Twin Souls – A Guide to Finding your True Spiritual Partner* by Patricia Joudry and Maurie D. Pressman, M.D., published by Element Books, Shaftesbury, Dorset.
7. See *Jesus and the Essenes* and *They Walked with Jesus* by Dolores Cannon, published by Gateway Books.
8. See *Jesus and the Essenes*.
9. See: *Sai Baba – The Embodiment of Love* by Peggy Mason and Ron Laing, published by Gateway Books.
   Sai Baba – Man of Miracles by Howard Murphet, published by Vrindavanum Books, London.
   A Catholic Priest meets Sai Baba by Don Mario Massoleni, published by Leela Press Inc.
   Sai Baba- The Ultimate Experience by Phyllis Kristal, published by The Convenor, Sri Sathya Sai Books and Publications Trust.
   and many others.
10. Doris Stokes' books are published by Macdonald Futura Publishers Ltd.
11. See *The Miracle of Colour Healing* by Vicky Wall, published by Aquarian Press.
12. See *Cutting the Ties that Bind* by Phyllis Kristal, published by Samuel Weiser Inc., USA.

Chapter VIII

TWIN SOULS ALWAYS CATCH ONE ANOTHER UP SPIRITUALLY
The story of Oliver and Polly

"I was in Australia," said Polly. "I had gone there to see if the better climate would make my MS go into remission. The friend I was staying with was a devotee of Sai Baba, and somehow he just wouldn't leave me alone. I was being plagued by visions of him. I had been brought up a good Sikh, and I thought to myself, "Who is this man?" I thought he was weird at first, and I just wanted him to leave me alone. In the end I decided to give him a test. I asked him to prove himself to me. Well, that very night I had a dream in which Sai Baba was standing on a balcony and there were hordes and hordes of people below with their arms outstretched. He was holding a very small vase. He rolled up his sleeves and then he turned the vase upside down and started to shake it. This grey ash kept pouring out of it. It went on and on coming, and I just carried on and on watching, wondering to myself, 'How can all that possibly have come out of that tiny vase?' Eventually I heard this voice asking me, 'Have I proved myself to you yet?' So after that I was hooked! I felt as though I'd come home. I felt as though I'd always known Sai Baba."

Polly's story seems appropriate immediately following that of Mary, whose spiritual development has leapt ahead since starting a Sai Baba group! This book is, however, not about Sai Baba but about twin souls, so I will simply refer readers again to the very many good books already written about this avatar[1]. I will, however, just mention in passing that the "grey powder" which Polly saw in her dream was *vibhuti*, the healing ash which Sai Baba materialises all the time. What is relevant to Polly's story and to our subject is the fact that, just as twinsoulship is the domain and the essence of every human being, irrespective of their belief or lack of it, so Sai Baba can be seen as the voice of God today, over and above all religions but at the same time embracing all of them as well as all of humanity in the immensity of his Love. Jesus Christ said, *I am the Way . . .* ; Sai Baba (who in my personal view may well embody the Christ just as Jesus did from the period in between his baptism and the crucifixion), as Polly points out, says, *Don't get attached to the form. Look beyond.* She says, "When I first discovered Baba, I kept seeing him – his face, his red-robed figure, his extraordinary fuzzy hair – but now I just see the Light. I just keep picturing God. Sai Baba is leading me directly to God. I get this wonderful warm feeling inside. It's hard to explain. It's the most wonderful feeling I've ever known. It's so beautiful! Oh I love the spiritual path!"

Polly, as will be clear from the above, is very wrapped up in spirituality and soaring in her spiritual development. It is this that enables her to regard her MS not as an impediment, but rather as a challenge. It is this that makes her such a joy to meet, her wheelchair being transfigured almost into a golden throne, emanating peace and light. Indeed she reminds me of one of the musicians whom I have most admired in my life: Jacqueline du Pré, who died of the same disease at the age of only forty-two. In Jacqueline's case her spirituality manifested itself through her 'cello and the divine sounds which she was able to draw from it right up until very near the end. Her soul was in her music, and her recognition of the eternal nature of both enabled her to make light of her illness, even to joke about it. In 1981, six years before her death, when the young American 'cellist Gerard Leclerc started lessons with her, she said to him gravely, "I have a terrible illness, you know. A very, very serious illness whose only possible outcome is death. Do you know what it's called? It's called *glissanditis!*" (I heard Gerard Leclerc himself perform some wonderful glissandos recently, in a Shostakovitch sonata, during a concert he gave in Geneva, where he lives.)

In early Egypt, Polly had a real golden throne. Oliver, her twin soul, and she were Pharaoh and Queen, and their reign was a very harmonious one, emanating peace throughout this great land. Late in that lifetime, however, she became ill and he was unable to bear the thought of her dying before him. So they decided both to take poison, and they died together, locked in an embrace, leaving their land to their children.

Later on they shared a Mayan lifetime as priest and priestess, and later still – in the Middle Ages – they were again priest and priestess of a Pagan coven in England. In both those lifetimes they had gifts and power which they used to bring healing to the Earth. Together they brought energies into the Earth of a divine nature. Energies which were needed to be brought down from Heaven in order to continue and promote the Earth's evolutionary cycle and process. So they have played very important roles in maintaining the flow of the Earth's evolution.

In their present lifetime, too, they have the potential for valuable joint work in the field of healing. As so often happens with twin souls, however, one partner has gone temporarily backwards in his development, and so reconnecting with his twin soul on the physical plane has been necessary in order to pull him back up again.

For whereas Polly, though born in England, is Indian and incarnated into a very loving Sikh family who did much to make her secure in her self-esteem, Oliver was born of parents who somehow managed to make him believe that he would never succeed at anything. It is not that they were inadequate in the physical care they gave him, nor even that they were uncaring, but they did nothing to foster his faith in himself and had low expectations for him. This led, inevitably, to his not being very successful in school, and to his growing up with something of an inferiority complex. His innate nature as a healer and carer was nevertheless not squashed by any means, and he eventually decided to go in for nursing, training at a hospital in the Midlands, where his home still is many years later.

Twin souls, as we have seen, so often follow similar paths, and Polly also trained as a nurse before the illness struck her. She is considerably younger than Oliver and exceedingly attractive. Arranged marriages are still the norm for Sikh families, even those who have settled permanently in England, and Polly was for a while much sought after by her parents' friends and acquaintances as a wife for their sons. Her parents had, however, not yet made up their minds between the prospective suitors when the MS came to her rescue. That is how Polly herself sees it anyway. She firmly believes that one of the reasons for her disease was to keep her free for her soul partner in order that they should do together the work that they had jointly agreed to do before incarnating this time. For, however attractive and intelligent a young Indian girl may be, a disease such as MS renders her immediately undesirable as a partner in a Sikh marriage.

Oliver, however, being, as we have said, a number of years older, was already married when they met, and this marriage is at present the major obstacle in his development. We have said that his parents conditioned him to failure. Well, just as his natural abilities might well have enabled him to qualify, say, as a doctor yet he settled instead for the less well paid profession of nursing, so in marriage he dared not aspire to the "perfect love match" that the majority of people yearn for. His wife is far from being an unpleasant person, but she is not spiritually inclined, they have fairly little in common, and they have stuck together over the years more from habit and for security than for any other reason. Cannot the same be said of countless marriages? In Chapter III we quoted Joudry and Pressman when they discuss the limitations that can be put upon one partner by another. Oliver's case is very comparable to Dan's, and, like Dan, he needed to meet with his twin soul in order to be alerted to the stagnant nature of his marriage relationship.

His spiritual catching up had in fact already begun some little time <u>before</u> they met. Remember how we are saying over and over that the physical connection is secondary in importance, since the spiritual connection between twin souls is always there even when we are not aware of it? Though he still felt his vocation to lie in the field of caring and healing, Oliver had begun to weary of nursing and the rigours of hospital rules and regulations. His long-held knowledge of traditional healing methods began to resurface, and he developed an interest in Aromatherapy (an art which was of course much in use in Ancient Egypt, where he and Polly, as we have said, have strong roots). He trained initially in that on a part-time basis, as his nursing duties allowed, and eventually – despite much scepticism on the part of his wife – he plucked up the courage to resign his job and embark on a new profession as an aromatherapist.

Here Polly's and Oliver's respective guides were obviously doing their jobs efficiently, as it is thanks to this new work of Oliver's that he and Polly became acquainted. Though reared, like Oliver, on conventional medicine, her illness combined with her subconscious knowledge soon led Polly to seek alternative therapies. And what might look to the uninitiated like chance but you, the readers of this book, now know better, which "alternative" did she choose first but aromatherapy, and which therapist did she "happen" to select "at random" from the telephone directory (even though she did not live in exactly the same part of the Midlands) but Oliver. The attraction between them was instantaneous, but of course they also experienced the proverbial "guilt and confusion" owing to the fact of Oliver being married. We have mentioned this as being an obstacle for Oliver, but it is also something of an obstacle for Polly on account of the fact that in her culture the parents expect to choose partners for their children. Polly's parents were beginning to come to terms with the fact that she was no longer considered eligible by the parents of the prospective sons-in-law they would ideally have chosen, but firstly a white man, and secondly one who was potentially a divorcee, was rather much for them to have to swallow.

As we saw in the case of Iris and Joe, difference in race is never a barrier to twinsoulship. (Nor should it be to any human love, for on this Earth there is only one race – the human race.) Oliver in his forty plus years had never had any true experience of love, and the feelings generated by and for Polly immediately began to transform him. He tried at first to conceal what had happened from his wife, but it soon became impossible. To start with they only met when Polly came to him for her weekly treatment, but even that was enough for Olivia to notice a change in her husband and consequently to question him about it. He is by nature a very honest man, and the depth of the connection with Polly was making him increasingly aware of the emptiness and shallowness of his married relationship, and so he began tentatively to talk about it with Olivia. This was difficult for him as the two of them had never been in the habit of talking openly with each other about anything at all, least of all about their own relationship, but one thing that twin-soul connections must and will always do is force the truth out into the open. Olivia was not hurt about Oliver's feelings for Polly because she too was well aware of the inadequacies of their relationship. She had, however, no means of appreciating the power of the connection, and fear of change and upheaval held her back from encouraging a separation.

Oliver, as we have said, is the one who has fallen behind spiritually and who consequently needed Polly's light to reawaken him. In *Messages from a Doctor in the Fourth Dimension,* Dr. Karl Nowotny speaks of the connection made between twin souls when one is in spirit and uses the other as a medium. Although he is referring to mediumship, I feel that his words can be applied equally well to the case of Oliver and Polly (not to mention many other twin-soul couples who are both incarnate). *The harmony of souls achieves a consonance that can lead to identical trains of thought, but must not necessarily do so. Because the development of two spirit entities and souls destined to complement each other need not necessarily have reached the same stage, one can still be educated and instructed by the other. In such a case intensified productive power is provided*[2].

Well Polly, with her intense spiritual interests, has undoubtedly been able, despite her illness, to provide Oliver with <u>very</u> *intensified productive power*. Indeed the chances are now that her power will be increased still further. During the course of the visit to Australia mentioned at the beginning of the chapter, Polly was introduced to a clairvoyant, from whom she sought a reading. This clairvoyant saw a past life in which he himself had done a great wrong to her and taken some of her power from her. In order therefore to protect himself from a karmic return, he told Polly that she had had a previous lifetime in which she had had great power and had abused it, and that he consequently advised her against looking into her past as she would run the risk, if she gained knowledge of her previous powers, of again abusing them.

Polly did not find out the truth of this story until some time later, in England, when she met another clairvoyant, who was able to see the reality of the story and explain it to her. This second clairvoyant also felt that she would in due course be able to remember something of this previous life, and that doing so would be beneficial to her and enable her to retrieve the power that she had held in that particular lifetime. Although this incident may not seem directly relevant either to our story or to the general concept of twinsoulship, I feel that it is very worth while recounting. For it is easy for people who do not have such gifts as that of reading the Akashic Records to imagine that those who do are in some way "superior". It is undoubtedly true that clairvoyants with this particular gift do tend on the whole to be advanced souls who would not normally be expected to behave amorally. Clairvoyants are nevertheless just as human as anyone else, and consequently not immune from the temptation to abuse their power if it appears to be in their self-interest to do so. Such a story reinforces the importance of finding a counsellor one can trust, and also perhaps of seeking confirmation of the facts which one regards as the most important.

From this English clairvoyant Polly received, too, confirmation of the fact that Oliver was her twin soul – a confirmation which she did not really need, so profound was the empathy and so frequent the telepathic communication between them. She says, "When we're not together I feel there's this great big hole which hasn't been filled, but when we come together there's this appeasement, as though we've interlocked again. And when we're not together we seem to be tuned into each other all the time. Recently I was in hospital with pain in my lower back. Oliver didn't even know that I was in hospital, yet he experienced pain in exactly the same place. I tune into his headaches when we're not together, and when I'm feeling bad and frustrated he feels the same without knowing why. Then, just the other day, I wasn't eating, yet I found I was tasting chips in my mouth. I made a note of the time and later I found out from Oliver that he had been eating chips at that precise moment!" Another interesting feature of this couple is that they each have a scar on their arm and a spot on one hand, which, when they put his left and her right arm together, match exactly! It is indeed as though they were, at least in that area of their bodies, two halves of a whole.

As the months went by, Oliver and Polly began gradually to meet more frequently, and her parents are now beginning to accept the situation. They were impressed, during Polly's recent stay in hospital, by the amount of caring that Oliver showed through his frequent visits to her, and in any case, when twin souls who are ready for one another are together, the "rightness" of the match is always so glaring that it would be difficult for even the most biased person not to recognise it.

Polly still has some problem with her parents with regard to her interest in Sai Baba. Last year the family made a visit to India, and Polly of course would greatly have liked to take the opportunity to visit Puttaparthi. Since, however, she is in a wheelchair, it would have been impossible for her to get there on her own, and no member of her family would have been willing to take her, since they have not yet recognised that Sai Baba in no way contradicts their Sikhism. Polly's strong faith enabled her to accept this without argument, and she is now confident that Sai Baba himself will see to it that she gets to meet him when and if the time is right. In fact she is hopeful that Oliver, who through her is beginning to become interested also, will eventually take her to see him.

Despite Oliver's immense caring for Polly in her illness – he has recently started to take her for treatment to the psychic surgeon, Dr. Kahn, who works through Stephen Turoff in Essex – he is no doubt a trifle plagued subconsciously by his memory of her fatal illness when she was his queen in Egypt, and is consequently reliving to a large extent his immense fear of losing her. It is therefore understandable that this should at present be another thing holding him back from making a full commitment. One of the hardest things that we all have to learn in life is the importance of taking risks. A life completely free from risk – if it were possible at all (which I doubt!) – would be an immensely uninteresting one, and it is partly through taking risks, chancing our arm, that we firstly learn Trust (such a vital element in our spiritual development), and secondly gain the full richness of experience.

As we said nearer the beginning of the chapter, Oliver and Polly have the potential for doing important work together. He is at present enjoying his aromatherapy work and finding that it suits him better than nursing, but he has a feeling that something more is being asked of him and that he has yet to find out exactly what it is. Meeting Polly who, as again we have seen, had leapt ahead of him in her spiritual development, has helped to reawaken him to his power – the power that he manifested so beneficially in earlier lifetimes, the power which his upbringing in his present incarnation had largely stifled. She is teaching him a great deal and he is learning fast, but he still needs to overcome his indecisiveness. Even the Catholic Church, renowned for frowning upon divorce, recognises that certain marriages are not valid and permits an escape for such couples through official annulment. Where two people are actually holding each other back through staying together, as is the case with Oliver and Olivia, separation is clearly the only sensible course, and Oliver's only real problem at present is his above-mentioned indecisiveness. The chances of their discovering the exact nature of the work that they should be doing will be greatly increased once Oliver has broken with his wife in order to make a new life with his twin soul.

Some people might be tempted to accuse Polly of selfishness in wanting, as it were, to "steal someone else's husband", but in reality this is not the case at all. For someone as spiritually advanced as she is, marriage is by no means of primary importance. God is the most vital element in her life. It is her love of God that makes her such a delightful person to meet, her faith in God that gives her not only an acceptance of her illness but also the recognition that it has been sent to her as a teacher. For, besides being thankful to the MS for having kept her out of an arranged marriage and available for Oliver, she realises that she has various lessons to learn form it. "What all these lessons are," she comments, "I have yet to find out, but I am confident that Oliver and I have been brought together for a reason, that we have something to bring to the world together in this lifetime. Again, what that something is time will no doubt reveal and, while Oliver is busy trying to sort himself out and reach a decision, I am just thankful for the joy of having found Sai Baba, and thankful for the sheer joy of being alive in God. And I know too that, if it is my karma to be healed of this disease, Sai Baba will in due course see to that also!"

Notes
1. See: *Sai Baba – The Embodiment of Love* by Peggy Mason and Ron Laing, published by Gateway Books.
   Sai Baba – Man of Miracles by Howard Murphet, published by Vrindavanum Books, London.
   A Catholic Priest meets Sai Baba by Don Mario Massoleni, published by Leela Press Inc.
   Sai Baba – The Ultimate Experience by Phyllis Kristal, published by The Convenor, Sri Sathya Sai Books and Publications Trust.
   and many others.
2. *Messages from a Doctor in the Fourth Dimension*, channelled from Dr. Karl Nowotny by Grete, published by Regency Press (London and New York) Ltd.

Chapter IX

IF ONE PARTNER GETS LEFT BEHIND SPIRITUALLY, THEIR POWER MAY BE TRANSFERRED TO THE OTHER PARTNER
The story of Quentin and Rosie

It was a couple of days before Christmas and Rosie's mother's car had broken down, so Rosie volunteered to pick her up when she had finished work at the nursing home. No sooner had she passed through the entrance than what should she see but a figure in a wheelchair. The accident had left Quentin looking sadly different from the attractive young man Rosie had known in her youth, yet, despite his brain damage and loss of memory, they recognised each other instantly. Rosie's mother came downstairs for her lift to find her daughter deep in conversation with the patient who had put himself into the nursing home in order to give his mother a break over Christmas. Putting aside her thoughts about the presents she still needed to wrap, the cake to ice, she watched the pair patiently and with interest. A few moments later she had a flash of intuition: "Twin souls!"

Rosie's mother, who is very psychic, deeply spiritual and undoubtedly an old soul, was brought up very strictly Methodist but, being a very strong personality and naturally rebellious, she soon rejected her parents' religion and got married when she was only seventeen. She bore three sons, of whom Rosie (originally "Roland") was the middle one, and always very obviously "different". This marriage ended in an amicable way when Rosie was only six, but a second marriage, contracted as soon as the divorce had gone through, lasted over twenty years, brought her many trials and much heartache, and for Rosie was totally disastrous.

For Rosie, from as far back as she can remember, had an irrefutable feeling of having been born into the wrong body. She, too, is an old soul, and one who has had a large number of incarnations – particularly masculine ones – in which she was very adventurous, very brave, frequently losing her life in dangerous situations. "And when," she says, "I wasn't scaling mountains or fighting battles, I was quite brazen. I've seen a few of my past lives in hypnotic regression, and in one of these I saw myself as a servant girl in a mediaeval dining hall. I remember the pig roasting on a spit, but most of all I remember noticing that I was very brazenly dressed. In another life I was a brown-skinned boy aged only about six. I had a spear and I was undergoing initiations. They were very painful, but I was brave."

Through our lifetimes balance has to be achieved. Although our <u>essence</u> never changes, our personalities have to become fully rounded. The perfect balance (Plato's Androgyn – the "third sex", which is the combination of man and woman) is only attained when each soul – each masculine or feminine energy, which also contains within itself the essence of its twin – having rounded and completed <u>itself</u>, fuses with the twin in preparation for the final return to God. Although basically androgynous, each soul will manifest either its feminine or its masculine side more strongly in a given incarnation. This masculine or feminine side will normally – BUT NOT INVARIABLY – coincide with the sex of the body chosen. We are living in a time of gender confusion. Far preferable of course to the times when women were universally oppressed, but difficult nevertheless. Rosie, having experienced in the past so much adventure and violence in a masculine body, chose this time another masculine body, but one with strongly feminine characteristics. Having been conscious from an early age of her very feminine characteristics, she felt a strong desire to "go the whole hog" and spend as much as possible of this lifetime in a feminine body.

Lilla Bek observes that in the past it was easier in a way, because those who felt their internal gender to be different from their apparent one were simply put into a monastery or convent in order to spend that particular lifetime concentrating on their spiritual development. Now, with the availability of hormone treatment and sex change operations, there are more choices open to people. All are simply different ways of being human. All may be experiences that we ourselves have gone through in the past but have forgotten.

We have said that balance is our aim. If a soul has been through many lifetimes of adventure, a quieter incarnation will sooner or later be called for. If a soul's masculine side has been dominant over and over again, the feminine one will need to reassert itself. It was with this knowledge that Rosie's soul came in this time. This is why, finding herself in a boy's body, she decided that she could never really be <u>herself</u> until she had changed that. Following lifetimes of fighting the enemy, conquering newly-discovered mountain slopes, for this incarnation she gave herself an even more challenging task: scaling the spiritual mountain, climbing the difficult slopes inside <u>herself</u>. For it is easy, in a sense, always to be "out there", where the action is all taking place, with little or no time for reflection. Sorting out the <u>inner</u> life, finding out exactly who one is, and where precisely one is going, can often be a harder task. And this is the task Rosie has set herself this time. This lifetime is for her largely a "within" life, following up other earlier lifetimes in which she was very intuitive, very creative, very much in tune with nature.

Quentin and Rosie, like all twin souls who are not new to the Earth's plane, have been together many times in the past, and a salient lifetime was spent as

135

priest and priestess in an Egyptian temple. It was the custom in that culture (and also occasionally in Greece) sometimes to castrate people in their position. In their temple Quentin and Rosie, despite being castrated, had what is known as *Tantric Exchange*. This may seem curious, yet Joudry and Pressman, in their chapter on Sex, explain how the true, spiritual union between twin souls is both deeper and higher than the mere physical, bodily union. When the highest realms of communication are reached, sexual exchange becomes almost irrelevant. In fact Joudry and Pressman cite a case they encountered of a couple (Alexandra and Leroy) who did not have a sexual relationship because they felt that their love had progressed beyond the physical. Such a case is obviously extremely rare, but these authors believe that *it is written on the future*[1].

But alas, as has happened to so many of us over the centuries, Quentin has retrogressed quite a long way since those days of enlightenment in the temple. Exactly what happened to him during the interval our story does not relate, but something (or no doubt several things) caused him in this lifetime to incarnate into very unfavourable circumstances. Born in a depressed area of Hull, to a mother for whom prostitution is a normal way of life, his childhood and youth were turbulent. His mother complained to Rosie's mother when she brought him for a stay in the nursing home, and has complained to Rosie herself many times, that Quentin has always been a trial to her; but she is herself partly responsible for that, having domineered him for all of his thirty-nine years. He was in constant trouble in school, and in due course became a heroin addict. This caused him to become involved in crime and to go in and out of prison. Rosie knew him for a while at this point, as he was friendly with the man she was living with at the time, but they had completely lost touch before his accident. Rosie says, "When I met him over Christmas, some time after he'd had the accident which had put him into a wheelchair, I wasn't surprised. It came as no shock to me to see him in the condition he was in, because I realised that it had been sent to him to stop him, to pull him up in his tracks . . ." For the accident had happened when Quentin was in a drugged state and had got caught up by a van. This had forced him to give up the heroin, but rendered him dependent on his mother for his physical care.

We have seen that twin souls often have similar experiences and difficulties prior to their meeting. One thing that Quentin and Rosie have in common is, both having been born boys, having been given the same Christian name at birth! While, however, Quentin incarnated into a very tough, working class background, Rosie was born into a middle class family in an attractive little town and spent her early years first there, and then in a pleasant, middle class suburb of Hull. Her difficulties were emotional ones, and they stemmed from always feeling different and not being understood either at school or by her stepfather. Her stepfather simply could not understand why she was so different from her brothers, with whom he regularly enjoyed a game of football, took a dislike to her from the moment they met, and was constantly cruel to her. At secondary school she was regarded as a "pansy" and mocked relentlessly, which caused her to play truant regularly.

Only Rosie's mother, with whom she has always been close, gave her any real support. She sensed all along what her trouble really was, but never felt able to put it into words. So depression was the chief feature of Rosie's early years, and she was also constantly troubled with migraines, which she sees now that she used as an alternative to truant for avoiding school. The doctor gave her *Migralief* tablets, and on one occasion in her teens depression drove her to take a dose which she thought was large enough to kill her. She was clearly, however, not meant to die so young, as the only effect it had was to make her feel ill and drowsy throughout the next day. This was not the "cry for help" so often made by would-be suicides, as she never told anyone about it. Both then, and some years later after she had left home, she genuinely wanted to die, and she says, "Even now I sometimes have days when I wish that that had happened."

Needing to find her niche while settling on her own, Rosie, not unnaturally, got in with a group of gay people. This, however, she explains, "didn't work out because that wasn't the way I was," and, being very unhappy and having already, at the age of thirteen, started smoking cigarettes stolen from her stepfather, she was soon introduced to Cannabis, which rapidly led her on to other, stronger, drugs. After a little while, following the youth who had led her into the drugs, she went off to Manchester, not telling her family as she thought it would be only a brief visit. In Manchester, however, she immediately got drawn into a group of transexuals (men who were dressing and living as women), and under their influence and because of her dependency on drugs, she got led into prostitution, and her "day trip" to Manchester lasted about two years.

Rosie's lifestyle in Manchester was so diametrically opposed to both her true nature and her upbringing that she could not bring herself to contact her family. Her mother, however (whose constant unconditional love has been the greatest support of her entire life), soon traced her through the DHSS and turned up on her doorstep with her younger brother. Seeing the way in which she was living made her at last able to tell Rosie that she had always understood what her problem was, and Rosie feels that she owes her mother an enormous amount for seeing and supporting her through the transition to full womanhood. Though her own pain at her would-be daughter's lifestyle must have been immense, her mother accepted it from the start as something that Rosie had to go through, never uttering a single word of reprobation.

Still unable either to come to terms with her situation or to escape from it, Rosie, as we said earlier, made another serious attempt at suicide. She was put under a psychiatrist, to whom she expressed her wish to undergo surgery for what she describes as "merely cosmetic changes", but in Manchester she was told that surgery would not be possible until after she was twenty-one. She returned to Hull for a number of reasons, and there by good fortune she came to hear of a doctor who was willing to refer her to a surgeon in Leeds, who, in view of her suicidal condition, accepted her as an emergency in spite of his three-year waiting list.

On returning to the Hull area, Rosie went first to her family home (where the relationship with her stepfather had improved once it had been made clear what her problem was), and then to a house which she bought for herself. The operation, performed when she was twenty, of course transformed her life, but she was still not able instantly to extricate herself either from the drug scene or from the life of prostitution which funded it.

It was at this point that Rosie first made the acquaintance of Quentin. She says, "I got to know him shortly before my operation because he was a friend of the man I was living with at the time. He was on the periphery of my life then for about four or five years. He was always involved with some girl or other, and anyway I was very much in love with the man I was living with, even though he beat me up because of the fact that the drugs made him violent, but I remember Quentin's cheeky, attractive eyes. I suppose I always found him attractive."

Eyes must surely be – for sighted people, that is[2] – the most important human instrument in the initial forming of a relationship. We (and dogs too for that matter!) express <u>everything</u> through our eyes, and if we are refusing to express ourselves, that will show up in them too. Stern, impenetrable eyes make a person so unattractive! Lucinda, it may be remembered, describing in Chapter VII her first meeting with Ken, used a similar phrase to Rosie's ("I remember his very strong eyes."). And Angela, in Chapter II, whose story had to be edited drastically as she had so much to say about her lessons, told me that it was Bruce's "lovely, pale blue eyes" that had always most attracted her to him. She said that he looked best to her when he was wearing a shirt which not only matched the colour of his eyes but also enhanced it, and that – before he took fright about where the relationship was going – she used to feel that he expressed his love for her entirely through his eyes. ("He would, at every opportunity, hold my eyes in his for what seemed like minutes, though it can only have been split seconds and, when I was at Church gatherings with him, though I never dared, I often longed to thank God aloud 'for eyes which express feelings when words will not come easily'.") Rosie herself has gorgeous, sensuous, deep brown eyes, which sparkle with vivacity when she laughs.

Quentin and Rosie lost touch when the former moved to London to start a new life. We have seen that, when twin souls are apart, they often have similar experiences. Both of them came off the drugs, but whereas with Rosie it was her strength of character that enabled her to do it for herself, Quentin in this incarnation is less strong and consequently this step was forced upon him.

Rosie says of her surgery that it was a "a wonderful, enlightening period of my life, which brought about many changes and revelations – not just physical, but also psychological – and it enabled me to develop a greater respect for my mind as well as for my body." As we have hinted above, however, the total transformation took some time. Rosie had started the relationship with Quentin's friend six months before the operation – she says that she loved him unconditionally and felt accepted – but after the surgery he became jealous and possessive. They stayed together nevertheless (despite the increasingly frequent beatings, which often left her with broken bones as well as black eyes) for three years, until he was arrested and imprisoned for drug dealing from Rosie's house. This of course got Rosie into trouble too but, being the strong character that she is, what happened gave her the necessary impetus for change. She got herself off drugs, did a counselling course, and started a self-help group for drug abusers.

Looking back now on that period of her life, Rosie feels more or less as though it were a different incarnation and wonders how, with her "good, middle-class upbringing" she could have allowed herself to become so "corrupted". No one, however,who still needs to be on Earth, can be totally immune to human frailty, and anyone who condemns prostitution or addiction of any sort has very likely been a victim of it themselves in a previous incarnation (or if not, may well fall into it in a future one). Alcohol, like sex, is not harmful in moderation, and many claim that Cannabis can actually be beneficial. Danger only lies when a person allows any of these things to take over their life, and it is normally people who are already victims of one sort or another that fall prey to such addiction. (And do not many "normal" people, too, have addictive tendencies?) Quentin was, and still is, a victim of his class and upbringing. Rosie was a victim of the body with which she was born. Of course reincarnationists know that there is actually no such thing as a real victim, since the circumstances of each of our lives are dictated by our conduct in previous ones, but we nevertheless often temporarily take on necessary "victimhood" as part of our learning process, and victims must always be viewed with compassion.

Though Rosie found both the drug abuse counselling and a subsequent post in Hull caring for the disabled "rewarding", she decided to move to London, where she felt she could be both "anonymous and autonomous". At this time she was working hard on her self-esteem and self-respect, and she says of her time spent in London, "My past was my past and had nothing to do with anybody. It wasn't mentioned more than once or twice in the whole ten years I was there." From starting as a home help and then a day-time social worker, she moved after a couple of years "into sales – basically for the financial rewards it would bring."

Rosie was still at this time, as might be expected, trying both to establish her femininity and to find her true self. She was both attractive to, and attracted by, many men, and each time that she embarked on a new relationship she thought that it was going to be "the one" but, being a person who has always greatly needed her own space and very easily feels invaded, she tired of each new boyfriend quite quickly. Eventually, however, she settled with one who she is quite sure is a "karmic soulmate" and, although she sent him packing at one point, they have recently got together again in a relationship of less proximity.

Rosie was very successful in her sales career and soon became accustomed to comfortable living. When, however, we deviate in an incarnation from our previously chosen spiritual path, something will normally happen to bring us back to it. In Rosie's case, having had minor back problems for a number of years, she was suddenly stricken with a disability which forced her to give up her job. Being the innately spiritual being that she is, she came to terms with this remarkably quickly, recognising that it had been sent to her "as a lesson" and to force her away from materialism. She decided to return to Hull, where her family all still lived, exchanging her London flat for a pleasant one in the northern city, and it was shortly after her move that the "chance" meeting with Quentin occurred.

So disability is now another thing that Quentin and Rosie have in common. While, however, the latter has a certain amount of brain damage, which makes living alone difficult for him if not impossible, Rosie is still a very strong and independent character and adept at getting about in her wheelchair or on crutches.

Quentin's karmic link with his mother is clearly very strong, but the relationship is anything but a happy one. That is why he decided himself to give his mother a break by putting himself into a nursing home over Christmas, and also, on learning that Rosie was buying herself a flat, he promptly asked if he could move in with her. She says, "I'm always impulsive and so I said, 'Yes of course you can.'" And then, for the first few weeks until her flat was ready, they saw each other most days. Rosie says of those weeks, "I felt inspired. For about two weeks I was writing and writing – little poems and bits of prose and stuff, which has never happened to me before – and I felt close to him." After only one week, however, of living together in Rosie's flat, they had sadly to admit that it was not working, and Quentin returned to his mother's. Rosie explains that this was partly because of the fact that he refuses to do anything for himself – even the things of which he is capable – but even more "because of the darkness in him. I felt like he needed some sort of love, someone to hold him and enable him to see that there's something beyond the darkness he's currently living in, but I don't think it worked. Initially it did change him. He sort of brightened up and became more responsive, but I think that was quite superficial because the darkness in him is too strong." And she adds, "That's not just because of the accident. The darkness has always been there, but now he just feels that he's lost everything."

Rosie really wanted the relationship to work when they moved in together initially. She was prepared to make a total commitment and dedicate the rest of her life to Quentin, but his problem now is that, having been forced off drugs by his accident, he has developed a taste for alcohol. Rosie says that "basically he just wants to drink himself into oblivion." She feels extremely sad about it, because she is aware of the potential within him, "if only he had the courage to bring it out", and aware, too, that he is a very sensitive person. (His mother has told her about his love of animals when he was young – a love Rosie shares with a vengeance, currently keeping house with a dog and six cats!) "But," she says,

140

"he puts up a huge defence barrier because where he was brought up it isn't considered manly to show one's sensitivity! He has never been permitted to show his own person." She is sad above all because she feels that the accident was sent to him as a lesson, but that "he hasn't got the awareness to see it. So he basically now just has a death wish because he hasn't got the capacity to learn his lessons. It doesn't matter what you do or say, or what light you try and give him – he doesn't want it. Maybe it's fear. I suppose he's got used to what he knows and can't see anything beyond it."

Quentin's disability does not make him unattractive to Rosie. She feels she could cope with that if only he would let her help him to advance spiritually. And the fact of his refusing even to bath himself, means that, in view of Rosie's own disability, much of the burden would fall on her family were they to continue living together. She says, "I suppose it's his way of exercising control. I would still find him attractive if he weren't so difficult to deal with, but he's so rebellious!" In the end it was Quentin's own decision to return to his mother, and Rosie would carry on seeing him more often if she did not find his mother so disagreeable. ("She's such a limited woman that I just don't want her in my orbit.")

All is not totally doom and gloom, however, because, Rosie says, "Since meeting me he's learnt about independence. Now he wants to rent his own house with a friend and be away from his mother." She believes that, if forced to do so, he would do more for himself. And she is sure that they met recently for a reason. "Because what were the chances of Mum's car breaking down and me going to the home just at the time when he was there?" He seems still to want to see her from time to time despite his desire to "drink himself into oblivion", and at the time of our interview Rosie was tuning into Quentin telepathically and knew that he needed her to phone him.

Though the broad outline of our lives is planned each time, there is always room for manoeuvre. When Quentin met Rosie he clutched briefly at the straw which could possibly have saved him, but instead of grasping it more firmly, he sadly let it go again and now his immediate future looks fairly bleak. Nothing in life, however, is ever completely wasted and, while Quentin appears at present to be drowning in beer and misery, his spiritual power is apparently being handed over to Rosie, who is at the moment soaring ahead in leaps and bounds. For, when one twin soul stubbornly refuses to keep up with the spiritual development of his or her partner, his or her power may sometimes be taken from them and transferred to the one who is equipped at the time to make better use of it. This seems sad, but it is temporary and, since they are so closely linked, *every effort of one twin* (in Joudry and Pressman's words), *is a gain for the other*[1]. Rosie is at present working hard to "confront my life issues, which in the past I have always evaded."

Being the feminine energy of the pair, Rosie is concentrating on developing that in preparation for what she hopes will soon be the end of her necessary incarnations. Though it is only in recent years that she has discussed such things as reincarnation (mainly with her mother), she says that she has always known that she has lived before. Having rejected the strict Methodism of her youth, her mother joined the Mormons for a while and the three children were all blessed in the Mormon Church. She was, however, excommunicated for "living in sin" prior to her divorce, and subsequently the family had no formal religious upbringing. But Rosie says that she has always known that God was to be found within and, now that she is intent on "confronting her life issues", she is more ready for the search.

Rosie says, too, that she has always known that she had psychic and mediumistic abilities, but that until recently it was something she resisted "because it didn't sit well with me". She has over the years often made predictions for friends which have come true, and sometimes she has had the experience of looking at someone she has only just met and being able to tell them all about themselves. She has not made a habit of this either, since "people find it disconcerting". Seven years ago, however, she started to practise Tarot, and she had developed the art of psychometry some time before that. Now, without making any attempt at advertising, Rosie is gradually finding that people are coming to her for Tarot readings or psychometry, and it seems possible that a future career for her lies in that. She says, however, that she is "not a person for working out a plan. If something happens, it happens."

With regard to the relationship with Quentin, Rosie feels that she will always be there for him if he needs her. She feels that she is on her last incarnation, though in my experience clairvoyants do not often agree with people who have such feelings! Though still young, she says that she would at present be happy for this lifetime to end sooner rather than later, but she knows that she must stay for as long as it takes to do what she has to do. For the distant future, she welcomes the idea of being Quentin's main spirit guide "because then I could guide him through on a better path, giving him the more positive direction which he obviously needs." Her mother's conviction that they were twin souls was confirmed by a clairvoyant reading, and Rosie, though reluctant to accept the idea at first, now finds that it makes a lot of sense to her. My personal guess is that it may take Quentin several more incarnations to catch her up, but catch her up he must and will. In the meantime, may God bless both of them!

Notes

1. *Twin Souls – A Guide to Finding your True Spiritual Partner* by Patricia Joudry and Maurie D. Pressman, M.D., published by Element Books, Shaftesbury, Dorset.
2. In this connection I strongly recommend *Touching the Rock* by John Hull, Professor of Religious Education at Birmingham University. Published by the SPCK, this book consists of his diary account of, and the most moving reflections on, the gradual onset of total blindness.

Chapter X

TWIN SOULS ARE SOMETIMES THE SAME SEX
The story of Susie and Tessa

In their otherwise truly excellent book[1], Joudry and Pressman make what is, to my mind, the astounding assertion that twin souls are always of opposite sexes. They give no reason for making this assertion and, since I find it hard to imagine that it is based on extensive research, I can only assume that the point is pure conjecture on the part of these authors.

Another disagreement with Joudry and Pressman is one that I have already mentioned: their assertion that twin souls never incarnate into the same family. I cited previously the example of Gertrude and her son, Hugh Lynn Cayce. Joudry and Pressman say that it is on account of the sexual dynamics which normally operate between twin souls that incarnation into the same family is undesirable, and indeed I have myself heard of two instances of father/daughter twin-soul relationships in which the daughter was raped by her father. (The first of these instances was a past life to which I shall refer in a later chapter. The second was a pair whose inclusion in the book it was clearly not appropriate to seek.) Besides these three unusual cases, I have a friend whose twin soul is her adopted son, but I am keeping her for the book I plan to write in the future on *Adoption and Karma*! Such cases are, however, clearly very rare, and I am therefore on this point not taking issue with Joudry and Pressman very strongly.

Where I <u>do</u> take issue with them strongly is over the same sex question. It is a well-known fact that the soul is androgynous and that most of us regularly change the sex of the bodies we choose. How therefore could we possibly expect all our lives to be so minutely organised that we would <u>never</u> arrive on the planet in a body that was the same sex as that of our twin soul? I myself am at present a woman and my twin soul is a man, BUT I am younger than he is. When he was a young boy I had not yet finished the life which I had immediately prior to this one, and in that life (though we lived in different countries and never met) I was the same sex as he is.

Angela in Chapter II learnt in regression of a life in which she and Bruce were missionary priests together. Graham and Helen found through meditation one lifetime in which they fought together as knights, another in which they lived together as Tibetan monks . . . Quentin and Rosie started this lifetime as the same sex. I have been told of two women friends who live together and believe themselves to be twin souls, of a pair of twin sisters who are also twin souls (thus refuting both of Joudry and Pressman's assertions!), of a man whose marriage was crumbling and who left his wife in order to live with his twin soul, another man, because they felt that they had work to do together . . . (In this latter case I have been given no reason to believe that the pair are homosexual.)

So, when my friend, Susie, told me that she believed her twin soul to be another woman, I was not in the least surprised. (On the contrary, I was delighted, since it filled the gap I had at the time under this chapter heading!) Perhaps the reason why Joudry and Pressman make their conjecture is the fact that, since the majority of humanity is heterosexual, most of us can normally only visualise total fulfilment in a relationship with a partner of the opposite sex. It is, however, perhaps worth reminding readers here that, while we may vary our sex from incarnation to incarnation, each one of us is always in essence either the masculine or the feminine of our particular pair. Thus Dan, in Chapter III, incarnated in Lemuria as the feminine energy, which means that Carol must have been the masculine, and – even in her present life in which she is very much a woman – she feels herself to be the masculine energy of that pair. The point that it is important to realise is that the sex we happen to be manifesting in any given incarnation is immaterial. We experience lives as both sexes, just as we experience lives with different coloured skins, different backgrounds and circumstances, in order to broaden and enrich us as fully as possible before our final return to spirit. The relationship between twin souls, as we have said again and again, is a spiritual one, and the spirit is both deeper and higher than either sex or sexuality.

Susie and Tessa, who are in their early seventies and late sixties respectively, have been life-long friends, having first met at boarding school when Susie was fifteen and Tessa thirteen. Susie recounts: "Tessa was newly arrived at the school, while I had been there for a whole two years. She saw me across a room and immediately said to herself, 'That person is going to be very important in my life.' We made friends extremely quickly and became very close." This is interesting because, although in most people's terms a two-year age gap is very small, at thirteen and fifteen it tends to seem large. Just as a thirteen-year-old would not normally aspire to the friendship of a girl apparently so much her senior – and particularly one newly arrived at a school – so an average fifteen-year-old would tend slightly to look down on anyone a whole two years her junior. But twin-soul bonds, as we have seen repeatedly, often defy conventions.

Susie says, "Our backgrounds and families were very similar in many ways, though hers was, outwardly at least, more stable than mine. We both had difficult childhoods and neither of us related well to our mothers. Tessa was very frightened of her mother. But she did have a good relationship with a nanny, whereas I had no one at all. My family was chaotic. Both my parents

144

were always having affairs with other people, and they finally separated when I was sixteen. My mother was an artist and my father was very eccentric and excitable. Tessa's household was rather more conventional. They were four in their family – three girls and a boy – but the only one she was at all close to was her youngest sister. I just have a younger brother, with whom I have always been close, so there's another similarity between us there. I hardly relate at all to the stepbrother and sister I have from my father's third marriage."

So through school, despite the age gap, Susie and Tessa were more or less inseparable, and their interests then, as now, were virtually identical. Both were, in Susie's words "intensely artistic", and both "spiritual seekers". In their teens both were very religious and both came under the influence of a high Anglican priest. It was Susie who first met this priest, shortly after leaving school, and she introduced him to Tessa. Susie explains, "Despite being unsure of myself, I've always been the dominant one, the one who has the ideas. But that doesn't mean that Tessa isn't very strong minded; on the contrary, she is. I feel that she grounds me, while I inspire her, though it's a bit the other way round too."

This is interesting, for here once more, though the relationship is not a sexual partnership, we see the complementarity typical of twin-soul relationships. (Remember how Graham said, "We both give and we both receive . . ."?) Anyone who has lived for a number of years will have observed innumerable marriages or partnerships. So often does one notice, does one not, relationships in which one partner is completely dominated by the other? This is not, either, a question which has anything to do with sex. Despite centuries of oppression of women, I believe that there are probably nearly as many "hen-pecked husbands" as there are battered wives. Even in cases which are much less extreme – cases of quite happily married couples – it can often be noticed that one partner is more dominant than the other. Not so normally with twin souls. This can apply too to companion soulmate relationships – indeed it must – but a particularly noticeable hallmark of twin-soul partnerships is complete equality. Remember how Fred said, "If someone comes wanting figures and contracts, I deal with that, whereas if there's someone wanting to unload their problems, I hand them over to Ellen." And Kenneth said, "I think up the things to do and she does them!"

Susie comments – the phrase we've heard so many times – "I feel complete with her." And she adds, "We have everything in common. We're like one person." This despite the fact that, until recently, Susie thought of herself as "the one with the problems", while Tessa appeared to her to be "more rounded". Now, however, that she is a lot older, Tessa has confided to Susie that her life too has been very full of problems.

From boarding school Susie went into the Wrens for a while, but then she went to Art College in London, where Tessa joined her a little later when she left school. So through most of their Art College training they were again always together. Susie was the first to marry, by several years, and "Stuart", her husband, was at the time studying for the Anglican priesthood. Gradually, however, the

145

spiritual direction of all three of them changed. Stuart abandoned his intended career for another, while Susie and Tessa both left their church for alternative spiritual interests, and at the same time both developed an interest in psychology.

Here we come to another point of great relevance in our study. Susie says that in the early years of her marriage she and Tessa saw much less of each other, and in any case Susie and Stuart left London for their native Yorkshire, while Tessa stayed on and went to study Stained Glass at another London college. "But the bond is so strong that we don't need to meet a lot. Once we didn't see each other for about three years, and when we did, we found that our spiritual interests had been developing exactly side by side – we had both been studying Gurdjieff, for instance – and we also found that we had both quite independently got interested in alternative medicine."

This is not the "coincidence" it may superficially sound. It may be recalled that Chapter V partly concerned the fact that twin souls often do similar things at the same time. In the case of Graham and Helen the period of separation was much shorter, but it makes no difference. For, whether they are living together or at opposite ends of the globe, twin souls are invariably influencing one another. If one is soaring, the other will be dragged behind willy-nilly. If one is plummeting, the other will have to make extra effort, or be extra strong, not to be dragged down also. (Rosie, in our last chapter, is an exceptionally strong character.) Then there is also of course the noteworthy fact that twin souls meet up at night when out of their bodies. Though only very advanced souls tend ever to remember what they did at night – and that only normally as the result of much training – it is all nevertheless stored in our subconscious. Let us for a moment imagine a possible nightly out-of-body conversation during those three years in which Susie and Tessa did not meet on the Earth's plane:–

Susie: How lovely to see you! I was thinking about you today, and I was going to phone, but then little David had a bad fall and I had to rush him off to Casualty.

Tessa: Oh, I'm sorry to hear that. Was it serious?

S: No, thank goodness. I was afraid he'd broken his arm, but it turned out to be just a bad bruise. Anyway, the other reason I wanted to phone was to tell you about this wonderful book I'm just reading. Gurdjieff. Have you heard of him?

T: Yes, I have. He's a White Russian, isn't he? So you think he's really worth reading, do you?

S: Definitely! I really recommend him. I'm sure you'd find his line of thought coincides beautifully with yours, and it should give you some interesting new ideas too.

T: Right, I'll go and look him up in the library tomorrow. You know, I've just been reading some fascinating books on homoeopathy and aromatherapy. I started because I found that some tablets the doctor had given me for stomach ache were making me worse, so I decided to try a homoeopath. He gave me something which seemed to clear up the trouble instantly.

146

S: Really? Do you think a homoeopath could help with my chronic insomnia?
T: Almost certainly. But why don't you just try lavender first? You could put some in your bath, or just a couple of drops on your pillow . . .

Well, I am not claiming that Susie would have woken up the next morning and immediately said to herself, "I must go to Holland and Barratt and buy some lavender oil," but she might have been back to the doctor's with little David and picked up a magazine containing an article on aromatherapy, or passed a health food shop advertising lavender in its window, and either such event could have triggered her subconscious memory, causing her to act. Similarly, Tessa could have been in a bookshop and noticed a book by Gurdjieff and been immediately prompted to buy it.

Susie has been told in a clairvoyant reading of two previous lives in which she was close to Tessa when they were both men. In one, they worked together as priests in Tibet; in the other – though their country was unclear – they were both political prisoners. Susie found what she was told about a Tibetan lifetime particularly relevant to her present life, for she says, "Even though I have never read anything about it, I always feel I know it! And sometimes an inner vision comes to me of being high up in very steep-sided mountains, looking out of a monastery window and seeing a deep valley with sharp blue light." And she adds, "Tessa, too, has been deeply involved in the Arcane school of the teachings of Alice Bailey, which were channelled through a Tibetan."

In this lifetime such affinity between them has persisted despite the fact that they have never lived together. Both have pursued artistic careers, neither has had a totally successful marriage. In fact Tessa's marriage, although she had six children, has been very unhappy. Now she and her husband co-exist in the same house, but that is all that can be said of the relationship. Perhaps she stays with him for security and material comfort – Susie says that they are very well off – but in any case, Susie says, "She doesn't seem to need people the way I do. I've always been very gregarious, always wanting to join groups, whereas Tessa has tended rather to shun groups. Though she always performed the role of mother to perfection – baking bread and so on for the family, for instance – she's always been rather detached from her children, and recently she confided to me that she never really enjoyed her maternal role very much. Apart from her youngest daughter. Her youngest daughter is about thirty now, single, and always travelling abroad. She and Tessa are extremely close and recently they've taken to having long holidays abroad together a couple of times a year."

Susie's own marriage, however, was an entirely different question, and it brings us to a completely new aspect of the whole twin-soul question. It is an oft-repeated saying that there is an exception to prove every rule! Well, Edwin Courtenay explains that, while in the majority of cases each spirit in the beginning sent out two separate souls, in a few instances, instead of the usual two, three were sent out: a masculine, a feminine, and a "balance". Although this is rare, Susie and Tessa's is not the first such case that Edwin has come

147

across. In Susie's reading he explained that she was the feminine energy, Stuart, her ex-husband, the masculine, and Tessa the balance; i.e. instead of being "twin souls", one can say that the three of them are "triplet souls". In their beautiful book, rather than talking of two souls which originated from the same spirit, Joudry and Pressman speak always of two halves of the same soul (which need to be together in order to be complete). While not disputing the ultimate "complete completeness" to which we all aspire and which we shall all eventually attain, I personally prefer Moshab's vision of two separate souls, which – remembering our yin/yang analogy used in Chapter III – can, when all is as it should be, fit perfectly together into their "case" (the spirit).

I prefer Moshab's picture because it confirms one of the most important themes of this book: the fact that each one of us can and must be whole on our own – that we will only be ready for the final fusion when we are whole on our own. Because each soul is a whole, not dependent on its twin, for a worthwhile incarnation, we all can, should, and so often do have fulfilling relationships with other people (companion soulmates like Edgar and Gertrude Cayce, for instance), and also spend useful and happy lifetimes in which we never meet with our twin soul.

Going back to Susie, Stuart and Tessa, the reader may now be wondering, "Why, if Susie and Stuart are really twin souls too, was the marriage not successful? Why are they now divorced?" Well, the answer is certainly neither uncomplicated nor easy, but once more this case is valuable for our study because it is an example of one of our most important points: the fact that life is not necessarily "all roses" if we meet our twin soul. Unlike Tessa's marriage, which was unhappy more or less from the start, Susie and Stuart made quite a good beginning and they had three sons, with whom Susie is still close. (In fact she is now selling her house in Yorkshire in order to live permanently in London, where she can be nearer to her family.) She explains that she and Stuart "grew apart", and that – though he agreed to it – it was she who suggested twelve years ago that they separate and "see how it goes". The divorce was then precipitated because, after the separation, Stuart very quickly fell in love with somebody else.

Stuart's second wife is now dead, but during the years in which they were married, Susie suffered great pain on account of the fact that he made it very clear to her that they could only meet at family occasions. She says, "His wife was very jealous of me, and in any case it wasn't appropriate for Stuart still to have meetings with his ex-wife, but I found it very difficult to cope with, as ever since we parted I've become increasingly aware of the closeness that exists between us. That's why – although of course it surprised me in a way – I found it quite easy to believe Edwin when he told me that both Stuart and Tessa were my twin souls." (It is doubly natural that the deceased wife should have been jealous of Susie, for she would no doubt have been aware subconsciously of the twin-soul link.) During this time, however, on an occasion when Susie was feeling particularly down because she could not see Stuart at all, she confided in a friend who is psychic. The friend said to her, "I can foresee a time when you will be really close again with Stuart and be able to see him a lot and it'll be like your relationship with Tessa." And this, Susie says, "is exactly what has happened. We do see each other a lot now, we're really good friends, and there's a wonderful closeness. But it's missing something. It's missing any expression – any physical expression. Once I tried to give him a sort of hug, but he didn't like it. We've both changed radically during the years since we first separated and now I feel much closer to him than ever before. He's very caring – he came to see me when I had my operation for instance – but he's very detached. I'm sure he feels the closeness too, but he finds it difficult to admit to things. He finds it very difficult to put feelings into words. He's always been like that, and I think he'd be frightened of showing affection to me for fear of being rejected. I think he did feel rejected when we split up, even though he agreed to it at the time. Now I'd really like us to get back together again, but I'm afraid it's not on the cards. Anyway, he told me recently that there was somebody else."

How one can empathise with Susie! How frustrating it must be to share children and grandchildren with someone, see them regularly, feel the closeness of the twin-soul bond, and yet not be able to live with them any more! She says, "I've never in this life been very fulfilled in a relationship, and I'd love to achieve that. I feel I probably could with him, but . . . I could imagine a fulfilled relationship with Tessa too if we were different sexes, and Tessa and Stuart are very alike."

Perhaps the reader is again wondering, "Why, if they are twin souls, were they not fulfilled when they were married?" but let us reiterate that we have to be ready for our twin soul. A point made in the Introduction was that broken marriages so often engender in the offspring further broken marriages, and it may be remembered that Susie was given no model at all by her own parents. An unstable childhood and lack of good parenting almost invariably cause severe emotional problems, and Susie says that she has had her full share of those. Only having met one of the partners, and not being clairvoyant, it is impossible for me, the author, to make any true assessment of Stuart, but there can be little doubt that he has had difficulties too, and that these will have rendered him also not fully ready for his twin soul.

Susie has been told also of a couple of previous lives that she shared with Stuart. In one of these he was a pioneer in the Wild West, searching for gold, and she was an entertainer – a singer – who lived in a sort of shanty town that had been set up in the area. It is no doubt thanks to her art that they met, and their life together then surely knew much joy. In the second incarnation that she has been told about, they were man and wife and served together during the First World War, he as a doctor and she as a nurse. So in that, fulfilled if painful incarnation, both showed great caring – a characteristic that Susie continues to

149

display in her present lifetime, not only towards her close family and her pupils (for she still teaches Art though, as we said at the beginning of the chapter, she is in her seventies), but also to all those with whom she comes in contact.

We come to Earth not primarily to find happiness, but to learn. (If happiness were our sole aim, we would do better not to come, for it sounds very much pleasanter "up there"!) And have not all the great teachers of all time pointed out to us that pain is also a great teacher – that it is, perhaps chiefly, through suffering and pain that we learn? It is perhaps difficult for Susie at the moment to see clearly what it is that she has come to learn, and what she is at present learning through the pain of her separation from Stuart. As a person with profound spiritual interests, however, she is in no doubt that she is here to learn. It is my belief that, though she was not fully ready for Stuart when they met and married (and how many people marry when they are not really ready for each other!), she may well be ready for him now (now that she has realised her mistake of suggesting that they part, learnt more about the spiritual life, and also learnt, through other relationships, more about the nature of her relationship with him), but that he is not at the moment ready for her. Their story is full of hope, however, as they are at present so much in touch that every worthwhile thing that Susie does will be of benefit to him as well as to herself. (Even if they were not in touch on the physical plane, all her actions would still be influencing him.) It is still possible of course – even though she herself at present does not foresee it happening – that they will get back together in this lifetime. If not, they are both undoubtedly paving the way for future incarnations together, and their being good friends will help this immensely. If there were acrimony between them, this would induce negative karma for them to work out next time they came together.

Another point in this story which makes it so different from any of our others, is the "triplet" aspect of the influential activity. Any work that two of the three do together will inevitably affect the third party, eventually raising them too to a higher vibration. For many years, while Susie was single and Tessa unhappily married, both lived in the depths of Yorkshire. Despite being near each other geographically (only about three quarter of an hour's drive), the fact of each living in a separate "depth" has meant that they have not tended to bump into one another. Consequently their meetings have always been arranged. They have been going to stay with one another about once a month and, even though Susie is now moving to London, there is no reason why such visits should cease. (Particularly for Tessa, for whom money is never a problem.) Though neither is fulfilled in a relationship, both now live at least partially fulfilled lives, what with their Art (Tessa painting, Susie painting and teaching), their families and their spiritual and esoteric interests. (Susie says that Tessa, who has never previously wanted to join groups, is now greatly enjoying going to a class in Circle Dancing!)

Being able to discuss their mutual interests helps them each along (also influencing, even if he is not consciously aware of it) Stuart, and making him readier for their final triple return to spirit. Susie also says, "But above all we're always there for one another. The only time I've really actually needed Tessa was recently, when I had to have an operation. Then she was an invaluable help and support. And of course she knows that I'll always be there too if she's ill. Though not so long ago I had a real shock because she had a nervous breakdown and she didn't tell me. It was her daughter – the youngest one with whom she's so close – who came to help her then, and it was she who told me about it. Tessa said she was so depressed that she couldn't bring herself to tell me. Maybe she was scared of upsetting me."

That of course is another aspect of the twin-soul bond. And, who knows, maybe it is part of the reason why Susie and Stuart are not together at the moment. For with the twin soul, the one being always the mirror of the other, we show as with no other being in the universe, our true selves. That is fine when things are going right! When the mirror reflects a beautiful soul, a soul of which to be proud, a soul in which to rejoice. But, if we are not happy, if we have allowed ourselves to sink into negativity, then what will the mirror show us but that which we do not want to be shown. So then there will be fear; a fear of confiding because of what such confidences may make us see.

I feel sure that this explains Tessa's reticence about her nervous breakdown, but fortunately Susie was brought in nevertheless, and she no doubt played a big role in Tessa's recovery. Now they are again able "to have great fun together". Susie says, "We're neither of us the least interested in the Church any more, as we used to be when we were young, but we've both developed spiritually in very much the same way, and our interests are all still shared just as they always were. We've just recently been together to see Mother Meera. I think that was the happiest time of my whole life."

I have not personally yet had the privilege of a meeting with Mother Meera. Nor do I claim to have any real understanding of who or what she is. (Is she a minor avatar while Sai Baba is a major one? Of the latter I am sure; of the former I am unclear.) I have, however, met several people who have personal experience of *darshan*[2] with Mother Meera and who have felt a tremendous spiritual upliftment from it. What is clear is that she – like Sai Baba – has come into our world at a time of great need, and that people who are drawn to her are already a good way along the right path. And, as we are saying again and again through the course of this book, it is being on the right path that matters, not whether or not we are with our twin soul.

Notes

1. *Twin Souls – A Guide to Finding your True Spiritual Partner* by Patricia Joudry and Maurie D. Pressman, M.D., published by Element Books, Shaftesbury, Dorset.
2. *Darshan* is a Sanskrit word, meaning *Seeing or beholding the Lord, or some other great person, and receiving his blessing.*

Chapter XI

WHEN TWIN SOULS ARE TOGETHER THEY TEND TO FIND THAT THEY GAIN ONE ANOTHER'S TALENTS AS WELL AS AMPLIFYING THEIR OWN
The story of Ursula and Victor

Ursula was going through a particularly low phase over her divorce, and a friend had consequently persuaded her to accompany her to a hypnotherapy weekend at Regent's College in London. She says, "We had only just walked into the refectory and Victor was already sitting there. I remember exactly how he was sitting, leaning back on his chair and reading a book, and I noticed his very long legs. I just looked at him, and I thought, 'Oh my God, I'm going to marry you!' So then I turned to my friend and I said, 'I'm going to marry him.' She screamed, 'What do you mean? He's <u>married</u>! I will introduce you to him, though. He's my friend. He's a doctor, you know, a <u>scientist</u>!' As much as to say, 'He wouldn't want anything to do with a psychic!'"

Ursula has been psychic all her life, and has for some years now been working as a psychic medium. She was born towards the end of the Second World War and, since her father was in the RAF and her mother worked in a factory, as a child she spent a great deal of time with her grandmother and a couple of aunts who, she says, "were quite intuitive and so didn't think it strange for me to see such things as cats who had died a couple of years previously." As a child she suffered the difficulty common to many psychics of not realising that everybody else did not possess this ability. It was at the age of about six, when she found people looking at her strangely if, for instance, she stated that something was going to happen, that she decided to keep quiet about things she saw, except to her understanding relatives. She has, like Joan Grant, always known that she has lived before, and at an early age she started to have flashbacks to a lifetime in the First World War which can only have ended very briefly before she was born this time round.

Victor, who trained as a hypnotherapist eleven years ago, has also had flashbacks to this same lifetime, and he says that a fellow hypnotherapist told him that over a long career of performing regressions, he had generally found that the gaps between people's most recent lives were much shorter than those

152

between lives which had taken place in earlier centuries. This man's experience led him to believe that most people alive today have already had a previous life during the present century. The recent population explosion is a common explanation given for this, and it is also widely recognised that people who die young – and Ursula and Victor feel that they were both only in their twenties – tend to come back quickly.

During this lifetime in the Second World War Ursula was a nurse and Victor was a bomber pilot, he thinks possibly American but more likely British. They met in London (probably at Regent's College – the same place as they met this time round!), but were both killed before they were able to get married. Victor, who believes that his name was John at the time, was shot down in a daylight raid over France, and Ursula was killed, probably shortly afterwards, in one of the London air raids. Victor says that it was the Americans who did most of the daylight bombing, but his intuitive feeling that he was British appears to have been confirmed by a visit that the couple made recently to a Spiritualist church. For the medium who was conducting a demonstration during the service, who did not know either of them, felt compelled to come over to Victor, and he said, "I don't know why, but I sense an RAF uniform around you and the name John. Does that make any sense to you?" Victor says that it didn't at first, but then Ursula reminded him about his most recent past life.

So, after an engagement which death prevented from being crowned by a happy marriage, Ursula and Victor clearly deserved to find their happiness together this time round, but it nevertheless did not come to them either quickly or easily. Life, however, is never meant to be easy (if it were we wouldn't grow!), and there is always a good reason for everything. Victor explains that at least part of the reason in their case this time was that he never wanted children, whereas Ursula did very much, and so, had they met at an earlier age, "it could never have worked".

When she was a child, Ursula knew that as a young girl in that First World War lifetime she had had long hair, and she consequently wanted this again. Her mother, however, would not let her grow her hair beyond her shoulders, and so she attached pieces of paper to an Alice band and wore it over her hair to make it feel longer!

Ursula left school at fourteen and went to work in a factory. Because of her psychic ability, she says that she always knew that she would marry and have children. "I always wanted children, and I knew that I would have two. I also knew that I would have two boys. From being very young I knew that these things would happen to me. I didn't know the time, because time is a funny thing to grasp, but I did know that my boys would be close in age." In fact Ursula married at twenty-one, had her elder son at twenty-one and the second one eighteen months later, when she was twenty-two. Although this was what she had always wanted, she says that she always knew too that it wouldn't be until her children were older that her life would "really begin"; that she was just "marking time until my life could begin".

Ursula's first marriage was hard because her husband was ill a lot of the time and, since he was constantly in and out of hospital, she had to be the breadwinner for the family. She worked nights as an auxiliary nurse in a cosmetic clinic. As seems to happen frequently with psychics, Ursula has heard the voice of her main guide from an early age, and when she got older and sat in a development circle, she started to see him as well. Ruth Montgomery says in her fascinating book on Walk-Ins[1] that she has been told that, since they are particularly sensitive, we all have at least one American Indian guide. Ruth wonders how there can be enough to go round, but I feel that she perhaps forgets that very many – if not most – of us will have had American Indian lifetimes, and that as spirits we can manifest ourselves in the incarnation of our choice. Anyway Ursula's guide is indeed an American Indian, whom she calls "White Cloud", and she reckons that he has been around her a long, long time.

After Ursula had been doing night nursing for some years, White Cloud told her that she must give it up in order to go into psychic work full time. Initially she resisted because of her need to support her family financially, but after a while the surgeon running the clinic moved to a better paid job and so it closed down. Ursula says, "I still thought I needed money, so I moved across the road to a fish and chip restaurant, but then that closed down. So I thought I'd do some nannying. I got a job with a family who had a little boy, but I'd only been there two weeks when the husband got posted abroad. So finally I got the message! Since each job I got folded, I realised that I perhaps ought to start listening to this little voice. I didn't know how to advertise, how to begin, but fortunately I had a friend who was a medium and she kindly offered to send me some of her clients. It was she who developed me, which was very good of her. To start with she sent me two or three of her clients, and it just went on from there. That's how it began, and it's always been taken care of. I've always been able to earn a living. People think that you can earn a lot of money from this sort of work, but you can't because it's very tiring and taxing and one only has so much energy. I've never been able to earn a lot of money, but I've always got by."

Nowadays people get in touch with Ursula either in person, by letter or by phone, for a wide variety of reasons. Many come simply because they want to contact someone who has passed over, while others seek guidance for the direction of their life or for important personal or business decisions. She also receives many enquiries regarding lost pets, objects, or even people (such as absent-minded elderly). "One woman phoned recently because she'd lost a ring that was of great sentimental value to her and she wondered whether it had been stolen. I told her that it was still in the house – in the child's bedroom in fact – and she was incredulous as they had already been through the house with a fine-tooth comb. But then, a few weeks later, she sent me a letter saying that they'd found the ring in the child's toy box!" Ursula doesn't charge for small telephone enquiries such as that, but she is also known as an expert in psychometry, which she is able to do from a variety of things, including a sample of the person's hair.

She only needs to hold the object in order to be able to tell a great deal about its owner, and so this is of course a useful method by which to carry out postal readings. She also, however, practises psychometry by this method on television, as well as doing radio work – all together an immensely busy woman!

Though twin souls often incarnate into similar circumstances and have similar upbringings and experiences prior to their first meeting, there are exceptions to every rule and Ursula and Victor are in this respect one of the exceptions. While Ursula was the first born to her parents and had just one brother seven years her junior, Victor had three elder sisters. He was born and brought up in Coventry, where his parents ran a shop, and, whereas Ursula did not have any strongly religious upbringing, Victor's family were strict Roman Catholics. He says, "My family were very religious. I was brought up very strict RC, and I was an altar boy." His mother died from multiple cancer while Victor was an undergraduate. This affected his father very deeply, whereas Victor himself, though he always considered himself to be close to his mother, found himself strangely detached from, and unaffected by, her death. He cannot explain this, and says that he has sometimes felt guilty about it. Now, however, that he has a wife who is a medium, his mother sometimes makes use of her to jog his memory about such things as his father's birthday.

It was during Victor's second or third year at university that he renounced his Catholicism. He says, "From an early age I was always interested in strange things – what nowadays people call the paranormal. I was always fascinated by all of that. My religion didn't make sense to me any more. I began to get extremely agitated and it struck me that if you wanted a neat and easy answer to everything you could conceivably ask, then it was there; while to anything the Catholics couldn't answer they would just say, 'We can't understand that because we're not the mind of God.' And I thought, 'This is a load of rubbish! I'm not going to accept all this.' I wanted answers, and I also wasn't very happy at not being allowed to think for myself. So I decided that Catholicism just didn't suit me. I thought to myself, 'I want to reason things out, and I want to adopt different ideas. I don't want to be limited to believing just this and nothing else.' After that I just kind of made my own way philosophically and never went to any other religion."

Victor did not only his first degree, but also a Ph.D., in Applied Chemistry, and after that he worked for some years for a major multinational chemical company. With his great interest in such things as the paranormal, however, he was clearly never a "typical scientist", and he gradually became dissatisfied with his work and desirous of finding a career that he felt to be more worthwhile. So he trained as a hypnotherapist and started working in that field initially part time, retaining his industrial career until after he had first met Ursula.

Concerning Victor's first marriage, he says, "My marriage had been terrible for a long time, and when I first met Ursula it was in its final death throes." Ursula comments that when something is meant to be, strange things can happen

155

in order to bring it about. She says that seven years before she met Victor, a new client had come to her for a reading and at the end of the day she had thought to herself, "I've really got to get in touch with that lady. I don't know why, but I need to make friends with her and I need to keep in contact." Ursula explains, "I've never done this before or since. I never make friends of my clients because it's normally just not a good thing to do, but this time I rang her up and said, 'Do you mind if we have lunch? I was really fascinated to meet you and I feel we have a lot in common.' I'd found out that she was an astrologer, and I'm really into astrology. So we met and became firm friends. We carried on meeting about once a month, and she was a great support to me when my marriage was breaking up. Her astrological predictions helped me a lot to get through it."

This friend is also a hypnotherapist and it was she who persuaded Ursula to go to the hypnotherapy weekend at which she first met Victor. With Ursula it was really an extreme case of "instant recognition"! With Victor, however, the initial feeling of recognition and attraction was less strong. Though Ursula went to that hypnotherapy weekend feeling depressed, her divorce was in actual fact quite amicable. Her ex-husband was only mildly interested in her work, they had drifted apart, their sons were already grown-up and accepted the separation without difficulty, and now her ex-husband (who has a new partner) and she are good friends. For Victor, on the other hand, the situation was different because his marriage, which had been up and down for years, was at the time, as we have already said, in its "final, agonising, death throes", and so the very last thing that was on his mind was another relationship. After the mutual friend had introduced Ursula to Victor, she took Ursula off to another table to meet some other friends, but then later, she recounts, "Victor came over to speak to me. He said, 'Hullo, I'm really interested in what you do,' and I thought, 'That's strange, a scientist being interested in what I do!' but we really got on. So you see this friend, who I'd decided a whole seven years previously that I'd got to keep in contact with, introduced me to Victor! Although we got on so well, I kept well away from him over that weekend because he was married and my divorce was only just going through, but I knew he travelled all over the country, so at the end of the weekend I gave him my card and said, 'Look, if ever you're in the area and need a psychic reading, just come down.'"

The following weeks were not, as one might have expected, agony for Ursula. She has an enviable acceptance of the fact that "when something is meant to be it won't happen in your time, but rather when the timing is right". "So," she explains, "I was quite prepared to wait for as long as it took. He'd got my number and I knew that at some stage he would get in touch with me." Well, the hypnotherapy weekend had taken place in January and it was during the following April that Victor was in Ursula's area on business and so decided to get in touch with her, "because," he explains, "I thought she was an interesting person". As soon as he arrived he began by saying, "I'd better tell you straight away that my marriage has just broken up." To his complete astonishment,

156

Ursula replied by exclaiming, "Oh good!" He asked, "What do you mean?" and Ursula again said, "Oh good!" and then continued, "Because I really like you and I think we ought to be together."

Victor says that he was "gob smacked", but Ursula explains, "I knew he travelled a lot all over the country and I didn't know when I'd have a chance to see him again. It's just one of those things. When you feel so powerfully strong about something . . . And I just knew inside that we were meant to be with each other, and so it didn't really matter. In any case he'd already shifted some ground since our first meeting, with his marriage having ended."

Victor takes up the story thus: "I said, 'Oh dear,' but then Ursula said, 'Well, I'll do a reading for you, but I can't really do a proper reading because of my involvement.' I hadn't felt anything at all when I first met Ursula – that's to say there was no feeling of any past-life tie-up or whatever – I was still married at the time, although the marriage had been difficult for years, and during those last six to nine months it was at a really critical stage and getting towards its absolute finality. I had far too much on my plate at the time to think about new relationships. That marriage ended in its own way, completely independently. Ursula's reaction to my news was a great surprise to me. I'd only gone to see her because I was in the area and had found her an interesting person. When she said that she'd like to see me again, I went into an absolute panic, because the last months of my marriage had been the most negative experience of my entire life and the <u>last</u> thing on my mind was pitching straight into another relationship. So I said to myself, 'Well, I've got two choices: either go along with it and see where it leads, or run like Hell <u>now</u>!' But anyway, there you go! In between the January and the April Ursula had phoned me a couple of times about a book she'd lent me, but it was my wife who spoke to her and I just thought, 'That was nice of her to phone.' We never actually spoke before I went to see her in April. However, we met again the very next day and within six weeks we were together!"

Ursula says: "During those intervening weeks he hadn't been on my mind all the time. In any case, I was very engrossed in my work. My work is more than just work; I consider it my life. I used to think about Victor now and again and wonder how he was getting on. It was natural that I should have wondered how he was because I had this very strong attraction to him and knew I wanted to marry him. But I also knew that if something is meant to be, the gods will make it happen. And sometimes they make it happen really quickly!" (This echoes Joudry and Pressman when, having said that the first encounter between twin souls was likely to have a *memorable quality*, being a momentous event on the spiritual level, they continue: *Events then tend to move swiftly, as though locking two souls into place, like the two spirit rings, which have always been interlocked in the heights.*[2]) Ursula continued, "In our case, soon after I'd told Victor that I wanted him, a friend came for a reading and I said to her, 'I see you've bought a house.'. She replied, 'Yes, do you know anyone who'd like to rent it?' and, to her great surprise, I said, 'I would!' So we went to look at it the

157

very next day and were in the following week. So sometimes when things come together, they come together very well!"

Now, seven years on, Ursula and Victor live in a pleasant, tastefully decorated house with an attractive garden, just a few doors away from the house in which Ursula was brought up. Victor has completely given up his industrial career and, in addition to Ursula's psychic readings and his hypnotherapy sessions, they work as a pair giving lectures, workshops, and leading local Ghost Tours. Since I had made contact with them not in my usual way through a friend, but via a little article about them in the magazine *Reincarnation International*, I greatly appreciated their giving up to a stranger, and at short notice, the large part of an afternoon which was their only free time in an extremely full schedule. While making me feel instantly at home and at ease in their comfortable living room, they answered my questions with clarity and precision, so that very little time was wasted.

One of the main themes of this book is the fact that, when twin souls are together, the purpose of it is normally to be a particularly strong force for good, because the strength of their combined energies enables them to bring more light into our troubled world. Ursula and Victor are no exception to this, and they are a good witness to the assertion frequently made by psychics that being together both enhances each of their talents and also enables each of them to gain something of those of the other. Victor, for instance, says that during the seven years of their marriage he has worked hard on developing his psychic abilities and, though he feels that he in no way approaches her ("In musical terms Ursula would be a Mozart while I would be just picking out a tune on the piano, which is better than not playing at all."), he is nevertheless making massive progress in this direction. Part of their joint work consists of running workshops on developing psychic abilities. Victor explains, "We think we all have psychic ability, just as we all have artistic ability, sports ability . . . , whatever. It's like anything else: if you never kick a football around, then you'll never be a footballer. To develop your psychic ability you have to concentrate on it and use it occasionally. I started to develop my psychic ability when I met Ursula, and we have regular circles and all kinds of things. I do my own Tarot readings professionally. Psychically I work through the Tarot. I find the Tarot suits me very well, and I've been doing it for two years now. I don't think I'm any more psychic than most other people. It's just that I've developed it because we work in this field full time and you tend to build up your sensitivity in that way. If you do anything full time you get better at it." Though they started off organising these particular workshops themselves, recently they have been run in a local Further Education College, each one so far being oversubscribed!

As for Ursula, she feels that living with Victor has enabled her to turn her dreams into reality. While Victor trained as a scientist, she has always been more artistic: she says that she gained from both her parents "because my mother is fairly intuitive and my father is very creative. He's a writer and a poet.

He's won lots of poetry prizes and has written historical books, detective books, and plays." Nowadays, her parents being in their seventies, Ursula isn't quite sure what they think about her psychism, but they accept it. "They accept that that's how I am. When I was young, when other children were playing with dolls, I used to try psychic writing. I would just sit with a pen . . ."

Victor says, "She will have dreams and ideas that are totally impractical, but she will feel free to have them. Whereas I'm very rational and logical and practical. So she will have all these grandiose ideas and I will put them into practice. I will say, 'You can't do this and you can't do that, but you can do this . . .'" Before they were together Ursula had a bit of a problem with realising what she wanted to do, because she would "go off at tangents, so things wouldn't work" but, thanks to Victor, she says, "I'm more structured now." And Victor says, "I can kind of channel her creativity into practicality, which it needs, and she's made me infinitely more creative than I ever was before." Here it is once more worth quoting Joudry and Pressman, who say, *In balanced proportion to twin soul sameness are the differences. These provide the necessary creative tension, the momentum for action and the fuel to lift the combined unit upwards.*[2]

Ursula, as we have said, had already been established in her profession for some years before she met Victor, but he has been able to enhance her work considerably. He explains, "When people have difficulties and problems in their life, some will chat to a good friend or a neighbour, others might go to a priest or a doctor, while a lot of people will come to a psychic to have their cards read or to be told what the future holds. They feel that if they can be told what's going to happen, it absolves them from making decisions now. Ursula is a very gifted psychic, but when you do one-to-one readings with people, foretelling the future isn't primarily what it's all about. What she's really doing is therapy. Ninety per cent of a psychic reading is actually therapy, and what I've been able to do, I think, for her, is to give her the benefit of all my therapy training and enable her to put that on top of her very gifted psychic ability. So that now not only can she see clearly for the person concerned in a way that no one else could, but she also knows a little bit better how to put it over, how to advise people. Because everyone comes to have their minds made up for them, and you can't do that. She never did do that, but now she's perhaps able to guide them a lot more professionally as well as being very strongly psychic and doing the mediumship and so on."

Psychic gifts vary from person to person just as do other gifts and, though Ursula is sometimes able to see people's auras when they are with her, her gifts do not include reading the Akashic Records. As a hypnotherapist, however, regression to previous lives is part of Victor's domain, and so that is another way in which between them they can make a more powerful team.

Team work is of the essence for them – "We lecture together. We run workshops together." – and now, since administration and publicity are so time-consuming and laborious, they prefer to work through organisations (such as universities and colleges) "rather than doing our own marketing". A certain amount of administrative work is, however, inescapable, and it is Victor, as the practical one, who runs "all our businesses. I run our Ghost Tours and I do all the research and all the administration and accounts," while Ursula says that he has "helped me in a lot of ways to see things in a different light from the way I used to, and to stand back a bit from certain situations. He balances me."

Ursula and Victor see one of the most important aspects of their work to be helping people who have relationship problems. They reckon that for about three quarters of the people who come for either psychic readings or hypnotherapy the biggest issue is relationship problems, and they say that, since they both had problems in their previous marriages, that is something that they can relate to and consequently be of help to others. Victor comments, "The question of relationship problems seems really to have been our biggest lesson in life, but now that we're together it's no longer an issue. Of course we have our ups and downs as everyone must, we don't always agree on things, but we're never upset with one another for more than, say, half an hour" – (and Ursula interjected, "We have our shouting matches, but he knows how to handle me!") – "and now the problem of relationship is never something that we think of. So this means that we've got a very firm basis with which to cope with other people's problems."

When I asked whether being together had enabled them to grow spiritually, they both replied, "Dramatically!" Ursula said, "I feel that now we're together we sort of empower each other – with all sorts of things, but certainly spiritually." Although they were married in a Spiritualist church, they are not members of any specific religion or denomination, and Ursula feels grateful for the fact that, although her parents attended Church of England services spasmodically, they never imposed any sort of religious practice on her and she was free to explore. She says, "I think Spiritualism is fine and it helps an enormous number of people, but in the end we're all spirit beings and it comes from within." And Victor adds, "We're very careful not to belong to anything, though most people would call us Spiritualists. What we think is what we think as a result of our experiences and our own thought processes, not because somebody's told us. These are the fundamentals . . . Victor, too, since renouncing his Catholicism in his teens, has explored other religions, retaining a very open mind and preferring, he says, to hold "theories" rather than categoric beliefs. (In fact, while happy to accept the fact that he and Ursula are "soulmates" of one sort or another, he prefers to retain an open mind over the definition of "twin souls". I, however, am firmly convinced that they are twin souls, not only from my meeting with them, but also from posing the question to my own spiritual director, who is a very reliable dowser.)

With regard to how they have changed through being together, Ursula says, "I've changed dramatically. I just feel as though I've got the other half of me. Before I always felt as though I was struggling on my own, while now I'm complete." As for Victor, he says, "My life's changed completely since I met

160

Ursula. I'm a hundred per cent different person – it's like another incarnation. I dress differently, I act differently, I speak differently, I behave differently. I'm totally different in everything. It's just like a new life really." And I sensed that this new life involved happiness, which was previously more or less unknown to him. He says, too, "She's toned me down tremendously. She's made me a lot more philosophical and laid back and relaxed. It's an ongoing process. I had lots of sharp edges when I met her and they're painfully getting knocked off as we go along. I've always been very controlled, very ordered, very logical, and Ursula's quite the opposite. She's imprecise, illogical, disorganised. We're total opposites." Ursula adds, "He's straight lines and I'm wavy. We're both learning to meet in the middle. He's straightening my lines out and I'm curving his a little!"

Of course no relationship on Earth can be a hundred per cent perfect – if it were we wouldn't still need to be here! – and Ursula and Victor both say, "There are <u>always</u> areas you still need to work on." Victor adding, "I think you are in deep trouble if there aren't things to work on. Perfect harmony would be boring! But it's not an issue for us. I'm the way I am and she's the way she is, and we're learning to meet in the middle." Ursula says, too, "Perfect harmony would be impossible if you're living with a psychic! Because we're two separate people, we're always going to have different ideas on things. It's a matter of working around until we're both happy with the answer to whatever comes up. We just have to work at that. It's give and take."

As is the norm with twin souls, Ursula's and Victor's tastes are very similar: they share a love of animals (until a few weeks ago keeping goats as well as a dog and some cats!), a love of walking in the countryside; they like the same sorts of art and music, of décor, and they both prefer to live in exactly the same sort of place. Their dislikes, too, are more or less identical, which is useful. ("What we most hate to do we both most hate to do, and what we most love to do we both most love to do. Of course we each have our individual likes and dislikes too, but we see eye to eye on all the most important things.")

Perhaps the most fundamental difference between them is the one mentioned earlier: the fact that Victor, unlike Ursula, never wanted children. He says, "I'd have made a terrible parent because of my lack of patience! I never, ever, with a vengeance, wanted the tie and the responsibility of having children." Since, however, Ursula's sons were both grown-up when they met, this has not created any problem, and Ursula says, laughingly, "Now he's learning to be a grandfather. He's leapt into grandparenthood having missed parenthood!" She of course revels in her six-year-old granddaughter, and Victor can enjoy it too "since it's not full time", and is finding it an "interesting experience".

Ursula and Victor travel a good deal with their work (which is why they reluctantly decided they had to get rid of the goats). They give psychic demonstrations for universities and other groups, and Ursula makes use of her talent for psychometry for people doing genealogies. By bringing her an object that had belonged, say, to a grandparent, people are able to obtain from her a good deal of information about its original owner. And Victor teaches such things as Tarot reading, self-hypnosis and stress management to groups all over the country. They find many young people coming to their courses "as people have much more open minds these days".

Victor says, "Although our work is commercial, because we need to eat, everything that we do – whether it's the Ghost Tours or the psychic readings or whatever – is raising people's awareness. We like to think that we're opening people's eyes a little bit, making them aware. We're not trying to preach at them or sell them an idea. We're just trying to get them to ask themselves questions. We feel that's a worthwhile way to live. When I was with my previous company, just working for profit – although it's a perfectly benign industry – it didn't satisfy me. I wasn't happy with that. There was no point in it, whereas I feel that there is a point in this." We have already said that they work as a team. When they give lectures, Victor is the main spokesman, but Ursula says that she "puts some frivolity into it" and that, when it's time for mingling after the lecture, some will go to him with their questions, while others prefer to talk to her.

Another feature of twin souls that we have mentioned in previous chapters is that they are often telepathic. Since Ursula and Victor are rarely apart, Victor has had little opportunity to test his own ability in this direction, but he recounted an extraordinary instance of Ursula displaying hers. It was soon after they had first got together, when he was still working part-time in industry, and his offices were in Newcastle. Since Newcastle was so far away, he used to go there for two to three days at a time, setting off early in order to arrive there late morning, then working till six or seven at night before going to the hotel. On one occasion, however, he was supposed to meet with a client on the way up, but the client phoned him in the car saying he couldn't make the agreed time and could he come later in the afternoon instead. So he went to the office first and then only finished with the client at about half past four. At that point Victor felt that it wasn't worth going all the way back to the office, and so he decided instead to go straight to the hotel. He recounts, "At about ten to five I was in my car on the way to the hotel, instead of being in the office as normal, when the phone rang. It was Ursula's voice and instead of saying, 'Hullo, how are you?' she said, 'Why are you in your car, at this time, going to the hotel? Why aren't you in your office?' So, if I ever wanted to play around, I'd have absolutely no chance whatsoever!"

Just as Victor hates scientific bigots, of whom, as a scientist himself, he has known many, so the couple have had their troubles too with religious bigots. There was an incident with a local vicar who tried to put a stop to their Psychic Awareness course at the College. Victor says, "I have no time for people like that whatever. If he were to book on a course and see what we do and then form a reasoned opinion on it, and then say, 'I don't think you ought to be doing this,' I'd have immense respect for that. But somebody who knows nothing at all

162

about what you're doing . . . And scientists are just as bad. They won't do the work, they won't chew the data . . ."

Ursula and Victor are obviously very happy in, and dedicated to, their present work, and see no reason not to carry on with it indefinitely. Victor points out, however, that "you have to go where you think your feet are supposed to tread, and if the path changes you have to decide whether to follow it or not. And paths tend to change with great regularity. So we're doing what we're sure we're supposed to be doing right now, and hopefully in six months or six years we'll be doing what we're supposed to be doing then, whatever that might be. Our idea is that it'll be the same as we're doing now but developed. But who knows?"

Ursula and Victor are clearly advanced souls and they are hoping not to have to come back after this lifetime. They are consequently working hard to try to see that they have paid all their debts, and Ursula says, "I remember when I was about five, standing in a beautiful field and the sun was shining, and no one had ever mentioned reincarnation to me at all, I didn't know anything about it. And I was just looking up and I was saying, 'Please let me get it right this time, because I don't want to come back again.' I remember that very clearly." Victor was surprised when I told him that some of the people I had interviewed did want to come back. He commented, "Who really in their right mind would want to come back here? It's too difficult! You've got a body that keeps going wrong, and it's cold in the winter, and you've got to grow up and learn things. Far too difficult! I'd dread coming back if I had to. No thank you!"

In the quotation from Moshab, the Essene monk, we saw that twin souls were "the right eye and the left eye", and that "they need to learn to look in exactly the same direction". Well, despite the fact that he says, "perfect harmony would be boring" and she says that "living with a psychic makes perfect harmony impossible", Ursula and Victor appeared to me to be coming as close to doing that as any other couple I have met. And Moshab says, too, that "their union seals the end of the pact that they needed to make with the world of flesh". So let us hope, for Ursula and Victor's sake, that this lifetime is their seal. On the other hand, we know too that evolved souls often choose to come back in order to be of help, and since Ursula and Victor are clearly dedicated to helping . . . As Victor says, "Who knows?" And in the meantime, I personally am looking forward to meeting them again in the spiritual realms, if not before.

Notes
1. *Threshold to Tomorrow* by Ruth Montgomery, published by Fawcett Crest, New York.
2. *Twin Souls – A Guide to Finding your True Spiritual Partner* by Patricia Joudry and Maurie D. Pressman, M.D., published by Element Books, Shaftesbury, Dorset.

Chapter XII

SOMETIMES TWIN SOULS HAVE TO
SEPARATE FOR THEIR GROWTH
*The stories of Winifred and Xavier
and Yvonne and Zachary*

Like Kenneth and Lucinda and Mary and Norman in Chapter VII, the two couples with whom this chapter deals are tremendously different in almost every way, though both of them have separated, and in both cases one partner is more spiritually advanced than the other. In the first case it is the man who is ahead spiritually, in the second case the woman; and in the first case it is the less advanced partner who has left her twin soul, while in the second case the more advanced partner realised the extent to which her twin soul was hindering her growth.

THE STORY OF WINIFRED AND XAVIER

"We met," Xavier says, "at a workshop on *Discovering the Western Mystery Tradition*, and there was with both of us an immediate recognition that we'd done this before, and there was too – although she was also afraid of it – a very powerful recognition of each other. So our courtship was very fast – only two or three months – and the feelings were so overwhelming that we both believed that she had succeeded in overcoming her fears. There was at that point an absolute confidence in both of us that we'd known each other before, and that we would spend the rest of this incarnation together."

We have seen – in Chapter VIII in particular, but also with several of the other couples we have looked at – that twin souls always catch one another up spiritually. A feature that all those involved in, or on the fringes of, the New Age movement will certainly have noticed is a predominance of women. The only explanation of this that has so far occurred to me (I would welcome others) is that women are generally more intuitive than men, and spiritual matters appeal to the intuition rather than to the intellect. It is always said, however, that there is an exception to every rule, and in this book Xavier is our exception.

The reason for this may lie at least partly in his and his twin soul's respective upbringings. For Xavier (who was born and brought up in London) was, he says, a member of a "large, joyous and happy family" in which he was allowed to "develop as a human being, with no sense of pressure", while Winifred was born into an upper-middle class family in Yorkshire, had just one younger brother with whom she has never got on, and was brought up, he says, with a "very strong sense of ambition, which caused her natural abilities to be put aside". Neither had any religious upbringing at all, but, whereas Winifred's family was very materialistic, Xavier's was poorer and much more spiritually oriented. Xavier, who brims over visibly with love for all humanity, explains, "I was brought up with love, but she inherited from her mother a great difficulty in giving love, particularly to children."

Another point which seems relevant is that Xavier (like Carol, who is conscious of her innate masculinity within a very feminine body) feels strongly that he is the yin half of his pair and says that they have both felt more comfortable in incarnations when their sex roles were reversed. Like a small handful of other advanced souls known to me, Xavier has a few conscious past-life memories. In one of these he and Winifred were wife and husband in Egypt, and their two children were taken away from them at an early age and brought up by the priests. One of these priests is Xavier's sister in his current incarnation, and the two children concerned are now her daughters. This sister is now repaying her karmic debt with regard to these children and Xavier, their former mother, but unfortunately it is largely this that has been the source of the difficulties between the couple, and which finally caused the break up of their previously very happy marriage.

Xavier explains that when he and Winifred first got together, they knew that they had a certain piece of karma to work out to do with responsibility – "though we weren't sure in what particular area it lay. We both assumed that it would be through our work, and were not at that point made aware that it would be to do with children." For, owing to Winifred's great difficulty "in accepting that if you give love you have to be responsible", her inability to give to children stemming from her own mother's inability to give to her, she decided right at the beginning of their relationship that they should not have children. Xavier accepted this on account of his immense love for her, but, a few years later, his two nieces (Xavier and Winifred's own lost offspring in their Egyptian incarnation) came into their lives in a very big way. This is because Xavier's sister made a disastrous marriage which did not last, and is now unable to cope with the children. To start with Xavier took to caring for them at weekends, but when his sister moved away, she put the girls into a school very near to where Winifred and Xavier lived, and he has now had more or less total care of them for the past seven years.

Xavier began his working life as a pharmacist and then moved into teaching. Though, as we have said, he had no religious upbringing of any sort, he began to find spirituality inside himself at quite an early age, and during his years of teaching, his work with, and love for, the children with whom he worked did much to deepen that. He has strong psychic gifts and tremendous perception, as well as a great interest in human relationships, and it was the combination of all these things that led him gradually to decide to give up teaching in favour of a career as a spiritual counsellor.

By the time that Winifred and Xavier met, he was very knowledgeable on esoteric subjects, she had also begun to learn, and she too believed in reincarnation. She, too, was a teacher (so often do twin souls go through similar experiences!), but in her case she had taken it up largely because her parents expected her to go into a conventional career. Her parents did not welcome their daughter's new relationship at all. She had had a previous boyfriend of whom they had approved because he was an engineer (like her father!), but Xavier's new work in spiritual counselling was not something they could even recognise as a career, let alone approve of. Though troubled by her parents' reaction, this did not deter Winifred from marrying Xavier forthwith, and they set up a home together in Brighton (which is a long way from Yorkshire!). Her parents' disapproval, however, was a permanent blot on their marriage (especially since Winifred was so much under the thumb of her mother), and her visits home on her own because Xavier wasn't welcome (even at such times as Christmas!), were naturally a great source of grief to both of them.

Despite this difficulty – or possibly even partly because of it – Winifred and Xavier grew together over the next few years and she, who had never really been happy in teaching, soon discovered in herself (with Xavier's help) abilities as a healer. So – to her parents' horror – she too gave up teaching, and now they were both endeavouring to establish themselves in somewhat precarious careers (though Xavier was by this time very highly respected as a counsellor and already fairly well recognised). Because of the fact that he is more spiritually advanced than she is, and because he gradually became more and more widely sought after, Winifred, though she knew that the karma she had to work out this time round was through a profession as a healer, found establishing herself quite difficult. He, however, gave her every support he could and never doubted that between them, and with the help of spirit, they could overcome any problems.

When Xavier's nieces first came into his care, they were young and had – not surprisingly in view of their parents' failed marriage – various emotional problems. They arrived just at the time when Winifred was endeavouring to establish her own career, and so they seemed to her to be a further hindrance in something which was already quite difficult. Although she recognised the karmic debt that she owes to the children from having previously been a father who failed to bring them up himself, she has always found the relationship difficult for the reason stated above. (While Xavier, on the other hand, now feels as much love for the two girls as he must have done previously as their natural mother.)

An additional difficulty for Winifred was the fact of Xavier – although, as we have said, he did all in his power to support her – becoming increasingly successful and well known. This led at times to a certain amount of jealousy on her part, because she felt that she had to catch up with him. Xavier, on the other hand, says that he could see that in their spiritual work together she was also teaching him something – gentleness. He has always been very passionate about his spiritual work, but he says that she helped him to see the importance, if one wishes to communicate with people, of being more considerate and gentle – "something for which Aquarians are not noted". "Aquarians," he says, "can at times be quite abrupt and direct, and this was sometimes quite disconcerting for her, as she is a Cancerian."

Winifred coped quite well over the next four and a half years, but then, with the children's demands on them both ever increasing, the realisation that she had to be responsible for them was too much for her. She found her awareness of the karmic debt to be overwhelming, and she saw in Xavier's sister a reflection of her own inability to cope and to be responsible, which aggravated the difficulty still further. She therefore suggested to Xavier that they live apart for a while. She was influenced greatly in this decision by her mother, "who had," Xavier explains, "never really grown as a human being, never allowed herself the beautiful opportunity of seeing the spiritual path, and whose purpose was really to negate – for herself and others – every opportunity of moving forward to happiness. She is one of those materialistic people who profess to believe in something, but really only believe in a lot of money in the bank. She and her husband are sensitive, yet they lack the awareness of, or the essential sensitivity to, the natural forces within life, which is quite sad really."

This decision was naturally a great blow to Xavier, but he accepted it, both on account of his love for Winifred and his commitment to the children; and so she moved away from Brighton, hoping to establish her own identity in her own career, as a completely separate entity from Xavier. Once Winifred had made the break, however, things gradually began to move for her in a way that neither of them had foreseen. After making the decision, she had again been alone to spend Christmas with her parents. They had greeted the news of the separation with alacrity, at the same time haranguing her for having abandoned a "good career as a teacher for this healing nonsense". Much though Winifred believed in her powers as a healer, she found her parents' disapproval extremely difficult to contend with without Xavier by her side. This, together with the well-known obstacles to entering a profession which many do not recognise and of which not all can afford to avail themselves, proved to be a contributory factor in Winifred's temporarily abandoning her vocation.

More or less at this same moment who should walk back into Winifred's life but the ex-boyfriend of whom her parents had originally approved because of his being an engineer. Without giving the matter a great deal of thought, and despite the fact that they are totally unsuited, for Winston (as we will call him) is completely unspiritual, Winifred plunged almost straight back into a new relationship with him. Before long, feeling a need for security, Winifred moved in with Winston instead of endeavouring to set up, as she had originally planned, a home/healing centre of her own. Xavier, who had anticipated that their separation would only be temporary, was of course devastated, and it was only his strong spirituality and his work that kept him going at all over the ensuing months.

Xavier's pain over the period which has elapsed since Winifred's departure can be left to the reader's imagination. Coping with two difficult children and an emotionally draining job is hard going even for someone who has a supportive wife at his side. Without that (combined with the constant thought of one's beloved having forsaken one for someone less worthy of such a beautiful woman!) the tasks must seem well nigh impossible. Xavier is, however (as is to be expected for an advanced soul), an immensely strong person and, simultaneously with being his main problem – the demands made on him by both his work and the children are endless – these two worthwhile things are what has kept him going. Another thing that has been of immense help to him is of course the knowledge that he and Winifred are twin souls and will inevitably come together again at some time in the future. (Initially he hoped – indeed was more or less sure – that she would return to him before very long, but now he has come to terms with the fact that this is unlikely to happen in their present lifetime.)

Now, three plus years on, Winifred and Xavier are "good friends". He has learnt, via mutual friends, that Winifred says that she doesn't love Winston, but she is nevertheless not ready to return to Xavier. One of the reasons for this is that she clings to the security of living with someone who is in a "safe profession". (Being less advanced spiritually, she has not yet developed Xavier's trust in being taken care of.) She has, however, recently returned to her healing work, and Winston, though he takes no interest and doesn't even try to understand it, "doesn't mind what she does just so long as she'll still go to bed with him". "That," says Xavier, "sounds awfully crude, but that's exactly how it is. His passion is his machines. Beyond that it's very difficult to make any sort of real contact."

Separated from Xavier, Winifred's personal development through her healing work has changed her view of her parents, and her own awareness of her karmic debt both to herself and to life has also, Xavier says, begun to change them. He explains, "Equally I made her aware that her parents were her children, and I encouraged her to see them as frightened children and have compassion for them. And when, over the last two years, she began to adopt that attitude and see them like that, her relationship with her mother and father changed dramatically. It's a whole aspect of giving to children. When you see a child, it's not just a physical child – it can equally well be an adult, and she's been made aware of that."

Another difficulty that Winifred has is that, despite being well qualified in a couple of different therapies, she has not yet achieved the confidence to initiate things for herself. She will always wait for somebody else to suggest and organise such things as workshops for her. Xavier's comment on this is, "Yet one of the beauties when you realise your spiritual path is that you have no need to be afraid because the universe will always look after you. She hasn't yet reached that point, but the therapies in which she is involved are beginning to enlighten her." I asked whether Winifred realised that they were twin souls, to which Xavier replied, "Yes, but she doesn't want to realise it completely, because once you have that realisation it does involve responsibility."

Winifred who, Xavier comments, has taken a step back in her spiritual development on account of her inability to give to children, does not at the moment want to face up to the responsibility of the life commitment that she made when she married her twin soul. Though they have met since she left him and are planning another meeting shortly, their communication since her departure has been almost entirely by phone and by letter. Xavier says, "Yes, the next meeting we've planned will be painful, but when you have a sense of vision, you realise that you're not trapped within that moment, that you're on a journey. . . Also, I am aware that part of my purpose is to help to motivate and inspire others to love, and to realise that it is essential to love themselves. I've begun to form an attachment with somebody whom I'm very much in love with at the moment, and with whom there is a very strong spiritual link, though we have completely different spiritual paths. Bella's spiritual path is with Sai Baba and I'm a Pagan, but she finds me very intriguing and there's a sense of buoyancy and lightness about it. One of the qualities I find in this relationship is a meaningfulness and a respect about communication of all types, and that's very elevating although I don't see it as permanent. We both know that the purpose of the relationship is to make us happy, perhaps for the next two or three years, but neither of us wants a commitment. We simply want to give each other friendship, support and spiritual love – human friendship and also human love."

So this new relationship, together with, as we have seen, his work and his love of the children and of friends, are the main things now keeping Xavier going. "Also the realisation that this is a beautiful world too. It's difficult for some people to understand that it is a beautiful world, but it's we who have made it difficult, and we have the awareness now, we have the power, gradually to change our world. If we change ourselves, we change our world." Xavier feels that he has grown and learnt through his pain, and no doubt it has further increased his ability to understand and empathise with the pain of the people who come to him for counselling. He says also that, while the learning to give love and accept the responsibility that entails is a "difficult chapter in Winifred's spiritual growth", the spiritual direction in which the healing work she has recently taken up again is leading her is now moving her towards that.

Like Angela in Chapter II and Carol in Chapter III, Xavier realises that his present period of pain is but a split second out of eternity, and that the separation will be more than compensated for by future lifetimes spent together more successfully. He puts it thus: "From a spiritual point of view, a death doesn't mean a death; it simply means that you're on a path, but the point of that path will always lead back to the same point. So, though she thinks she's going away, she can never go away. That sounds rather controlling, but it isn't; it's simply a realisation that if you recognise your twin soul, then fate will bring you back at some stage in order to communicate. Whether you like it or not, the walk you make will be a circular one, and you will be brought back to an opportunity where you are forced to communicate. The love between twin souls is a quality that you cannot contain. It's a spiritual condition which is eternal." In addition, he feels that enough has been done between them in this lifetime, and that Winifred's facing up to her spiritual responsibility now has to wait for a future one.

Another of Xavier's past-life memories is an eighteenth century one in which he and Winifred both lived in Cornwall and both were artists, he (who was the man that time) being a painter, she a musician (a singer), and so the connection was a very creative one. The link between the two of them in that lifetime was extremely close, and they were very telepathic. Winifred unfortunately, however, was married to somebody else, and she and Xavier had an affair. Much though she loved him, the social climate of the time was such that Winifred refused to leave her husband despite all Xavier's pleadings, and Xavier himself (who was a bachelor) was completely ostracised by their society on account of the affair. So here again we see an example of a repeated pattern. Then he was ostracised by society on account of his love; this time her parents refused to accept him. Awareness of the pattern will enable them both to break it for a future lifetime, but this will involve planning at the between-life stage, so that she in particular can choose a more suitable setting into which to be born.

Nothing in life, however, happens without a reason, and we have spoken of the lesson Winifred needs to learn with regard to the giving of love and taking responsibility for it. She is not unique in this. Remember how Bruce hurt Angela so deeply by denying that he loved her although he had previously done so much to show it? And how Dan went even further by declaring his love for Carol, but then shut it off and also denied it? I dispute Joudry and Pressman's assertion that *When one marriage partner strays from the marriage, we can be sure that the partners are not twins.*[1] To be sure, this is fortunately a comparatively rare occurrence, but while we are all still "frail human beings"...! Since Winifred is not now in a relationship of love, and is only staying with Winston for security, it seems likely that this lifetime will have taught her the lesson that happiness cannot be achieved without taking risks, and that financial security does not bring either personal or emotional fulfilment.

Just as they were closely linked and telepathic when they were artists in the eighteenth century, so now Xavier says that they are again equally closely linked and that he always picks up on Winifred's emotions. "When I think of her, she phones. If I dream about her, a letter will come the next day. When I talk about her, then my friends will say they've seen her." (So it seems that we might be hard put to find a pair of twin souls who are not telepathic!)

As well as enjoying the companionship of Bella, Xavier is now finding that his efforts with the children are giving him ever greater reward. He says that "though still insecure, they are now happy, buoyant, full of life, creative, spontaneous . . . They enjoy life, but the essential bridge of that relationship with their mother has been denied them, and I feel very angry about that for them." He says, too, that the death of his own mother – he shared with Winifred a strong relationship and strong affinity with his mother – has made him even more aware of the importance of the mother/child relationship, and so he is doing all he can to encourage his sister to see that being responsible for children does not necessarily mean that you have to negate or restrict all your own freedom. "And," he adds, "I know that part of my lifetime's work is making people aware that you can love and care, but there's a price to be paid. A price, however, which rather than destroying you, will enrich you and give you the feeling that you are part of this universe."

Xavier, as we have said, feels that he and Winifred will be more comfortable in a future lifetime when their sex roles are again reversed, each returning to their essential feminine and masculine nature. He appreciates, however, the necessity for both of them to learn about the other. As Joudry and Pressman put it: *Through the experience of each sex, the male consciousness enters the female soul, and every development of the feminine nature is absorbed by the masculine counterpart. They learn of each other by becoming built into each other, as once they were*[1]. And this building can continue even while they are living apart. Although Xavier has for the time being shot ahead of Winifred in his spiritual development, her recent return to her healing work has, he explained, begun to open her up, and the fact that he is so willing to maintain communication despite her infidelity will inevitably be of immense benefit to her. She probably still has a good number of years to live, and who knows what further strides she may yet make in catching him up. Xavier is not only confident that they will be together next time round, but, despite his present suffering, he says that he wants to come back "because the Earth is my mother, and she's beautiful. And I'm part of her life!" Let us trust that this separation will prove to have been a valuable learning experience for both of them – a hurdle the overcoming of which will be a stepping stone to their final, permanent reunion.

THE STORY OF YVONNE AND ZACHARY

"We'd been married for over twenty years," explained Yvonne, "and I just couldn't take any more of the abuse. It was actually on our wedding day that I realised that he had a drink problem, and it got steadily worse. It was already quite a big problem when Jeffrey was only a baby, and then one night, when Caroline, the younger one, was only about three months old, he came home so drunk that he beat me physically. I had to take refuge with some neighbours, and of course, once he was sober again, Zach was horrified to see what he'd done. The neighbours were so concerned that the husband drove me to the gates of the Army Camp to see the medical officer, but I just couldn't bring myself to go in. You see, the conflict was so great: my injuries against his career and the dependence of the children. And that's how it went on – for years – the conflict. Looking back now, I really wonder how on earth I stuck it for so long. But when you're married to your twin soul, it's incredibly hard to leave. The bond is so strong! After that night I stuck with him through loyalty – I had made my vows and that was all there was to it – and also, not having any qualifications, and not earning, I had nothing to fall back on. I hadn't heeded my mother's warning. But something – my love for him I suppose – definitely died that night, never to return."

Yvonne has gained (from a regression) knowledge of just one previous lifetime which she sees as relevant to her relationship with Zachary this time round. This was in a farming community round about the sixteenth century, somewhere where the land was very flat – possibly Lincolnshire. During that lifetime Zachary was Yvonne's father, which, as we have mentioned already, is fairly unusual for twin souls. In the regression she found herself giving birth at a very young age – possibly as young as thirteen – and she saw herself on a wrack, numb from the waist down, with figures around her in dark garments with large cowls. During the birth process she left her body, flew through the window and diagonally across an expanse of ripe green to a farmstead with a wall and a large gateway. As she did this she looked back, saw that the building she had left was a monastery, and realised that she had been banished to the care of the monks on account of her pregnancy. She needed, however, to understand the reason why she had been banished. So, travelling on, she went towards some houses with half doors and to a woman who was standing at one of the doors, who she recognised as her mother. To her great distress (because she didn't know that she was out of her body), her mother didn't see her. She then went into the house and saw Zachary, who was her beloved father, sitting in a chair. At this point the realisation came to her that she had got pregnant by her father, and that that was the reason for her banishment.

This regression caused Yvonne to see that, having failed to do so as her father in the sixteenth century, Zachary's duty in this lifetime was to provide her with a home. Yet – (another repeated pattern!) – he has again failed in this. So often through the course of our lives we are given opportunities to redress the balance,

172

to pay a debt and thus free ourselves from a piece of our negative karma, yet so often do so many of us miss these opportunities and force ourselves to remain tied to the relentless wheel. Even if – as Yvonne has determinedly done in her present lifetime – the person to whom we owe the debt forgives us and sets us free from it, we will still not be able to forgive <u>ourselves</u> until such time as we have found another way in which to put right what to the Ancient Egyptians were known as the *Scales of Tahuti*.

Yvonne had a happy childhood. She was born and brought up in Nottingham, where she still lives, and her family were staunch Presbyterians and very loving. She was the third of four children (two of each sex), and it was not until after her father's death that she found out from her mother that she had been his favourite. She always felt particularly close to her father and was very proud of him. He had been the eldest of six, had his own business, and was always very dutiful. Yvonne and her mother are both Geminis. She says that they press each other's buttons, but also know how to get the best out of each other. The three older children of the family were close in age and are still all close to each other. After Yvonne there was a five-year gap to the younger brother, so he never really felt "part of the gang".

Zachary was also the third child, though of five boys, and he was also brought up mainly in Nottingham. He is, however, a Cypriot, and his family only moved to England when he was eleven. He is tall, dark and rugged – quite a striking contrast to Yvonne, who is on the short side and of typically English complexion. In Cyprus Zachary's father was employed on the RAF Camp, and his move to Nottingham was to a similar position. Feeding and clothing five sons in England, however, was far from easy, and so Zachary's mother supplemented the family income by running a little corner shop (where Yvonne has memories of visiting her).

Zachary is two and a half years Yvonne's senior, and they first met when she was only fourteen. Her elder brother and sister were both at the same school as Zachary, while Yvonne's two younger brothers were at the same school as she was! He had a bit of a chip on his shoulder as the "middle one", being a bit young for the older two and bit old for the younger two, but he always gravitated towards the older ones. His great passion was rugby, from which game he earned both a reputation for skill and the nickname of "The Smasher". It was, however, his reputation for running a protection racket against bullies that drew Yvonne to him even before she met him. Zachary's demeanour as the "tough guy" terrified Yvonne's elder sister, but Yvonne herself regarded it as a challenge.

Yvonne, who says that she has always been a "very social animal", started dating boys at the age of only eleven, and her first meeting with Zachary was organised, at her request, by her brother. They met in a group at first, in a restaurant used regularly for local social gatherings, but it was not long before Zach started asking to walk her home. She was attracted to him at first sight,

173

and there was also, she says, an "instant feeling of familiarity". He is, however, very shy, and he consequently appeared very guarded. She took this as an immediate challenge – to find out what was behind the façade – and, owing to his inability to talk very much, their communication was on a different level. They soon started dating regularly, but after about nine months Yvonne got bored and went off on holiday with some friends to a local seaside resort.

Yvonne and Zachary, though very aware of the strong attraction normally experienced early on between twin souls, were clearly not at this point ready for the uniquely fulfilling relationship that only twin souls can give one another. Firstly, they were both of course extremely young to make a permanent commitment, but also this time round they do not appear to have the ability to complete one another. (The distortions on the *yin/yang* symbolism in Chapter III evidently do not quite match in their case.) While away on holiday with some other girls, Yvonne found herself wondering whether there was life outside her relationship with Zachary, and also feeling an intense need for freedom. So she decided to end the relationship, and told Zachary so on the phone shortly after her return home. She didn't want to see him – perhaps because of her subconscious awareness of the pull – but he insisted and, though she found the meeting very hard, she was unwavering in her decision.

Over the next five months or so they saw one another only at social gatherings, and Yvonne found it quite hard to break other people's habit of seeing them as a couple, to get rid of the feeling of being "owned". This is understandable, since twin souls who are together normally present to the outside world an appearance both of total compatibility and indissolubility. But at fifteen Yvonne felt too young to be owned (if indeed it is ever right for anyone to be owned!). She wanted to be free to mix with lots of people and enjoy life to the full; yet at the same time quite a large part of her was missing Zach.

Yvonne had more or less decided that she wanted Zachary back, when he started playing hard to get. He was a member of the Air Force Cadets and, when she went to one of their "dos" and saw him there with another girl, she felt an intense jealousy (not knowing that for him there was nothing in the friendship with the other girl). This experience of jealousy gave her some insight into Zachary's possessiveness. During the evening she had a little "snogging session" with one of the other Cadets, but he told Zach afterwards that she had done nothing but talk about him, and that they simply must get back together again. So when they got home, they got talking on the phone, and soon it was all "back on again".

Yvonne describes Zachary's family (who were also Presbyterian) as "rather strange". Unlike hers, they were not affectionate, and they never used Christian names, addressing each other simply with a "Hey", or with eye contact. When he was young Zach often helped his mother in her "village shop" in the suburbs of Nottingham, and after they were married and he was only thirty-two, she died very quickly of stomach cancer. He was devastated, and he told Yvonne that one of the things that distressed him most was the fact that he had never told his mother that he loved her, never hugged her. Yvonne did her best to convince Zachary that the guilt was not his but his mother's, since she'd never told him that she loved him either – they weren't that sort of family. Yvonne says that being part of her family, who are very loving, was a learning experience for Zachary.

Yvonne says that they learnt their sex together when she was only sixteen. Her family, despite their strictly religious outlook, "turned a blind eye", recognising the depth and strength of the relationship. In fact she says that such was her father's recognition of the bond between her and Zachary that, when she was still only sixteen and he went off to Newcastle University, her father paid her fare to Newcastle so that she could spend her summer holiday near him. In Newcastle she worked as a waitress.

While Zachary was reading for his degree in Engineering, Yvonne sat at home in the evenings doing needlework because his possessiveness would not allow her to go out. Her parents felt that she ought to have some social life, but she herself says that she "felt grown-up" and was "condescending to her friends who weren't in steady relationships". She left school at nineteen with the intention of going to Domestic Science College and becoming a teacher, but on account of a sudden change in the system, she was told that she did not have the right number of "A" Levels. She took this very stoically, and until she was married at twenty, took a job as a housemother in a school for Spastics. This experience she has found invaluable both in fostering her innate interest in care for people, and in moulding her subsequent career, for she is now newly qualified as a brain surgeon.

As already mentioned, it was actually on their wedding day that Yvonne first became aware of Zachary's problem with alcohol. "Because he got drinking with his brothers and didn't want to go off on honeymoon!" It was October and they went camping in Northern Spain, greatly enjoying the dramatic drive through the Pyrenees. Yet she says that she was bored by the end of the trip. Just as at fifteen she had become temporarily bored with the relationship, she found on the honeymoon that they simply weren't fulfilling one another. This may seem strange in a case of twin souls, but (remembering the *yin/yang* symbol analogy) it is understandable if one partner has got temporarily left behind in his spiritual development.

One of the problems, Yvonne explains, is that Zach has a high libido, while she is more romantic and has strongly intellectual needs. He has an extremely good brain, and is in fact an intellectual snob, but "arrogant – always wanting to be the best at everything", which she finds immensely irritating. While he, as an engineer, is very left-brained, she is very much more rounded intellectually, has very wide interests, and much more feeling than he has for the Arts as well as for people.

175

They got married as soon as Zachary graduated, he became an RAF engineer, and his first job was in Germany. He was aware of his problem of lack of control from an early age, but the Air Force encouraged the use of alcohol, and the Mess was always Zachary's first home despite being married. In fact Yvonne feels now that he was not really cut out for marriage and would probably have remained a bachelor if he had not met her.

Jeffrey was born two years after Yvonne and Zachary were married. Though she has always been strong and healthy, there were some problems with the birth, which caused her to have to have a hysterectomy many years later. Zach was absolutely thrilled about Jeffrey's birth, yet never gave him enough attention. He has, however, because of not having had a sister, always adored Caroline, who was born two years later.

Since Zachary spent so much of his time in the Mess bar, the children were Yvonne's life while they were young. They did not get them baptised as, though Zachary had been brought up very strongly Presbyterian and attended all the RAF church functions, he has never been a great church-goer. As for Yvonne, she says that she had started on the "dark night of the soul" when she was sixteen, having refused to take communion. She has always been an ardent seeker, always wanted to find out the truth, but could not accept Christianity. (She knows now that in a previous lifetime she walked alongside Christ at the time of his crucifixion, but that he wouldn't let her help carry the Cross. Like Lucinda in Chapter VII, this close contact with Jesus has doubtless left her with the opinion that the Churches have strayed somewhat from the original message.) Jeffrey, however, asked to become a Christian when he was five. He is very like his father and has consequently always aroused his wrath, whereas Caroline can say the most cruel things to him and he takes it. (Yvonne comments that nowadays, "She whips him with her tongue!")

The years following the night when she refused to see the medical officer were little short of Hell for Yvonne. She says, "The drunkenness and beatings just became part of my life, and I felt unable to confide in my own family because I didn't want to worry or upset them. But years later, when I finally plucked up the courage to tell my parents of my decision to divorce Zach, they expressed immense relief, because they'd been made aware of the situation I was in by neighbours. Once Jeffrey brought a friend home to play and found me pinned to the floor for a beating. He was so upset that he asked me afterwards why on earth I didn't divorce him, but both children seem subconsciously to have been aware of the strength of the bond, and I suppose that's why they mostly accepted the situation, at least on one level."

Besides her great love for her children, Yvonne says that, together with meditation, it is Yoga that has enabled her to get through life. (In fact her suggested title for this chapter was "The Biography of a Yogi"!) Her seeking led Yvonne to Yoga quite early on in her marriage. She started on her own, but after nearly breaking her neck on falling out of a headstand, she sought a teacher and has studied continuously ever since. Air Force acquaintances asked her to teach Yoga, but she waited until she was in a settled environment and then did the necessary training for teaching it.

This "settled environment" came when Zachary took early retirement from the RAF and they returned permanently to Nottingham. Though Yvonne's ability to love Zach had ended with the first beating he gave her, they did at this point still occasionally have some good times together, and he, with her help, now made a real effort to give up both smoking and drinking. This effort failed dismally, but she was nevertheless still determined to make a go of the marriage, and to keep Zach's friendship for the sake of the children. Their plan was to buy a house with his annuity, but the money soon all disappeared into drink. Yvonne says that Zachary's capacity for drink is quite staggering, and that it is only his ox-like constitution that has kept him alive. (Twin souls are quite often akin in their health, and Yvonne says that the two of them share basic excellent health, only that his has been marred by drink, hers more recently by her hysterectomy.)

So they took out a mortgage on a house, but now they owe even more on it than they did then. Retirement as an RAF engineer did not for Zachary mean giving up work, and he has been fortunate in finding jobs in Nottingham. As the children grew, Yvonne's desire for independence – including financial independence – increased. In Nottingham she was able to train as a Yoga teacher and, with the children at school, this teaching soon became for her a source of some regular income. Her great interest in Yoga, together with the friends she made through it, led her very naturally into the field of healing and alternative therapies, and she also joined a meditation group.

All this gave Yvonne much meaning to her life, but she was still very troubled by Zachary's possessiveness. One of his unusual characteristics is an ability to leave his body very easily – a thing that Yvonne has often noticed happening unintentionally. Once she took him along to a health fair where he had a Kirlian photograph taken which showed him to be totally out of his body. He was told by the photographer that part of the reason for his addiction was to help him stay earthed. Yvonne feels that this ability to leave his body so easily is a sign of a fairly advanced soul and that, had they been able to work on his gifts together, "it would have been dynamite". Unfortunately, however, the lack of control has always made Zach panic, he has always blocked his energy, and he chose a different path from hers.

Anyway, Yvonne actually going away from home for Yoga courses caused a big problem for Zachary's possessiveness, and the first time that she went away he followed her astrally. He told her on her return that he had seen something he hadn't liked, and the next time that this happened, he managed to tap on her window. Yvonne immediately realised that the tapping was caused by Zach while out of his body, and told him in no uncertain terms to ". . . off home", which he promptly did!

Now it became Yvonne's ambition to enter a full-time career, feeling that it would be her only salvation from the abuse, the possessiveness and from financial insecurity. We have already said that, when she first met Zach, who was both shy and guarded, Yvonne's great desire was to understand "what made him tick". This, she says, has always been her passion in life: understanding how things, as well as people, work. As a young child her parents gave her a beautiful doll one birthday with eyes that shut when she laid it down. To their horror she took the head to bits in order to fathom the mechanism!

With her friends from the meditation group Yvonne studied various therapies and began to make use of such things as Aromatherapy and Aura Soma, but before long she decided that she would really like to be a brain surgeon. (Normally people who are interested in holistic medicine tend to spurn Western medicine, but it is Yvonne's interest in understanding mechanisms, together with her desire to heal, that gave her this ambition.) When she mentioned the idea to Zachary, he pooh-poohed it totally – not because he minded if she went out to work, but because he thought the study it would entail was totally impracticable. However, as we have said, Yvonne is a very determined woman. She had already done one Science "A" Level at school and, having obtained a couple more at night school, she enrolled for a medical degree with the Open University, paying the fees from her Yoga teaching.

We have said that Zachary was arrogant intellectually. Not wanting to be outwitted by his wife, he decided to study with her, and so joined her in the Open University one-year Science Foundation course. Cribbing everything that she did, he succeeded in getting higher marks for all the work that they did throughout the year, but when it got to the exam, he failed and she passed. They both went to a summer school, now that the children were old enough to be left, and he wanted them to go to the same one, but she was determined to be independent. So, on a different summer school from hers, the tutors realised that Zachary was a cheat.

Jeffrey, on leaving school joined the Army, which did not please Yvonne too much, but she didn't believe either in opposing her children's wishes. As both her children were growing up and needing her less, as her Yoga teaching was never full time, and as Zachary's drunkenness and abuse troubled her increasingly, Yvonne's determination to complete the studies necessary to become a brain surgeon began to override almost everything else for her. She thought often of leaving Zach, but so many things (including of course the twin-soul bond) kept her bound to him. One was the financial question. Her teaching enabled her – just – to pay her Open University fees, leaving her otherwise totally dependent on Zachary's earnings. Since so much of that went on drink, and since they had a mortgage to pay, the housekeeping was an immense struggle and a constant worry for her. Had it not been for her courage and strength, her Yoga and meditation, and the support of Caroline and friends, she would doubtless not have kept going at all. Zachary, though she knew that he often said good things about her to others – for instance what a good housekeeper she was – not only failed to express appreciation for anything she did, but also constantly criticised and ridiculed her. She sees this as a symptom of his insecurity.

One of the friends who came to Yvonne for Yoga lessons was training as an Aura Soma therapist. Knowing that Yvonne was also fascinated by this, she suggested one evening bringing her set of bottles round to the house and giving her a reading. When the friend had done her reading, Yvonne felt an inner prompting to call Zachary into the room and persuade him to make a choice of bottles too. It so happened that he had not yet been to the pub that evening and was consequently sober when he made his choice. He rather pooh-poohed the whole thing and left the room without waiting for Yvonne's friend's reading, but when he had gone the two of them just looked at one another. Eventually Yvonne said to her friend, "His choice of bottles was virtually the same as mine. That must mean that he's my twin soul!" Her friend (who is quite clairvoyant anyway) simply replied, "Yes, I realised that some time ago." Yvonne then asked a trifle fiercely why she hadn't told her before, to which the reply was, "It isn't always the right time to be told things."

The more Yvonne thought about this new revelation, the more she realised that in her heart of hearts she had always known it, and that that was the main reason why she had stayed with Zachary for so long. Things by now, however, were becoming more and more intolerable. She had long since (following a large number of injuries) cleverly developed an art of tricking Zachary out of the physical abuse before it started, but the drink and the verbal abuse were frightful, and Yvonne was finding that she was losing Yoga students through his behaviour. So, with Jeffrey still in the Army, and Caroline, who had just left school, temporarily in America, she made the decision to file for divorce. The knowledge that she and Zach were twin souls actually intensified her realisation that this was essential, because she knew that staying with him was holding her back seriously in her spiritual development. She also knew that she was the person who could ultimately help Zachary the most, but that the suffering he inflicted on her was at present rendering her totally ill equipped to do this.

Getting a divorce, even in such extreme cases where it is so obviously the only solution, is not always as easy as it sounds. Zachary, as we have said before, is extremely possessive, and he has never wanted to let Yvonne go. Her petition was one of truth, but Zach, not wanting the truth to be out, planned to take Jeffrey and Caroline to court to speak for him in the witness box. Resisting this, and feeling that she had time, Yvonne decided initially to go for separation under the same roof. One of her reasons for this was that, since Zachary had always kept her books from her Yoga teaching and refused to release them, she could not be assessed for legal aid. Yvonne has always admired Zach's brain, but always found too that he uses it negatively. From the moment that she started the divorce proceedings, he contested the lawyers, continually trying to show himself to be their intellectual superior.

When Caroline returned from New York, she wanted to go to university. Zachary's refusal to release Yvonne's books, however, meant too that Caroline could not be assessed for a grant. So she did a degree at Nottingham, funding herself by working through every vacation – another very strong minded and determined woman! (Now, having obtained a degree in Fashion Design, Caroline has a good job as a wardrobe mistress and is a pride and joy to her mother.)

The divorce eventually went through after four and a half years of blockage by Zachary, and Yvonne at one point almost walked out of the door into nothingness. Friends, however, who were aware of her potential in the career she desired, persuaded her that she must see things through and get all that she was entitled to. So, increasingly absorbed in her studies, she tried to adjust to a life which was separate from Zach's yet still in close proximity to him. Her family (who, as we have said, were relieved at her decision), gave her a little bit of financial support but were not in a position to give her enough to enable her to find separate living accommodation. She now refused to clean or cook for Zach, and he allowed the house to deteriorate appallingly. She just used one bedroom to sleep in, having all her social and work life outside her home. (Nottingham Medical School had by now accepted her for the final part of the medical and surgical studies which are of course impossible to do just with the Open University, and she had managed to obtain a loan for her fees.)

The house, Yvonne says, was a "black hole" in which she was the only light, and the necessary energies were unable to get through because of all the negativity. Suddenly the internal trouble caused so many years previously by Jeffrey's birth flared up to such an extent that, though she had for long resisted the idea of a hysterectomy, she could no longer do so. Her uterus burst, she became very ill indeed, and feels that she could well have used this as a means of exit, but one of her friends, who is a healer, knew that she had work to do here, and Yvonne feels that it was she who saved her. Having come through the operation, Yvonne returned to her studies, and made a serious attempt at cutting the ties with Zach, using Phyllis Krystal's method[2]. The ties between twin souls, however (as we saw particularly in Chapter III), can never be cut at every level – a thing that Yvonne increasingly realised. Abuse suffered by wives from their husbands has been a topic of much discussion in the media in recent years. There are no doubt several books on the subject, and I have seen at least one television programme about it. Psychiatrists and others try to understand the various things that make women put up with abuse for so long. One aspect, however, that I have never seen discussed in this particular context is the possible spiritual links between such couples, and this may well frequently be the principle reason for their staying together.

Yvonne was coming very near to completion of her studies and qualifying as a doctor, when suddenly another trouble beset her. Jeffrey, after a few years in the Army, went AWOL one summer – a thing which Yvonne admired more than she deplored it – but after getting into trouble for that, he informed his mother one day that he was taking up a career in petty crime. She realised later that part of his motive in this was to gain his father's attention (Zachary visited Jeffrey in prison, while she herself refused to), but it is easy to imagine Yvonne's initial feelings.

Just at that time, however, Yvonne happened to attend a channelling/healing session with some of the other members of her meditation group. Though one of the other people present was the one apparently being healed, the voice that came through singled out Yvonne as the person present who was in the greatest need at that moment. It is important here to note that she had not confided her predicament to anyone else, but the spirit who was coming through assured her that she had no need to worry about her son – that it was simply "part of his karma", because he had had previous lives in which he had been working strongly on the side of the law and now needed the experience of "the other side of the coin". She was told that her son would come through this phase of his life successfully, and indeed Jeffrey is now, at twenty-nine, though at present unemployed, a great joy and support to Yvonne, as well as the proud father of her first grandchild.

Once Yvonne was qualified as a junior doctor, her salary enabled her to repay her loan, and she embarked on the surgical studies with enthusiasm despite her horrendous living conditions. Looking back now, she wonders how she managed to get her surgeon's qualification in the circumstances, but anyway she did and, after performing her first operation and receiving her first handsome salary cheque, Yvonne felt that at last the time had come for her to be able to move into separate accommodation. She had already tried to persuade Zach to put their house on the market, but it was two years before he finally did this. It was a bad time for selling, and the house had dropped in value because of Zach's failure to look after it, and at the time of writing it is still unsold. Yvonne was therefore not yet in a position to take out a mortgage of her own. She did not yet feel ready, either, to live completely on her own, and so leapt at the offer of sharing the rent of a house with a friend of her daughter's. This man, who is not much older than Yvonne's own son, is also a dress designer, has a very strong spiritual link with Caroline (who is now settled with her own partner), and is at present excellent company and support for Yvonne, sharing many of her artistic and therapeutic interests.

Yvonne says that besides the financial aspect and the difficulty of separating oneself from one's twin soul, one of the reasons she took so long to get away is that she was determined not to incur any bad karma in the process. Her children both felt that they should have stayed together, and so, difficult though it must have been, she has made immense efforts to make everything as harmonious as possible. Yvonne found that Zachary's "Leo pride" was severely wounded once he finally realised that her only reason for leaving was him, and so he has put obstacles every step of the way, refusing to settle or to answer solicitors' letters. Though he has given her absolutely no reason for doing so, she has always been determined to maintain friendship – for the sake of the whole family.

Now, though she is only a very few months into her surgical career, Yvonne is already beginning to feel well established, and she finds her work tremendously fulfilling. Remarkably, she is able to see a positive side to all she has been through, for she says that Zach has served her as a teacher, the abuse she has suffered at his hands having helped her in her healing approach. Another thing which served as an important pointer on her path was the work she did with the physically handicapped when she was first married, and she says that without her marriage to Zach she would never have done that. In fact really she sees Zachary's whole life as her lesson, and knows that she would not be doing her present job if it were not for him. "One can help one's karmic discount through another's learning," she says, "and then others can learn through you. But it's hard when your children choose not to learn from your mistakes. Jeffrey has made a lot of Zach's mistakes, but fortunately he's wakened up sooner."

Yvonne's experience with the physically handicapped has also heightened her appreciation of her own generally good health, and she says that Zach would have excellent health too if only he had not so abused it. She also has the odd positive thing to say about Zachary. For instance that, because of his good brain, he is good at sorting out other people's problems, and that (before getting drunk!) he often helps people in the pub. Though he didn't want her to do so, she has kept his surname because she prefers it to her maiden name – perhaps another indication of her awareness of the indestructible bond between them.

Now that Yvonne has achieved the career she had so set her heart on, she has two other ambitions still remaining. Firstly to get a house of her own, but this cannot materialise until the house she has been buying jointly with Zachary has been sold and that debt cleared. Zach says that she will never get a penny out of him, but now that she is in a well paid job, that no longer bothers her. She sees the time coming when she will need to be completely on her own, and she also both wants and needs to live rather nearer to her work than she does at present.

Her second ambition is to embark on another relationship, though at present she feels that the house, which is so much theirs, is causing a blockage to her freedom to do that. As we have said, she has done various tie-cutting exercises already, but only the sale of the house will constitute the final break, and only after that will she feel totally free to be fully herself. And she feels that only when one is completely oneself and complete in oneself, can one form a truly satisfactory relationship with another person. Being full of life, attractive, intelligent, interesting, and easy to get on with, Yvonne should not have much difficulty in finding the "right man". And it will be a lucky man who can win the heart of such a caring and dependable partner!

As for the more distant future, Yvonne is quite determined to make this her last incarnation! This was one of her reasons for taking a gentle approach to divorce, doing all in her power to maintain friendship with Zachary – so that she would not have to come back to sort out any more karma with him. At present, though she has not given him her new address or telephone number and they communicate mainly through their daughter, they are on quite reasonable terms. She says that she will be more than happy to serve Zach as a spirit guide for just as many times as he may need to come back. We have seen that twin souls always have to catch one another up spiritually, and Yvonne feels that it might not in fact be too long until he does so: "Because all he'll really need to do is to forgive himself . . ." Alcoholics do, it appears, often have trouble escaping from their addiction even after they have passed over into spirit[3], but with Yvonne watching over him and being ever ready to help him, let us be optimistic!

Notes
1. *Twin Souls – A Guide to Finding your True Spiritual Partner* by Patricia Joudry and Maurie D. Pressman, M.D., published by Element Books, Shaftesbury, Dorset.
2. *Cutting the Ties that Bind* by Phyllis Krystal, published by Samuel Weiser, U.S.A.
3. See *At Peace in the Light* by Dannion Brinkley, published by Piatkus, and *Dead Happy* by Lance G. Trendall, published by Lance Trendall Publishing, both of which describe how the spirits of dead alcoholics hang around alcoholics who are still in their physical bodies in order to inhale the alcohol fumes from their auras.

Chapter XIII

TWIN SOULS WHO ARE VERY EVOLVED SOMETIMES COME TOGETHER IN ORDER TO DO IMPORTANT WORK

When you dispense with the idea of soulmate as an entity who will bring
you happiness, and when you understand soulmate as the rest of
humanity, then the entity – your soulmate, who will allow
you the experience of happiness – will appear[1].

Although we have already looked at some examples of twin souls who are doing important work together (particularly Ellen and Fred and Ursula and Victor), I want now to discuss a few couples whose names have become widely known in certain circles. The fact that I have been unable so far either to interview any of them or to get them to write to me about themselves is, I believe, indicative of features which are common to such couples: firstly modesty, and secondly the fact of being <u>exceedingly</u> busy (working with their understanding of twin soul *as the rest of humanity*!).

I will begin with a couple to whom I personally owe a great deal because it was thanks to attending an Edgar Cayce conference at which he was the speaker that I first began on the "spiritual venture" which has led me into writing books: Harmon and June Bro. Harmon is one of the few people still alive today who knew Edgar Cayce personally, and to hear him speak about that great man is an experience which I would recommend more than almost any other. To those, however, who are not privileged in this way, I strongly recommend his biography of Cayce[2], which, of all the Cayce biographies, I feel is the best.

Harmon and June were among the first disciples of Jesus (very likely, I imagine, among the hundred and eight of whom Anne and Daniel Meurois-Givaudan write in their books about the Essenes). After the crucifixion they worked together spreading the gospel – work which they have continued to this day, for in their present lifetime they are both ordained ministers. We have seen in previous chapters how repeated patterns are so often a feature of numerous incarnations. Well, fortunately these patterns are not necessarily bad ones, and in a case such as that of the Bros, "trapped" is not the appropriate word to use. Rather, as twin souls who two thousand years ago were open and ready both to

184

be inspired by the wonderful words of Christ and for the fulfilment of love in each other, Harmon and June have come together repeatedly since that time, and who knows but that their present life may be the culmination, the last stage in their preparation for fusion.

Another important fact of reincarnation already discussed is the carrying over of our talents from lifetime to lifetime. In the Bros' case one of the talents they made use of at the time of Christ was for music, and in this lifetime Harmon is very musical and June is trained as a professional musician. Harmon is both a very powerful writer and a very powerful speaker, and his forcefulness is beautifully complemented by his wife's quieter, *yin* characteristics. They make a truly perfect team, and many years of their present life have been devoted to the running of a Christian educational institute. The work this has entailed must be immense, and so theirs is a very clear example of what can (probably uniquely) be achieved by twin souls working together, supporting one another.

It was the Bros who, when I had only recently been converted to belief in reincarnation and was seeking my first past-life reading, put me in touch with Aron Abrahamsen. And it was Aron who told me, in that reading, that I had come this time "partly as a writer – to disseminate information on the spiritual life". This book (plus any subsequent books I publish) therefore owes its life to him!

Aron has just retired after a long career of giving readings from the Akashic Records. He has told his story himself in *On Wings of Spirit*[3] – another book that I recommend most heartily. He is rather unusual in that he was born (in Norway) into a Jewish family, and his conversion to Christianity came about largely through his relationship with his wife and twin soul, Doris (whom he met after emigrating to America). Although we have not yet met, I already feel as though Aron and Doris are good friends of mine, as we have corresponded quite a lot during the four and a half years since I received the reading which, I can say in all honesty, changed my life radically. Aron's own book makes clear the extent to which the two of them have based their lives and work on God, praying and reading the Bible together daily.

Like those of his predecessor Cayce, Aron Abrahamsen's past-life readings have given help to vast numbers of people the world over, and, now that he and Doris are in their seventies and enjoying a well-earned retirement, we just have to be thankful that younger people who also have this unusual gift are gradually incarnating on to our needy planet. Aron (who incidentally is still producing a quarterly newsletter on Earth Changes[4]) reads the Akashic Records in what he calls an "altered state", out of his body, and he does not believe in giving people pats on the back for the great achievements he might come across in their past. On the contrary, he is of the view that the principal reason for looking into one's past is to see where one has gone wrong and needs to make amends in one's present lifetime. This does not mean either that his readings were unduly judgemental. He has a great talent for finding the perfect balance, for following the thread of a person's lives and indicating to them the ways in which this thread has led them in a good direction but also where they have twisted it wrongly. Such readings give food for thought for many years, and I know that I am not alone in feeling that my life has been very much changed for the better by receiving one.

Although they themselves say that they have a rather different view from most people on the whole subject of soulmates, and make no claim to be twin souls, I have had my intuitive feeling on the matter confirmed by dowsing, and I am quite sure that Aron and Doris are another example of a twin-soul couple who are very spiritually evolved and who were brought together in their present lifetime with the purpose of performing a certain task which they would have been quite unable to carry out separately. In fact Aron says himself in his book that, when Doris is out of the room, he does not function so well doing his readings. May the Lord bless them in their old age and hasten their final reunion in spirit if that is what they now desire.

Reading the Akashic Records is, as we well know, by no means the only method of finding out about past lives. Another of those most commonly used is regression therapy. Many good books have been written by regression therapists, but one of the most interesting I have come across is that by Dr. Michael Newton, entitled *Journey of Souls*[5]. This book is different from the majority of those written on this subject, in that Newton recounts in it not regressions he has performed on his patients to past lives, but to the periods spent in between their lives. From this he has been able to gather much useful and interesting information on realms beyond the physical one we all know so well, and his research in this domain has led him to categorise souls – both incarnate and discarnate – into five levels of evolution. Of himself he writes little, but he does recount the interesting way in which he met Peggy, his wife and twin soul (whom he describes as his *soulmate* – this is another instance in which I have had my own intuition about the nature of their relationship confirmed by dowsing). Peggy Newton does not work quite so directly with her husband as do June Bro and Doris Abrahamsen, but it is nevertheless clear to my mind both that his work is greatly enhanced by her support and that they are themselves what Newton describes as *Level Five* souls. Level Five is the level to which we must all aspire, and it is not until we are there that we can hope to achieve perfect reunion with our twin. For Level Five people – these are my observations not Newton's – are complete in themselves and in love with God (whether or not they recognise Him consciously). Level Five people may or may not be living with their twin soul (probably more frequently not), and if not, they have no concern about looking for him or her.

My fourth and final evolved couple are the French authors Anne and Daniel Meurois-Givaudan, whose definition of twinsoulship I translated for the Introduction. Only two of their thirteen books have to date been translated into English (though it does look, fortunately, as though I have just succeeded in finding someone to translate more of them. Translation is a rather special skill, for which neither a degree in French nor the ability to write good English renders one automatically qualified!) Although we have corresponded, Anne and Daniel and I have yet to meet, but I feel nevertheless well acquainted with them now through their wonderful writings.

As Essenes, Myriam and Simon, as their names were then, grew up in the same village as Jesus and consequently came under his influence at a very early age (Simon having been just a year older than Jesus). They married, too, at an early age but had no children, devoting their entire working lives firstly to following Christ and learning from him, and secondly, after the crucifixion, to spreading the gospel in the country they knew as Kal, which is anyway part of present-day France. *De Mémoire d'Essénien*[7], (which has been translated), covers more or less the whole of that shared lifetime, while *Chemins de ce Temps-là* (Paths of that Time) recounts in much greater detail their work as evangelists, also bringing into the story in vivid detail such renowned figures as Joseph of Arimathea, Mary Magdalen[8] and St. Paul. A third volume in the series, written by Daniel alone, has been published in 1996 under the title *Visions Esséniennes*[9].

Myriam and Simon would appear to have been almost if not quite ready for fusion and their final return to spirit at the end of that particular lifetime, so great was their love of the Master and of all that he taught and witnessed to, and so apparently perfect the harmony and unity between them – already the "perfect model" of a twin-soul couple. After they had been travelling and preaching alone together for some little time in Kal, Myriam caught a fever and Simon, despite his knowledge of and practice in healing, was unable to save her. The link between twin souls being so strong, very often if one dies the other follows very shortly, but in that lifetime, despite his intense grief described so poignantly, Simon knew that he still had important work to do on Earth and so he soon gained the strength to carry on alone, at one point joining forces with *Myriam de Magdala* (Mary Magdalen), who was also a very powerful healer. In due course, however, he is put to death, and so he and Myriam are immediately reunited in spirit.

Joudry and Pressman make the point that, even when the final reunion has been achieved, twin souls sometimes opt to return to Earth, either together or separately, in order to carry on spreading the light. A clearer example of this could not be seen than in the case of Anne and Daniel, who this time, two thousand years later, incarnated in the country in which they had both died as Jesus' disciples. Indeed they now live in the Dordogne, parts of which are the scene of the action in *Chemins de ce Temps-là*. Once again their life together appears to be one of perfect unity and harmony. They have both perfected the ancient art of astral projection, which they use for the purpose of reading the Akashic Records. They work together astrally, and they write their books together. The first two Essene books are divided into sections, each of them giving their own version of the story, but one would not know which of them had written which section were it not for the interjections of "I, Myriam" and "I, Simon", for their style of writing is identical. Also, in the books such as *Les Neuf Marches*[10] (The Nine Steps) and *Chronique d'un Départ*[11] (Chronicle of a Departure), in which they help respectively someone preparing to be born and someone preparing to die, they act as one being, using only the words "We" or "Said one of us", never the singular personal pronoun.

In their chapter on how to recognise a twin, Joudry and Pressman explain that while in a normal good relationship – let us say one between companion soulmates – harmony is achieved by the couple reconciling their conflicting views, in the case of twin souls there is a *fundamental sense of oneness: oneness of vision, oneness of purpose, oneness of feeling*. It is this oneness that enables their advance to be *so swift once the connection has been made*[12]. Anne and Daniel's books give witness to that to an even greater extent than all the other happily married twin-soul couples I have studied during the course of writing this book. In Moshab's definition, it may be remembered, the analogy was used of the two fusing into a single eye. Well, Joudry and Pressman say that *They see with one eye, the third eye, the instrument of spiritual vision*[12]. "Spiritual vision" is indeed an apt description of what Anne and Daniel manifest throughout all their writing.

The title of this chapter refers to the "important work" carried out by twin souls who are very evolved, and it is firstly because I consider their books so important, and secondly because of the fact that most of them have not yet been translated into English, that I am keen to write something about them. A summary of every one is of course beyond the scope of this book, but I feel it to be worth while picking out a few of the salient points.

The Essene books are to my mind invaluable because of the fact that they give not only an eye-witness account of Jesus in action, but also because they quote many sayings of his which are not to be found in the New Testament as we now have it. (Much of it is, however, in accordance with the contents of the Gnostic Gospels, e.g. the Gospel of Thomas[13].) I feel that I know Jesus much better, and love him more than ever, for having read these moving accounts, and one of the things that struck me most is Jesus' expressed wish to get away from dogma. (Would that the Churches would pay heed to it!) I mentioned in an earlier chapter that another thing that is very evident in the accounts – and one which has been suppressed both by the "official evangelists" and subsequent theologians (who have almost all been men!) – is the important role of women in the early Church (for want of a better word, though it does not really seem the most appropriate description for Jesus' followers as they were then).

The books mentioned in Chapter VII give historical evidence for Jesus having survived the crucifixion[14]; *The Way of the Essenes* gives the evidence from the Akashic Records (to my mind even more reliable, since not written by human beings!). Does not having died at the tender age of thirty-three make Jesus any less great a person? I cannot see that it does, and indeed I personally like the idea of our planet having been able to benefit from his physical presence for longer. Edgar Cayce enumerated the previous lives of Jesus (thus showing him to be indeed truly a man, albeit a very exceptional one), and Anne and Daniel clear up this tricky theological question still further by explaining that Jesus and the Christ are two quite separate beings, the Christ energy having entered Jesus' body at the time of his baptism and left it ("died") at the crucifixion. This reconciles Edgar Cayce's assertion that Christ did indeed die on the cross with the historical evidence that Jesus himself was healed by Joseph of Arimathea. (I also personally find it useful, having always in my youth been totally baffled by attempts to explain the "Mystery of the Trinity"!)

Visions Esséniennes is different from the two previous volumes, not only in that it is written just by Daniel, but also because he alternates chapters describing scenes and quoting words of Jesus with others applying these words to the present day. One of Jesus' most important messages quoted in this book is: "If you walk exactly in my footsteps, all you will do by treading in them is distort or erase them. What matters is you, your voice, your actions. I want you not simply to have faith in me, but – even more importantly – to have faith in yourself." It is perhaps fitting, too, that this book is written exclusively by Daniel, for another of its important messages is that we are just now entering into the age of the feminine, the age in which women must come into their own. There are so many books written by feminists, but how many are there with that same message written by men?

Récits d'un Voyageur de l'Astral (Tales of an Astral Traveller)[14] and *Terre d'Emeraude*[15] (Emerald Land), its sequel, give an enormous amount of fascinating information about the "realms beyond", of great interest to any spiritual seeker. And in *Terre d'Emeraude* Daniel recounts how it was that he embarked on his life's work, following an involuntary out-of-body experience.

Chronique d'un Départ is a moving account of a woman who is coming to terms with her imminent death, and also of the various stages of the whole process of death (an invaluable handbook for anyone who works with the dying). It differs from the many books on NDEs in that the account begins much earlier (and also of course because Elisabeth doesn't return to Earth to tell her tale).

Of equal interest – and even greater originality – is *Les Neuf Marches*, the story of a soul who is preparing for birth (each *marche* or step being one month in the pregnancy). Here again the message is an educational one which is of immense importance: that the greater the numbers of people who are reborn consciously, with their prior knowledge acting as a compass for them throughout their new life, the more it will "help to give back to the Earth, which is getting destroyed, her shape and her strength". Rebecca, the incoming soul, says, "My greatest hope is that you should be born to the Earth not as someone in a state of torpor. That your return should not be a shipwreck, but rather a desired and a well prepared landing . . . I want to be born consciously. Those of us who want and are able to come back in this way are becoming more and more numerous."

189

An important feature of both Elisabeth and Rebecca is that neither is a particularly advanced or exceptional soul. What they achieve with Anne and Daniel's help – dying and being reborn consciously and joyfully – is something well within the reach of all of us, even those of us who consider ourselves to be the most ordinary sort of people. Anne and Daniel's great achievement is in bringing "ordinary people" to this awareness, and it is only after we have reached such awareness that we shall each be ready, as they are, for working in unison and harmony with our twin soul.

Anne and Daniel's other books include a guide to reading auras – *Robes de Lumière* (Clothes of Light) – a fascinating one about the nature and functions of the animal spirit world and group souls (*Le Peuple Animal*), and works in which they relay beautiful words of wisdom from a great being (*Wésak, Par l'Esprit du Soleil* (By the Spirit of the Sun), *Celui qui Vient* (He who is Coming)[16]. With these latter three they point out that the books have not been written (as are so many at the moment) by "channelling", but again as a result of encounters made during astral projection.

Anne and Daniel know – indeed have experienced ever since the publication of their first volume (*Récits d'un Voyageur de l'Astral*) – that they will always be derided by sceptics, but that does not deter them in continuing in their mission. Twin-soul couples must have courage as well as a desire to seek the Truth and to spread their love towards all humanity, for they know that bringing more light into the world is what they are here for and that this may well entail difficulties for themselves. Life was never meant to be easy.

Although Anne and Daniel explain that the technique they use for astral projection (which they describe as a "simple method of breathing") is a very ancient one, to many of us the idea may seem impossible – even frightening – and we might prefer to leave reading the Akashic Records by this method to people such as them. Yet, as we have said, fairly ordinary Egyptians trained themselves to remember the work they did at night while out of their bodies, and this is important from the twin-soul point of view because even when we are not living with our soul partner on the Earth's plane, we frequently work with them astrally at night. Is it therefore not now time for us (most of whom have probably <u>been</u> Egyptian!) to retrieve this lost skill, which can be so useful in – for instance – helping the dying[17]?

Joudry and Pressman say that *When twin souls join they generate a vortex of energy that may be seen as light in the darkness of society's unconsciousness . . . a force of light and love at an extremely pure level. This kind of energy, which partakes of the energy of both twins, is different from that of individuals or even groups of people working together. It is the special offering that the twins have to give to each other and expend in service to mankind.* Anne and Daniel are such a light now. What a wonderful place our world will be when it has become filled with countless numbers of them!

Notes

1. St. Germain channelled by Azena Ramanda and Claire Heartsong – see *St. Germain: Twin Souls and Soulmates* published by Triad.
2. *A Seer out of Season* by Harmon Bro, published by Thorsons.
3. *On Wings of Spirit* by Aron Abrahamsen, published by ARE Press, USA.
4. *The Abrahamsen Report* is available at $25 p.a. from Aron and Doris Abrahamsen, P.O. Box 840008, St. Augustine Beach, Florida 32084-008, USA.
5. *Journey of Souls* by Michael Newton, M.D., published by Llewellyn, USA.
6. *Chemins de ce Temps-là* (Paths of that Time) by Anne and Daniel Meurois-Givaudan, published by Editions Amrita, Plazac, France.
7. The French edition is also published by Amrita, but it has been published in English by Destiny Books, USA, under the title *The Way of the Essenes – Christ's Hidden Life Remembered*.
8. Mary Magdalen has quite unjustifiably been portrayed as a prostitute. This image, according to her own account in *Chemins de ce Temps-là*, was created by men who did not believe that a woman should show as much independence as she did!
9. *Visions Esséniennes* is published by Amrita.
10. *Les Neuf Marches* ditto.
11. *Chronique d'un Départ* ditto.
12. *Twin Souls – A Guide to Finding your True Spiritual Partner* by Patricia Joudry and Maurie D. Pressman, M.D., published by Element Books. Shaftesbury, Dorset.
13. *The Gospel of Thomas* presented by Hugh McGregor Ross, published by William Sessions Ltd., The Ebor Press, York, and distributed by Element Books, Shaftesbury, Dorset.
14. See: *Jesus Lived in India* by Holger Kersten, also published by Element Books.
    The Holy Blood and the Holy Grail by Baigent, Leigh and Lincoln, published by Corgi, and the words of Sai Baba in
    Sai Baba – The Embodiment of Love by Peggy Mason and Ron Laing, published by Gateway Books.
15. *Récits d'un Voyageur de l'Astral* (Tales of an Astral Traveller) is being translated and published by Vent d'Ouest, USA.
16. All these are published by Amrita.
17. See *Winged Pharaoh* by Joan Grant, published by Ariel Press.

Chapter XIV

TWIN SOULS DO NOT NEED TO BE TOGETHER PHYSICALLY

Although in the previous chapter I described some wonderful examples of very spiritually evolved twin souls who have come together in their present lifetimes in order to perform a valuable task, thus bringing more light into our needy world, one of the most important points (if not <u>the</u> most important) that this book is aiming to make is that twin souls do not need to be together physically in order to achieve their life's purpose and be able to do a great deal of good. So here, as my final "case histories", are some examples which can serve to illustrate this vital point.

I should like to begin with a friend of mine who is a counsellor, and who (like Edwin Courtenay) spends some of her working hours helping people who are suffering either because they don't know their twin soul or because they do! For herself, however, the question presents no problem at all. She says that she knows that her twin soul is not incarnate and that they practise fusing when they work together at night, and during the day she is normally far too busy to think about it. She says, however, that she is aware of the other person's energy inside her, and she knows that this increases her strength.

Very similar to the above case is a healer friend of mine whom I shall call John. While perhaps the majority of people who work in the field of holistic medicine have come to it through overcoming difficulties and traumata in their own lives, I see John as an example of a very evolved soul who may not have actually needed to come back to Earth this time, but chose to do so in order to be of help. (Joudry and Pressman make the point, too, that twin souls who have reached the point of union sometimes opt to do this, sometimes together, sometimes incarnate in different parts of the globe, and sometimes with just one of them incarnate and the other remaining in spirit.)

John's youthful appearance, soft voice and gentle manner mask a strength of character, a wisdom and a maturity which can only come from much meditation and prayer in this lifetime, crowning many previous lifetimes of service. His early years were happy and relatively problem-free, he both matured and married young, and his marriage was an ideal one from the point of view of leading him at an early stage in the direction of the healing work for which

192

he had so obviously come. Feeling very "complete in himself", John has always regarded his wife as a companion soulmate, and until quite recently he believed that he did not have a twin soul. In fact it was only my writing this book that prompted him to look into the question, and he has now found out that his twin soul is one of his spirit guides. Clearly his feeling of completeness comes from his strongly spiritual nature combined with the awareness (both conscious and subconscious) of the support that spirit – including of course his twin soul – is continually giving to him.

Edwin Courtenay's case is slightly different since, having become so embroiled in the problems of people who are either searching for or cursing their twin souls, he is rather hoping that he will never meet his! "At least," he says, "I certainly can't spare the time to go looking for her (assuming that she is a 'her' and incarnate!), and if I did happen to bump into her, wooing her might be too much of a distraction from my work."

"But supposing," I asked him, "that one day she just walked into your life, shared all your spiritual and other interests, and had secretarial skills?"

"It's true," he replied, "that I could do with someone to handle my paper work and help to organise my workshops, but I trust God and my guardian angel and guides to provide for all my real needs. If marriage turns out to be part of the Plan for my life, then that's fine, but for the moment I simply haven't got time to bother my head about it. There are just too many people out there needing help!"

Another friend of mine who works as a healer is Ann Evans. She was married for ten years, until his death, to her twin soul, Ken, who is the most wonderful artist. (His pictures are amazingly varied, and he said, "I paint the beauty of nature so that people will stop destroying it before it is too late.") Ann is "special" in a different way from the above-mentioned healers, as her normal work is not on Earth at all, but in spirit, and her present lifetime is only her seventh incarnation. (It is a mistake to believe that all the souls in God's creation incarnate on this, or any other, planet. In the beginning, while so many of us opted to take on physical bodies and experience the difficulties and joys of Earthly existence, others elected to stay behind and act as vital bridges and go-betweens, remaining continually aware of the fact that we are all really part of God.)

Ann's spiritual work is helping people to choose the settings for their lives[1]. Since, however, she explained to me, life in the spiritual realms is so different from the physical one, she needs to come to Earth every now and again in order to remind herself of just how difficult it is being here, and thus be better equipped on her return to empathise with the people whom she is advising. Ann believes that she incarnates roughly every three to four hundred years, and she says that this is the first time that she has come as a woman. This is probably because the climate nowadays is more favourable for women; in previous centuries she would only have been able to do her important work in the body of a man. Sometimes she is aware of meeting people on Earth whom she had directed before they came.

"So I suppose these people are always older than you?" I asked naively.

"No, not always," Ann replied. "I think there are two possible reasons for this. One is the very obvious reason that when one is beyond the physical plane one is outside time. The other possible reason is that I am still doing the same work when I am out of my body at night." Interesting!

Ann incarnated this time as the elder child of a well-to-do Catholic family, her brother being just eighteen months her junior. Though there was never any question of financial deprivation (they always had nannies, and both children went to boarding school), the setting she chose for this lifetime gave her many difficulties and challenges to be overcome. "My mother," she says, "is eccentric, talented, interesting, difficult and artistically most inspiring. (She won a scholarship to the Royal Academy Schools.) Being born in 1940, we were caught up in problems caused by the war. My father was killed in action, and my brother and I were even sent to boarding school for a term when we were only two and three. I have memories of constant homesickness."

Ann is clairaudient and, to some extent, clairvoyant. As a child she had a "secret garden" where she met Jesus frequently, both seeing and speaking with him; and from the age of about nine she had dreams which she would have liked to have been able to talk about but couldn't. Her family did not understand her at all, nor was it easy for her to discuss her communications with spirit in her Catholic boarding school. Now her communications with spirit are audial rather than visual, but her clairvoyance does enable her to help people by seeing a past life which sheds light on difficulties they are having in their present one.

Her lonely childhood did nothing to deter Ann from the purpose for which she came: helping other people. In her youth, while her mother was in hospital, she kept house for a while for her young half brother and sister and her step-father, at the same time as studying for exams. Then, after a year spent working on a farm looking after horses and teaching riding, she went to teacher training college with the aim of learning to teach the blind. One day, however, after completing the teacher training course, she was listening to God, as was her practice each morning, when these words came clearly: "I want you to be a nun." She says, "I was horrified! But knowing that this was what was required of me, I took up the challenge whole-heartedly and entered the Convent of the Assumption in Suffolk."

Ann was a nun for nine and a half years, three of which were spent working in Africa. Though happy in her religious vocation, Ann gradually became aware that God was telling her that it was time for her to move on. She left the convent and now she is a Quaker.

Reflecting on her life now, Ann says: "Looking back I can see why I needed to become a nun; it was an incredible teaching in contemplative prayer, awareness and gentleness. In ordinary life it is very difficult to be calm within; an inner silence is much harder to achieve. In the religious life we can concentrate on awareness of the divine and tune in to God's love and wisdom.

My next trainings after this – caring for people in Africa and learning to be a partner/wife and mother – depended greatly upon the spiritual training I had received in the convent. I use this training all the time in my life. Without it I would be distracted and swept hither and thither much of the time; it is like a living rock that sustains me.

My secret is that I know to the depths of my being that I cannot possibly cope with life. I have to lean upon God; I have to listen at every turn. I am part of the whole and kept alive by all creation, which is filled with God, so that I am filled with that love and truth which can flow outwards all the time. This is only my doing in so far as I welcome this 'arrangement' and am content with it."

Ken, Ann's twin soul, also chose to incarnate into quite difficult circumstances, his mother (Ann says) "being eccentric in just the same sorts of ways as mine was, though her talents were in the field of music". He was loved, but his family suffered dreadful poverty, and this led to malnutrition which was responsible for constant ill health in his later life, and probably his early death from a stroke at the age of sixty-two. They met at an exhibition, the organisation of which Ann was involved in, and she says that her initial feelings were of pity for "this poor man, struggling to put up his paintings when he obviously didn't really want to be there". The feeling of familiarity with each other normally experienced by twin souls was nevertheless there from their first meeting; Ann and Ken's courtship was only three months and, for the ten years of their marriage, they were literally never apart. ("We even did the shopping together!") Besides difficulties in their early lives, another thing Ann and Ken have in common is being related to the martyr Margaret Pole, who was the last of the Plantagenets. (They found out that they are actually twelfth cousins!)

When their elder daughter, Jessie, was three years old, Ken heard a radio programme about Bruce MacManaway, and this gave him a desire to attend a course at the Fife Healing Centre. Despite having no money, they got in touch, and the MacManaways kindly said that the three of them could stay in their caravan without paying. Although she knows that she is here in order to find out about how difficult Earthly life is, Ann says that one difficulty she still cannot understand is why people worry about money! Never having had a penny (figuratively speaking) since the day she left school, she has never found herself able to be concerned about it. This, combined with the love of God and of humanity which emanates from her whole being, must be what gives her her wonderfully relaxed manner, and others the desire to spend endless time in her company.

It was on the MacManaway course that they did together that Ann discovered her healing ability. Since then she has never looked back, and has been known for many years now as a spiritual healer, often giving consultations on the phone, and often sending people absent healing. She does a great deal of healing work, too,

195

together with both her daughters (Jessie 17, and Christine 10), and recently the three of them went out to Tanzania to initiate a project for teaching people to make solar ovens. Jessie went to school until she was nine but never enjoyed it, and now both the girls are educated at home. (One has the feeling that they would be out of place in school, being exceptionally mature for their years and so obviously "different" and "special".) Jessie, just like Ann, normally works only in spirit, and she says that she is here now for the first time, because her group was needing a "sensor" – someone to let them know from first hand how the Planet is feeling. She has always had a great deal of work, but is at present waiting to be told exactly what else she has to do. Christine says that she has come "for the animals".

Although Ken had been unwell a lot of the time and had begun to feel "old" at 62, when Christine was only a year old, his death came as a severe shock. He died (Ann discovered later, when Jessie had a near-death experience in which she met him) in his sleep in hospital. As soon as she saw his body and recognised the fact that Ken was no longer in it, Ann felt his presence by her side, and he told her not to worry, that he was fine, and that what had happened was for the best. So she <u>didn't</u> worry! Nor has she done so ever since, (though she does have an advantage over many people suffering such a loss, being in the fortunate position of being able to talk to Ken whenever she wants to!). Both the girls are clairvoyant, and they see Ken from time to time. Since Christine was only a year old when he died, Ann (though she doesn't need it!) has proof of these sightings from their younger daughter's descriptions of his appearance and actions. "He was sitting in that chair and he stuck his tongue out at me." "That," says Ann, "is <u>exactly</u> the sort of thing that Ken <u>would</u> do!"

When Jessie had her near-death experience (at the age of eleven), Ken told her too about his work, and that he had promised before incarnating this time to go back as soon as he was needed. It is obvious why he was needed "up there" so much at the moment, because his job is helping people who do not believe in God or in an afterlife. Such people are unable to walk straight into the light when they die, and it can often take a great deal of time and effort to get through to them[2]. Souls such as Ken are often needed, too, at the scene of accidents, when death comes so quickly that the people concerned are completely unaware that it has happened, and wonder where "on earth" they are[3]. (Then it comes as a shock when they are told that they're <u>not</u> "on Earth"!)

Four months after he had died, Ken started asking Ann to write down the meanings of his paintings (sometimes getting her up at 4.00 a.m. to do it, which she says was the best time because then her mind was "a blank"). He is still painting as part of his work, but now he paints in light, and the souls he is helping can change the pictures if they want to[4]. The whole family has recently produced a book entitled *An Artist's Life After Death*, for which Jessie, who is also a talented artist, has written out her father's words in her own script[5].

Being myself a rather "earthy" sort of person, with much interest in spiritual things but little personal experience of direct communication, I was curious to know how, and from where or whom, Ann Evans has got all her information. She told me that, besides Ken, there are three main spirits whom she talks to: a Dominican priest, whom she knew in this lifetime and who comes from the same soul group as she and Ken do, her own grandfather (who, as a child, she always found very loving – "as was my mother, in her funny way!") and Ken's father.

With regard to the points about herself, Ann explains that she just has an "inner knowing". (She has not spent time looking into her previous incarnations because, she says, the listening it would involve is "all-pervasive" and she feels that there are more important ways in which she needs to be spending her time.) It is this "inner knowing", too, that tells Ann that she and Ken Evans are one being. Far from being limited to that, however, she feels the two of them to be – it was difficult for either of us to find words for this – part of something much greater, much more wonderful . . . "like being part of an ocean of love and wisdom". She is in fact, to return to Lilla Bek's words quoted in the Introduction, one of those souls who have become "much more collective" . . . who have reached "the higher levels, where we all merge into one fire", but Ann prefers the word "ocean" to "fire", which she feels suggests burning up. (I imagine Lilla is thinking of us all burning with love.)

The question of the ocean/fire into which we shall all ultimately be reabsorbed once we have become sufficiently evolved is a slightly tricky one, and I imagine that I am not alone in having assumed at one point that it implied a loss of our individuality (a thought which I did not find very appealing!). Further study and reflection have, however, led me to appreciate that the reverse is actually the case. For, looking around at people one knows, is it not obvious that the more evolved they appear to be, the more individual they are also?

The "deceased" Richard, in conversation with his friend Graham Bernard who is still on Earth[6], explains the paradox thus:– *We are all one in God. Remember, each fellowship will ultimately become a distinct organ in the augmented Body of God, each member contributing an individual, unique, and perfect element of that organ without which it would be incomplete . . . The more truly we are one with God,the more we become one with all. The more we become one with all, the more we are individual . . .*

So the image that one has to have is really of an ocean in which each single drop is visible and distinguishable!

Similarly, just as becoming once more one with God as we originally were, enhances both our own individuality and the richness and variety of the whole "God force of the universe", so the final fusion with our twin soul will not mean that we will become, as it were, lost in the other. Rather, the two separate halves will, by being together in their joint spirit, be able to bring out the individual characteristics of each one to the fullest possible extent, thus making us at last able to be, in the most profound sense, completely ourselves, each at the same time amplifying the other's wholeness.

Ann Evans is one such an "exceptionally individual" person, and I feel so very privileged to know her. Also (while accepting her assurance that I can talk to him now, and feel conscious of his agreement to my use of his picture to illustrate what "this twin soul thing" is all about) I am greatly looking forward, next time I am in-between lives, to meeting Ken, of whose individuality I am already aware through his paintings.

So that is four examples known to me of very evolved souls, who feel no need to be physically together with their twin souls, and the shape of whose lives stems from, and is enriched by, an enormous love of God and a desire to be of service to humanity. I should like now to conclude with someone whom geography at present unfortunately prevents me from being able to meet personally, as she is American, but we have corresponded. She is known to the world by her pseudonym of Marlo Morgan.

I regard the book *Mutant Message Down Under* as a "must" for anyone who has not read it already. The author is an acupuncturist who was called for a period of time to work in Australia. While there (without wishing to spoil the story for those who have not yet read it!), she is taken to a tribe of Aborigines, who inform her that she is to go on a walkabout with them, and for four months she lives exactly as they do, with the only one of them who knows English acting as her interpreter. This tribe claim to have been there since the world was first inhabited, reincarnating over and over among themselves, living in total harmony with nature, and doing all they can to preserve the planet from the plunders of their fellow human beings. They still have some of the gifts that were possessed by the Atlanteans, such as communication by telepathy and healing with sound. Now, however, they feel that their time is up, and they are consequently celibate. It is the turn of others to try to clear up the mess, they say, but before they finally leave this world they want their story to be told, and "Marlo Morgan" is the person chosen to do this (which she does in an extraordinarily moving and powerful way).

When "Marlo" first meets the Tribal Elder she has an instant feeling of affinity with him. Eventually they talk – through the interpreter of course – but they do not really need the interpreter to transmit their deep feelings and the awareness of their soul connection. She finds out that the two of them were born on exactly the same day, and also that, though they were at opposite ends of the globe, their childhood experiences were remarkably similar. The phrase "twin soul" is not actually used in the book, but it is obvious to the reader that the tribe all recognise the nature of the relationship between these two people. She describes her pain on parting with him very vividly, but never for a moment does it enter either of their heads that she should do otherwise. They both know that their present paths in the world were destined to be separate, and she, now back at work in New York, feels incredibly enriched by having made the connection, and aware that her spiritual link with him is an eternal one.

So that seems to be a fitting example with which to end my case histories!

Notes
1. See *Journey of Souls* by Michael Newton, Ph.D., published by Llewellyn Publications, USA.
2. See *Récits d'un Voyageur de l'Astral* by Anne and Daniel Meurois-Givaudan, published by Editions Amrita, to be published in English by Vent d'Ouest, USA.
3. See above, and also *Life After Death* by Neville Randall, published by Corgi.
4. See, when it comes out, Lilla Bek's book on Remedial Art, to be published by Thorsons.
5. This book, together with cards made from prints of Ken's pictures, and a book of Ann's poems with illustrations by Ken, entitled *The Light Within*, are all available from Ann Evans herself at Eggmoor Lane Cottage, Chardstock, Devon EX13 7BP.
6. See *Eternal Ties – The Reality behind Relationships: A Conversation with Richard*, channelled by Graham Bernard and published by Destiny Books, USA.
6. *Mutant Message Down Under* by Marlo Morgan, published by Thorsons.

Chapter XV

CONCLUSION – THE MESSAGE

I love you because you give without wanting.
I love you because you invite search without fear.
I love you because you smile for no reward.
I love you because you seek my depth without intrusion.
I love you because you are so alive without agitation.
I love you because you see but do not condemn.
I love you because you are strong without plundering.
I love you because you are gentle without guile.
I love you because you sing and invite participation.
I love you because in living you add my life to yours.
I love you because you are you and quite unique.[1]

This is of course the ideal model for each of us, and for all love relationships. How to achieve it has, I trust, been outlined in the preceding chapters. Only when we are whole in ourselves, only when care for others, care for the planet, and love of God are paramount in our minds, will we be really ready for <u>any</u> "perfect" relationship, let alone final fusion with our twin soul. Twinsoulship being, however, the subject of this book, let me now summarise the ways by which it can be recognised.

Readers may perhaps have gained the impression that, in order to be sure that someone is one's twin soul, one needs to consult a clairvoyant, and there can be no doubt that this is normally the simplest method. Firstly, however, clairvoyants of the necessary calibre are by no means yet very thick on the ground, and secondly, we are at present entering an age of "Intuition", in which people are increasingly taking responsibility for their own lives and actions.

Here then – for the benefit both of those who do not have access to a good clairvoyant and of those who prefer to work things out for themselves – is a list of the principal features to look for when trying to assess whether a relationship is indeed a twin soul one.

1. *Instant Recognition*

I have already quoted Joudry and Pressman in saying that first meetings between twin souls are invariably memorable events, momentous occasions. Though some were more dramatic than others, this would appear to have been true in all of the thirteen cases I studied. And even with the less dramatic instances, all the people with whom I spoke talked of <u>very soon</u> having come to feel that their partner was someone they had always known. Of course, in companion or karmic soulmate relationships too there will often, if not always, be a strong feeling of recognition on first meeting, but, as I see it, what distinguishes twin-soul relationships from any others is the feeling that the partners have, almost from the first instance, of not needing to <u>get</u> to know one another since they already <u>do</u> know one another, profoundly. Remember how Kenneth, who was convinced that he was "too old" for Lucinda, was surprised at finding himself on the occasion of their first proper meeting, which was a "business" one, talking at length to her and saying things that he did not know that he knew? And how Graham and Helen, who are of different nationalities, made their strong connection within the space of twenty-four hours? How Xavier said that their courtship was very fast and very intense, and how Ann and Ken Evans became inseparable within three months of their first meeting?

2. *Telepathy*

The extent of this depends upon the individual's level of psychic awareness, but I am sure that this study shows that it is an extremely common feature among twin-soul couples. Ellen, Graham, Polly and Victor all recounted quite dramatic instances of telepathy, while Kenneth and Lucinda, Rosie, and Xavier all experience it strongly too. (Angela often <u>feels</u> that she is experiencing it, but has no means of checking.) And Carol's experience is that her moods are intensely affected by Dan's even when she does not see him for weeks at a time, while even Yvonne, who had good reasons for cutting all her ties with Zachary (if it were possible!), found that the joint ownership of a house was blocking her from moving forward and being open to another relationship. The predictions are that, the further we enter into the New Age, the more telepathic we shall all become, and is it not to be expected that, the link between twin souls being the strongest possible between any human beings, it is they who will always be the most telepathic with one another?

3. *Incarnating into Similar Circumstances*

Although this is not universal, it is also a very common feature of twin souls and therefore one that it will always be worth looking for if certainty is being sought. It can happen even in the most apparently unlikely cases such as that of "Marlo Morgan", where the partners were born at opposite ends of the globe and into different races. Since the empathy between twin souls who are ready

201

for one another must always be intense, it is natural that their backgrounds should be similar; if they were _very_ different, such empathy would not be achieved so easily.

4. *Having Similar Experiences prior to their meeting*
This again helps the empathy between twin-soul couples to be felt when they first meet. And, like the above, it is also a natural result of the close link that exists between them. Remember how Mary and Norman, who could neither of them have been expected to make a relationship easily – he because of shyness, she because of the negative self-image that her mother had given her – were drawn together by the intellectual and artistic pursuits they had previously been following separately? This, however, as I pointed out in Chapter X, will also be a consequence of the astral meetings which take place between twin souls prior to their acquaintanceship on the physical level. Angela and Bruce were both "late developers" from the career point of view and then entered the same field of work; Oliver and Polly were both drawn first to nursing and then to aromatherapy; Quentin and Rosie were both addicted to drugs.

5. *Finding that they have been doing the Same Things at the Same Time*
Graham and Helen's more or less identical post cards crossing in the post to each other might be regarded as a somewhat exaggerated example of this, but it nevertheless did actually happen. Melvyn Bragg says in his biography of Burton[2] that Alan Jay Lerner reported Richard and Elizabeth relating a shared dream of a boat capsizing, each in panic looking for the other; and then waking up simultaneously out of the shared nightmare! Less dramatically, Kenneth and Lucinda had both joined their local *Universal Principle Support group* and both got interested in meditation (which was how they met), while Iris and Joe were both working in restaurants when they met. Again, this may well be a feature an increase of which will be observed in the future, as we all become more telepathic.

6. *The Health of Twin Souls is often Linked*
Bruce boasts of his exceptional good health and never having taken a day off work in his whole career, while Angela, despite various minor physical problems, says that she has never experienced any illness other than the normal "childhood" ones or 'flu. Graham's health caught up with Helen's as soon as he came under her good influence. Kenneth and Lucinda say that they share excellent health. Quentin and Rosie, though its cause is not the same, are both now victims of disability. Susie and Tessa discovered alternative therapies simultaneously though independently. Yvonne made a particular point of the fact that she and Zachary both have iron constitutions. So here is another common feature to look for, even though it must be appreciated that there will always be exceptions. (Carol says of Dan that his health is a good deal better than hers, as does Mary of Norman.)

7. *Twin Souls who are practising Fusing at night often experience Strange Symptons when they meet during the day*

This feature can only apply to couples who are apart most of the time, not to those who are living together. Angela, it may be remembered, described trembling and intense feelings of sickness on the comparatively rare occasions when she met Bruce, and Carol also told me that her experience was similar initially. In Carol's case, however, the symptoms were gradually reduced simply because she became accustomed to meeting Dan fairly frequently and had regular occasions for lengthy conversations with him, which Angela never had.

Among Joudry and Pressman's case histories they recount the experience of a person called Alexandra who, while still officially married to somebody else, had an out of body meeting with her twin soul, Leroy, whose astral presence she sensed and saw at the end of her bed. What happened to her can perhaps best be described as a "spiritual sexual encounter", and I imagine that it was similar to what Kenneth described as a "sort of spiritual orgasm" when he had a vision of Lucinda shortly after their first proper meeting.

Such experiences can best be understood when we appreciate that the ultimate destiny of each one of us is fusion with our twin soul, and that love-making on the physical plane is firstly the means we have at our disposal for procreation, and secondly the soul reaching out for that wonderful spiritual union that it subconsciously remembers from the beginning and yearns to regain. (The two are, to my mind, equal in importance, though of course totally different – something that the Curia of Rome has yet to understand!) Once this final reunion has been achieved, the bliss will not only be permanent, but it will be increased still further firstly by the joining with other pairs of twins (the "group soul" and "soul mate" aspects of our destiny described so beautifully in Joudry and Pressman's final chapter), and secondly by the return of us all to God, our Source.

In the meantime, as mentioned above and explained in Chapter II, twin souls who are coming in sight of their final necessary incarnations practise this astral fusion when they meet up for the work they do together while their bodies are asleep. The consequences, as described in Chapter II, can be uncomfortable – indeed embarrassing – but that is a small price to pay for the ultimate bliss that we have in store. I would advise anyone who experiences such symptoms on meeting a person of the opposite sex not to assume automatically that the person concerned is their twin soul – it may be simply a natural nervousness caused by feelings of sexual attraction – but to weigh it up as a possibility if most of the other features listed are apparent in the relationship.

8. *Twin souls do not try to Change One Another*

Just as the above can really only apply to twin souls who are not together, so this feature can only apply <u>fully</u> to those who are.

Chapter III showed how companion soulmate relationships can sometimes be more comfortable than those between twin souls, but this is of course before the twin souls have perfected themselves. Companion soulmate partnerships are often truly wonderful, often immensely beneficial to the world. In the best of such relationships each partner will accept the other as they are. Indeed, training ourselves to do this is part of the necessary preparation for reunion with our twin. Loving someone as much for their faults as for their qualities is essential for any good relationship. (*I love you because you see but do not condemn.*) Once, however, this preparation has been completed and we do unite with our twin on Earth, total acceptance will be natural – inevitable in fact – for the partner will appear to us in the very form the memory of which we have kept "locked in the depths of our hearts" for so long, and will consequently seem to us to be "perfect".

Even in the cases I studied in which the partners or partner concerned were not fully ready for union, I noticed an acceptance of them just as they were. Although Bruce was not ready to take responsibility after showing love for Angela, she blamed herself more than she did him for things going wrong. Carol got frustrated at first by Dan's being stuck in his empty marriage, but gradually realised the extent to which he needed to go through his own learning process, and became content to go on sending him love and to let him develop in his own time. Rosie soon came to terms with the fact that Quentin was not ready to change in his present lifetime and to withdraw, leaving him in the knowledge that she would always be there for him. Xavier, whose pain (together with that of Yvonne) is perhaps the greatest of any of our characters because of the fact that he has been abandoned by his twin soul apparently quite undeservedly, has gone on loving Winifred just the same, harbouring no bitterness, and waiting patiently for her return to him in a future lifetime. And finally Yvonne, who had the most reason of them all for bitterness, and although she could no longer love Zach since he had treated her so badly, was still able to speak of his good qualities.

9. *Physical Age is Completely Immaterial to Twin Souls*
Just as this book was being completed, an article on *Twin Souls* that I had in the magazine *Reincarnation International*[3] provoked a fascinating response from the wife of an Anglican vicar, who got married at the age of twenty-two when he (clearly her twin soul) was a widower of sixty-eight – an age gap of forty-seven years! People's prejudices being as they are, the couple were much criticised at the time, but now, twenty-eight years on, their marriage is still "perfect". At ninety-seven, Harold is at present "as sprightly as someone twenty years younger", but the couple now treasure each day as a gift, knowing that their physical separation could come at any moment.

This couple are an excellent example, too, of twin souls whose talents are enhanced by being together. Jacqueline is the parish organist, and she says, "I compose, or rather 'receive' music which I play extemporaneously to fit the mood during various parts of the service, and our congregations have found the spirituality of Harold's preaching combined with the music uplifting. I find that I cannot achieve such spiritually inspired music when I am working with other priests: the atmosphere does not vibrate in the same way."

Since twin souls will <u>always</u> be the same age spiritually, their respective physical ages are of no importance in their making of a relationship. Ken and Lucinda found very quickly that the fact of his being a lot older than her was immaterial; Graham did not even notice that Helen was fourteen years older than him until she mentioned it as being something that concerned her. Angela had no idea that Bruce was any more than a year or two older than her until they had known each other for a few years and he told her that he was about to have his sixtieth birthday.

Besides not feeling the large age gap between them, and despite his profession as a Church of England vicar, Harold and Jacqueline have both always believed in reincarnation, have always felt that they were "soulmates", and have had flashbacks to previous shared lives (both being very drawn to Greece and to Wells in Somerset). Also, she says, "We feel each other's moods, are very telepathic when apart, and Harold often speaks about what I am thinking."

So there are nine points we can look for when trying to identify twin-soul relationships. Another method, however, which I have also mentioned previously, is dowsing. Here it must be put on record (as Angela pointed out in Chapter II), that it is vital that the dowser should not only be a person with a very clear intuition, but also completely impartial. If you fall in love with someone, convince yourself that he or she is your twin soul, and then try to verify it by dowsing yourself, I can more or less guarantee that your pendulum will reply "Yes" to you whether or not it is true! Even for this book, where the cases I studied were in a sense never of particularly personal interest to me, I made use of a reliable friend for the dowsing as I could not be totally confident of not having a vested interest in whether a particular couple were really twin souls.

So that concludes my assessment of how twinsoulship can be established, but another point very worth noting is that twin-soul encounters force the partners concerned to face up to their own Truth. Richard Bach, the well-known American writer, has told his own story in *The Bridge Across Forever*[4]. Although he refers to Leslie, his wife, as his "soulmate", it is quite clear that they are twin souls. Prior to meeting her, he had a number of affairs and was in perpetual search for HER and the perfect relationship. Even after first making the relationship with Leslie, however, his own insecurities prevent him initially from committing himself, and it is her precise analysis of what he is doing that forces him for the first time in his life to acknowledge his true self. Years of having run away from this reality make this an exceedingly difficult and painful task for him, but once he has faced up to the Truth he is finally able to "let himself go" into real love and the "perfect relationship" which had previously eluded him for so long.

Carol in my study did not marry Dan as she would have liked, but she was the only person he ever met who had the insight and the courage to point out to him the ways in which he was wasting his life and his potential. Whatever happens in the future, he will have been changed radically for the better through knowing her. Similarly Angela, who like Richard Bach yearned for the perfect relationship, was forced by her twin soul to look into herself, and as a result she came to terms with the fact that she had come into her present lifetime not to achieve happiness in a selfish way but in order to learn and to be of service. The service that she is now performing should stand her in good stead for a future incarnation shared with Bruce.

Xavier, despite the pain of his separation, is teaching Winifred about the reality of her relationship with her parents and her need to learn to give love and to take responsibility for the consequences of so doing. And Yvonne has been patiently teaching Zachary that he cannot expect to get away with treating someone so badly, and that she is not his personal property even though she is his twin soul.

As for the happy couples whom I met through writing this book, all of them made it very clear that they were on a joint search for Truth, and that neither ever kept anything hidden from the other. Again, this is the model for all good partnerships, but, as Joudry and Pressman point out too, with twin souls it cannot be any other way since, as opposite halves of one being, they act as mirrors one to the other.

If it appears that much of the principal focus of this book has been pain, this is nothing other than an inevitable consequence of the fact that both the subjects of it and the readers are all <u>here</u>. Were I able to write such a book on a different level of existence, neither I nor the readers would probably be needing it anyway! Joudry and Pressman quote the Masters as saying that we evolve through suffering until we learn to evolve through joy. Had we all already reached the happy point of evolving through joy, most of us would not still need to be on Earth, for – apart from those evolved souls who come only as helpers – we come here not to find happiness but to learn. Once we have completed our learning, we shall discover – as Arthur Ford explained to Ruth Montgomery[5] that *The satisfaction . . . is far greater on this side (in spirit), for here it is a magnet which unites souls so closely as to be unknown in physical body, where each travels the road alone. Here it is possible to be truly united with each other in blissful oneness.*

Even Ellen and Fred, Graham and Helen, Iris and Joe, Ken and Lucinda, Mary and Norman, Oliver and Polly (we hope!) and Ursula and Victor, who are enjoying twin-soul union in their present lifetimes, have firstly already had their share of pain and know that the fact of being together will not even now shield them completely from that, and secondly will not be able to experience the perfect, permanent and total unity that awaits them until they have completed all their necessary incarnations. They may appear nearly ready for this at the moment, but no one's evolution is pre-determined, and it is alas never a continual progression, i.e. through our lifetimes we have all been up and down – taking perhaps three steps forward in one incarnation, but then two (or even four!) steps backward in subsequent one(s) – which is why the upward struggle is such a very lengthy process.

Another important point that I hope, however, to have made clear is that – just as nothing on this Earth happens without a reason – so all twin soul encounters, whether or not they lead to happy reunions, take place for a specific purpose and are part of the Divine Plan, the "lives tapestry" of the couple concerned. For that reason I should like it also to be noted that not one of our stories is without hope. So now let us take another look at each of the apparently "sad" tales in that light.

Angela, before her conversion to belief in reincarnation and her leap in spiritual development, believed that "Fate" had dealt her an unjust blow through not allowing her to meet Bruce until after he was already married to someone who probably loved him less than she did. Her chief problem was, however, her inability to love herself – one of the most vital ingredients in the "Recipe for Readiness for Twin-Soul Partnership" – and his love for her (even though he never declared it and subsequently denied it) transformed her. And it transformed her at the very point in her life when she was getting ready to move into her true vocation. He helped her to come fully into her femininity, to believe, as she had never been able to before, that a man could find her attractive. After that her growth was brought about through pain, but it was a growth far greater than she would have achieved if they had not met, and now she is able to see the purpose of it rather than feeling cheated by life. Similarly Bruce – if he once more allows himself to be receptive to her love (which does not entail infidelity to his wife) – could be enriched by it and realise that it gives him greater insight into the love of God for us. (There is still time for that to happen in his present lifetime, as he and Angela may well meet again.)

Carol's pain was even greater than Angela's, in a sense, simply because of the fact that she experienced greater proximity to Dan and they were in a position to express their real feelings to one another. Both of them too, however, after many years in very destructive marriages, needed the other to make them believe themselves to be lovable, and both of them grew and learnt through their pain. It was thanks to this growth that Carol became able to make a good companion soulmate relationship, and she is fortunate in having a partner who understands and accepts the more profound nature of the bond she has with Dan. Dan's development is taking longer than hers, and it may yet take him another lifetime or so to catch up, but the fact that they are able to maintain a friendship will serve him in tremendous stead both for the rest of this lifetime and for future ones. In fact their union in their present lifetime is by no means beyond the realms of possibility, for she might one day be widowed and he might in due course be either divorced or widowed. It is not that one would wish either of these things on to anyone, but firstly death is the happy culmination of life, and secondly we saw how Dan's development was being severely held back by his wife. Like Angela and Bruce, Carol and Dan are preparing <u>now</u> for their ultimate joining in a way that they could not have done so well if they had not met.

Oliver and Polly's future is still unclear, but what <u>is</u> clear in their case is that they were destined to meet and that she herself does not see her disease as an unfortunate disaster. Even if (like Dan possibly), he never succeeds in making the decision to end his marriage, Polly's connection with Oliver will continue to have a strong and valuable influence on him.

Quentin's and Zachary's must be the most difficult of all our cases, since both these men appear to have become trapped in their own darkness and to be impervious to the light offered them by their twins. Both women, however, Rosie and Yvonne, see their relationships as having been valuable learning experiences, and both are now soaring ahead spiritually. And we must remember that, in view of the indestructible link between each pair, all the work that one partner does on herself will also, inevitably, benefit her twin.

Susie's is an unusual case on account of the fact of her having two twin souls. With Tessa she has no problem – she is simply her closest woman friend and the relationship is of great benefit to both of them – but the pain lies in her divorce from Stuart. This, however, is another case of the assertion made in the title of Chapter III: that the ties can never be cut. Susie, having not been fully ready for the union when she married, took a long time to become aware of the strength of the bond she had with Stuart. Now she regrets the mistake she made when she suggested that they separate, but she probably needed that period of separation in order to learn to appreciate him. Fear of another rejection is preventing him at the moment from returning to her fully, but their friendship has deepened, and the closeness that they now feel for each other (even though he is unwilling to admit it) will again doubtless be an important part of the preparation for a more successful partnership in a future lifetime.

"Future lifetime" are the operative words, too, for Xavier, who has had to come to terms with the separation from Winifred which was not of his choosing. But here again we saw that the ties were not being cut, and he, being such a deeply spiritual and loving person, is able to carry on helping her despite the pain she has caused him. So thank goodness for karma, for in this case we know that he can look forward to the time when Winifred will become fully aware of, and repay, the immense debt that she has incurred to him!

I have referred many times in this book to the guilt and confusion that can be experienced by twin souls on account of the strong attraction between them. This is inevitable with upright people who are already committed to another partner, and one problem about it is the fact that the reason for the attraction is not always understood. In fact, since so few people at present know about twinsoulship, it is probably <u>usually</u> not understood, and the people affected may well see what they are experiencing as "sin" which must be conquered. Consequently, a man such as Bruce, who is strongly religious, will endeavour to suppress his feelings and emotions. This is understandable and natural, but it is not good for the health! (Suppressed emotion is generally recognised by "alternative" practitioners to be, for instance, one of the most common causes of cancer.) If, therefore, twinsoulship is acknowledged and the attraction seen as natural even when it cannot lead to emotional fulfilment, the pain can be sublimated (as Angela is now trying to do) and help our spiritual advance.

Perhaps an even greater source of guilt and confusion than that of being already committed to another partner is when the twin-soul relationship is that of parent and child. Fortunately such a relationship occurs very infrequently. Gertrude and Hugh Lynn Cayce apparently had no problem over it, but they must of course be very advanced souls. Yvonne, however, as we saw in Chapter XII, knows of a previous life which was ruined for her by the fact of her father having made her pregnant, and I have heard of a similar case where a woman was raped by her father, who is her twin soul. The counsellor who told me about this woman anonymously was sure that she would not want to be interviewed (understandably!), but he told me that the couple had been married in England in the Middle Ages, when the woman now in question, who was then his wife, left him. Because of the karma she incurred in that lifetime she had to reincarnate in this century as his daughter, and the love for each other which the two of them now feel – which they both really experience as a kind of sexual love – is naturally an immense cause of guilt and confusion. She, however, is apparently being enabled through the problem to take an immense step in her spiritual growth.

So, if "pain" is one of the key words of these chapters, "hope" is the chief key word of all! Hope for those who are suffering on account of their twin soul, since they can know that the suffering is simply a necessary part of the learning process essential to their evolution. Hope for those who have been searching for their twin soul and not yet found him or her. And hope for those who were not previously aware that they had a twin soul and were possibly thinking that "perfect love" was something completely beyond their grasp. So it is to people in all three of these categories that this book is particularly addressed. With, however, the important reminders firstly that it is not by searching to the ends of the Earth for our twin soul that we shall find him or her, but rather by doing the necessary inner work on ourselves, and secondly – what is really the primary message of this whole book – that whether or not we are acquainted with our twin soul is of little importance.

Experiencing Christ consciousness within yourself, loving unconditionally that which you are as you exist and abide in your reality, at this point in time, creates the resonance within your being that attracts the identical essence within the opposite body of soul energy – your soulmate will manifest in physicality as a natural progression and merge with your energy and you with it. And as you

merge together closer and closer and drink more and more of one another's
cups, you will become one, and you will become one another's strength and
one another's love. As this occurs, you experience what is called enlightenment.
So says St. Germain through Azena Ramanda and Claire Heartsong[6]. Learning
to love ourselves, learning to stand on our own, remembering that our primary
mission on Earth should be service (showing our love of God through serving
our fellows – *I love you because you give without wanting . . . I love you because*
you smile for no reward . . .) – that is what we are here for.

Notes

1. Freely adapted (by I don't know by whom – I saw it hanging on a wall in a friend's house) from
   Meher Baba on Love.
2. *Rich* by Melvyn Bragg, published by Hodder and Stoughton.
3. *Twin Souls or Soulmates?* by Ann Merivale (the author's real name) in issue No. 10 (November
   1996) of *Reincarnation International*, P.O. Box 10839, London SW13 0ZG.
4. *The Bridge Across Forever* by Richard Bach, published by Pan Books.
5. *Companions Along the Way* by Ruth Montgomery, published by Fawcett Crest, Random House,
   New York.
6. *St. Germain: Twin Souls and Soulmates*, channelled by Azena Ramanda and Claire Heartsong,
   published by Triad, Australia.

POSTSCRIPT

I have alas a rather sad postscript to add to Chapter IV. "Fred" died in a car accident, on 19th February, 1997, while on his way to Warwick University for a meeting of the Trustees of the Stratford Lifeways Centre. His car went off the road in a dreadful storm, hit a tree, and both he and his beloved German Shepherd dog died instantly. Readers can well imagine what an appalling shock this was for his wife and family as well as for those who knew him. "Ellen" is, however, coping wonderfully well, and has received a great deal of help from the Life Foundation. Much of the brunt of sorting things out and holding the fort at Lifeways has fallen upon my friend, Heather Burton, and prayers for them all would be greatly appreciated.

The funeral was apparently a most moving occasion, and on 16th April, what would have been his fifty-seventh birthday, a celebration of "Fred's" life was held at Lifeways. All those involved of course appreciate that there are no accidents in life and, difficult though it must have been, they were able to emanate much joy and positivity at this event. A bench to his memory has been erected on Welcombe Hill, where he used to go each morning to send absent healing.

When I received "Ellen's" letter giving me the news, I was of course devastated. My heart ached for her and everyone else who is close to him, but also I found myself thrown into a quandary at what had seemed one of the happiest chapters in this book being given such an unhappy ending. The whole thing has therefore been yet another learning experience for me. An integral part of life is that sometimes, when we think we've got everything "sussed" and know exactly where we're going, from one second to another the ground can be torn from under our feet and we have to make a completely fresh start.

We know that the broad outline of our lives is planned before we come in – particularly such an important event as the timing of our death – and we know that there is a good reason for everything that happens. Sometimes it is easy to see the reason; often it is much less easy. One reason for this sad event that has occurred to me is that "Ellen", who has never previously lived on her own at all in her present lifetime, had perhaps chosen to learn to stand on her own. Remember how the importance of that has been one of the chief themes of this book?

Another thing we have to remember is that, "indispensable" as "Fred's" work at Lifeways seemed, he clearly had even more important work to do on the other side. Since "Ellen" is clairaudient, perhaps in due course he will come through to her and tell her what he is doing. (I hope so very much for her sake!) In the meantime of course their separation is only physical, and only during her waking hours. At night, when she is out of her body, I have no doubt that they are still performing important work together. May "Ellen" continue to be a support to Lifeways and the Centre to her, and may her remaining years on Earth be a time of continuing growth until the couple's eventual reunion. May the Lord bless them and all their family, Heather and all those involved in Lifeways.

Judith Merville
June 1997